# Standards for Juvenile Justice:
## A Summary and Analysis

Institute of Judicial Administration

American Bar Association

**Juvenile Justice Standards Project**

*Standards for Juvenile Justice:*
*A Summary and Analysis*

*Second Edition*

Barbara Danziger Flicker

BALLINGER PUBLISHING COMPANY
Cambridge, Massachusetts
A Subsidiary of Harper & Row, Publishers, Inc.

This document was prepared for the Juvenile Justice Standards Project of the Institute of Judicial Administration and the American Bar Association. The project is supported by grants from the National Institute of Law Enforcement and Criminal Justice, the American Bar Endowment, the Andrew W. Mellon Foundation, the Vincent Astor Foundation, and the Herman Goldman Foundation. The views expressed in this draft do not represent positions taken by the sponsoring organizations or the funding sources. Votes on the standards were unanimous in most but not all cases. Serious objections have been noted in formal dissents printed in the volumes concerned.

This book is printed on recycled paper.

# IJA-ABA JOINT COMMISSION ON JUVENILE JUSTICE STANDARDS

Hon. Irving R. Kaufman, *Chairman*
Orison Marden, *Co-Chairman 1974–1975*
Hon. Tom C. Clark, *Chairman for ABA Liaison*
Delmar Karlen, *Vice-Chairman 1974–1975*

Institute of Judicial Administration, *Secretariat*

Nicholas Scopetta, *Director 1978–1980*
Howard I. Kalodner, *Director 1976–1978*
Peter F. Schwindt, *Acting Director 1976*
Paul A. Nejelski, *Director 1973–1976*
Delmar Karlen, *Counsel 1971–1975*

David Gilman, *Director of Juvenile Justice Standards Project*
Barbara Flicker, *Executive Editor*
Jo Rena Adams, *Legal Editor*
Mary Anne O'Dea, *Editor*
Susan J. Sandler, *Editor*

Barbara Flicker, *Director 1975–1976*
Wayne Mucci, *Director 1974–1975*
Lawrence Schultz, *Director 1973–1974*
Paul A. Nejelski, *Director 1971–1973*

One Washington Square Village, New York, New York 10012
(212) 598-7722

# Contents

# Introduction
# to the
# Second Edition

The first edition of this book was published in 1977, following the release of the twenty-three volumes of standards and commentary produced by the Juvenile Justice Standards Project sponsored by the Institute of Judicial Administration (IJA) and the American Bar Association (ABA). It attempted to provide a framework within which the overall pattern of recommendations for reform of the juvenile justice system could be understood, especially by the youth specialists and members of the legal profession who were about to review the published tentative drafts of the proposed standards.

As a synthesis of the series, it described the history and current status of juvenile justice in the United States, identifying the problems the proposed standards were designed to solve and the process by which they were adopted. It also presented the principles and policies underlying the various standards, explaining, if not always reconciling, apparent inconsistencies. In general, the first edition was prepared as a handbook to introduce readers to a new approach to the relationship between children and the law. It was intended to serve as a supplement to and not a substitute for the twenty-three tentative drafts being distributed nationally at that time.

This second edition marks the completion of the last phase of the project—the review, revision, and final authorization by the executive committee of the Joint IJA-ABA Commission on Juvenile Justice Standards of the approved text of all twenty-three volumes. This edition undertakes a comprehensive update of the process and the product in Part II, current legal developments in Part III, reproduction of the revised standards in Parts IV through VII, and a new assessment of their future impact in Part VIII.

During the four years that have passed since the first edition, the standards have been reviewed by nearly a dozen sections, divisions, and special committees of the American Bar Association. Comments and suggestions were received from the National Council of Juvenile and Family Court Judges, the National District Attorneys Association, the Legal Services and Defender Attorneys Consortium on Juvenile

Justice, the American Psychological Association, the American Psychiatric Association, the Society for Adolescent Psychiatry, the Citizens' Committee for Children of New York, the Judges of Rhode Island Family Court, the Pennsylvania Juvenile Court Judges Association, and many other groups. The executive committee of the IJA-ABA Joint Commission met in 1977, 1978, and 1979, considered the recommendations of the interested individuals and organizations, and agreed to revisions in the standards and commentary comprising twenty-one of the volumes. In February 1979, the ABA House of Delegates voted to approve seventeen of the volumes; in February 1980, it approved three more volumes.

Of the remaining three volumes, *Schools and Education* was withdrawn from consideration by the ABA House of Delegates by the executive committee of the IJA-ABA Joint Commission at its 1977 meeting on the ground that the issues raised by outside commentators were too technical for resolution by persons who were not education experts. The *Noncriminal Misbehavior* volume was tabled after the ABA House of Delegates meeting in 1980 as too controversial to gain ABA approval without major revisions and too fundamental to the series to be compromised. Finally, the executive committee directed extensive changes in the *Abuse and Neglect* volume, which were completed and approved by it too late for inclusion in the House of Delegates agenda during the life of the project. Therefore, twenty volumes have been republished as ABA-approved standards and three more will continue to be distributed as the product of the IJA-ABA Joint Commission.

Reactions to the standards have been highly favorable. Most of the revisions adopted by the executive committee were concerned with details rather than general principles. In instances in which concern was expressed that a standard was correct in theory but might prove too burdensome to implement in some localities, the executive committee voted to add brackets to indicate that the bracketed figure or phrase is the recommended position, but is permissive for individual jurisdictions. For example, in the *Court Organization and Administration* standards, modified rotation of judges and executive administration of juvenile intake and probation services are bracketed in the approved draft, as is the number, four, for the judges who must serve in a court before a full-time administrator is required.

Some changes resulted from the urging of the ABA Section of Criminal Justice and others to conform the juvenile standards more closely to standards and practices governing adults. Thus, in the *Adjudication* and *Prosecution* standards, dispositional concessions were added to the matters subject to plea negotiations; both the standards and commentary concerning admissions by juveniles were tightened in those volumes and in *Counsel for Private Parties*. Other changes were made in response to the charge that the standards were too lenient. As a result, the maximum durations for dispositions in *Juvenile Delinquency and Sanctions* were increased and bracketed; the range of offenses was expanded and the age lowered for waiver of a juvenile to adult court in *Transfer Between Courts*. Similarly, the original *Corrections Administration* standard barring routine searches of visitors was revised to permit nonintrusive routine searches, intrusive searches based on probable cause to believe contraband is present, and other searches based on reasonable cause.

The revisions in the *Abuse and Neglect* standards are described fully in Part IV. Most of the changes were to reconcile the procedures it contained with those in the other volumes involving judicial proceedings. More particularly, the permanent termination of parental rights was changed from a possible disposition following a finding of endangerment (child abuse) to a separate proceeding, with stricter criteria stressing exhaustion of family reunification efforts before authorizing termination.

For those familiar with the standards in the tentative drafts, this edition includes an Appendix consisting of the full Addendum appearing in each revised volume and describing the specific changes made. While most of the revisions entailed an augmentation of the commentary, some changes were made in black-letter standards.

The second edition also examines the impact that the dissemination of the twenty-three original drafts may have had on the law. Observable trends in juvenile law and practice, prospects for national implementation of the proposed standards, and suggestions for improving those prospects are discussed in Part VIII. It might be said that this edition expresses the state of the art in juvenile justice as of 1981 and offers its own prescription for the future of that system.

## PART I: NATIONAL STANDARDS
## FOR JUVENILE JUSTICE

---

## 1.1 Special Nature of Juvenile Justice.

The size and complexity of the task undertaken by the Juvenile Justice Standards Project of the Institute of Judicial Administration and the American Bar Association and the IJA-ABA Joint Commission of Juvenile Justice Standards must be understood at the outset of this volume. The formulation of standards to govern the juvenile justice system goes far beyond criminal jurisprudence. Juvenile offenders are only a portion of the population within the juvenile justice system. Neglected, abused, and dependent children, as well as their parents and other affected persons, also come within the jurisdiction of juvenile or family court. But even those parties and proceedings do not cover the full spectrum of juvenile issues. The mere fact of minority and its attendant disabilities and special circumstances present problems unique to a system for the provision of justice for juveniles. These standards attempt to cover every aspect of the laws regulating children in their contact with social institutions.

When we consider that age and dependency, conditions beyond the control of the principal party involved, can precipitate involvement in the juvenile justice system, whereas the commission of an unlawful act is the sole determinant in initiating contact with the criminal justice system, we begin to recognize major differences between the two justice systems. Nevertheless, each is a system of justice for which standards should be promulgated, compelling a commitment to shared principles of justice and administrative coherence. The standards for criminal and juvenile justice alike must provide procedures for all the agencies and individuals functioning as parts of the organizational whole to arrive at a fair disposition of the matters brought before them. Police, probation, courts, and corrections agencies must mesh into the criminal justice system. And the roles of the actors—defendants, victims, witnesses, law enforcement officers, probation workers, judges, prosecutors, defense counsel, and administrators—must be defined with precision.

1

The juvenile justice system includes the equivalent of all of the participants in the criminal justice system plus persons peculiar to the condition of youth: parents, guardians *ad litem,* foster parents, teachers. It also adds special problems and concepts: consensual and contractual disabilities; standing to sue; emancipation; family autonomy; age differentials for drinking, marrying, compulsory education, voting, curfews, sexual activity, driving and flying licenses, etc. National variations in the definition of juveniles by age, marital or parental status, living arrangements, and financial independence are significant in determining not only the court's jurisdiction but the youth's permissible range of private activities, life style, and liberty.

An additional complicating factor in the juvenile justice system is the question of developmental age. For the criminal justice system, that factor is acknowledged in some jurisdictions through the intermediary stage of a youthful offender category—usually for first or second offenders who are charged with lesser crimes and can be somewhere between the ages of seventeen and twenty-four, although most often under twenty-two. Youthful offenders may be treated more leniently or sentenced to special facilities to separate them from older, presumably more hardened criminals. The youthful offender category represents an effort to distinguish between incipient and career criminality. There is room for the exercise of discretion by the court in granting or withholding youthful offender status, but the criteria are specified by statute and are largely objective and provable. After a certain age, maturity and responsibility are presumed in the absence of compelling evidence to the contrary.

The juvenile justice system conscientiously attempts to establish age parameters, which vary not only from state to state but according to the purpose of the age limitations and the traditions of the community. Twenty-one used to be universally regarded as the age of majority. Recently, eighteen was substituted for most purposes. For other purposes, such as compulsory education, consent to health care, and the maximum age for juvenile delinquency jurisdiction, states have variously adopted seventeen, sixteen, and fifteen as the ceiling. The lack of consistency among state legislatures is not remarkable in view of similar disagreement among child psychologists. Since the maturity and capacity of an individual child are debatable, arbitrary lines must be drawn as close to the developmental norm as possible. As with most laws, rigorous efforts to be fair in adopting a norm should be expended, a rationale provided, and a mechanism developed to permit a chance for rebuttal or to prescribe grounds for appeal when the norm can be proven by objective evidence to be inapplicable to an individual case.

## 1.2 Reasons for Formulating National Standards.

The juvenile justice system stands in dire need of thorough dissection preparatory to the promulgation of a comprehensive set of standards. Standards generally are adopted for the following purposes:

1. *to achieve uniformity* in the law for greater fairness, efficiency, and predictability in the consequences of the same conduct, action, or behavior, regardless of jurisdiction;

2. *to develop linkages* within the system by: defining the roles of affected individuals and agencies; eliminating gaps and duplication in services; and coordinating the planning, operation, and monitoring of programs;

3. *to reexamine accepted concepts and premises* underlying the current laws in the light of objective findings derived from recent studies and other developments. Basic principles should be reaffirmed, revised, or replaced, as a result of taking a fresh look at the system;

4. *to codify* the relevant case law, administrative decisions, selected statutory innovations, and fundamental principles approved in the standards in a form readily translatable into a model act or acts.

With respect to the juvenile justice standards, the Commission deliberately sought to attain those goals. It voted to apply the standards to federal and local laws as well as to state laws.

## 1.3 Lack of Uniformity Among the Various Jurisdictions.

A major contribution by any series of juvenile law standards would be to establish a uniform scheme of age and offense definition. A 1974 study by the National Assessment of Juvenile Corrections at the University of Michigan, entitled "Juvenile Delinquency: A Comparative Analysis of Legal Codes in the United States," said:

> The philosophy of the juvenile court movement was premised on the assumption that children, because of their age, are generally incapable of criminal behavior. There is today, however, no agreement on the age at which a child is considered an adult. In fact, many recent statutory changes have occurred in this area—age limits have been both lowered and raised. *Id.* at 13.

The study found few minimum age limitations in juvenile court statutes, but adult penal codes generally conformed to the common law minimum age of criminal responsibility of seven. The maximum age for juvenile court jurisdiction varied greatly. As of January 1, 1972, the cut-off date adopted for the study, thirty-three jurisdictions (including the District of Columbia) treated seventeen as the maximum age, twelve states used sixteen, and six states limited the age to fifteen. The study also found disparities among the states in determining the point at which the juvenile's age fixes the court's original jurisdiction, i.e., the age at which the offense was committed or the juvenile was apprehended, and even greater disparity in the court's continuing jurisdiction, varying from seventeen to twenty-one, with several states setting no maximum age to continue jurisdiction for serious offenses.

The age at which a juvenile is considered within the jurisdiction of the court also is affected by the state's law on waiver to adult criminal court. Although other factors may be considered in some states, such as the seriousness of the offense, previous record, and available resources, transfer to adult court is mandatory for certain offenses for all juveniles in some states and for juveniles over a specified age in other states.

As indicated earlier, state laws vary widely on age limitations for minors in many matters other than juvenile offenses, such as licensing privileges, contract rights, consent to health care, statutory rape, voting rights, drinking, employment, and compulsory education.

It clearly is essential to a concept of fairness in juvenile law that an effort be made to remove inconsistencies in a juvenile's rights and liabilities that are caused by the accident of geography.

Another area in need of uniformity is the delineation of acts or behavior that will bring a juvenile within the court's jurisdiction as a delinquent or status offender or an adult as a neglectful or abusive parent. Definitions of child abuse, neglect, and dependency differ substantially among the federal government, states, and localities. Not only court jurisdiction, but program funding, eligibility for services, foster care placement, termination of parental rights, social service intervention, income maintenance, inclusion in a central registry, and an unparalleled assortment of other state actions, including criminal liability, can be triggered by statutory distinctions as vague and uncertain as any in the law of the land. The standards have attempted to clarify these classifications.

The definition of delinquency is a problem only to the extent that state penal laws vary in their exclusion of certain minor offenses, such as vagrancy and loitering. Traffic offenses also are treated differently among the states if the violator is a juvenile, in determining whether the cases are heard in juvenile or traffic court and in differentiating between felonies and misdemeanors, for offenders under and over sixteen.

But a much greater problem is the definition of status offenses.

About half the states include the numerous forms of noncriminal misbehavior constituting status offenses within the classification of delinquency. The others create a separate classification and attempt to provide differences in dispositions, detention, and other aspects of handling such juveniles. The statutory definitions of status offenses include several instances of clearly proscribed behavior, like truancy and running away from home, but other statutory status offenses rely on vague and subjective concepts of incorrigibility, unruliness, need of supervision, and being beyond the control of parents or other lawful authority. Here too the standards make a bold attempt to eliminate these inequities, in part by removing status offenses from the jurisdiction of the juvenile court.

Aside from delinquency, status offenses, child abuse, neglect, and dependency, the juvenile court's jurisdiction may include many additional family problems. Some juvenile courts are called family courts, as in New York. Family courts may have original or concurrent jurisdiction over such matters as support, custody, family offenses, adoption, paternity, and divorce. Most states limit their juvenile court's jurisdiction to juvenile offenses, neglect, abuse, and dependency.

There also are broad disparities in the organization of the juvenile courts independent of questions of jurisdictional scope. In some states they are separate courts, handling only cases involving juvenile misconduct and parental failure. These courts may be statewide, in the sense of covering the state by having courts in all geographic regions or political subdivisions, whereas other states have juvenile courts with jurisdiction over discrete areas only, such as larger cities, with juvenile cases elsewhere in the state heard in a division of the court of general jurisdiction. In most states, the juvenile courts are a special session of a lower court of limited jurisdiction and are "inferior courts," equivalent to the criminal court in New York City, which hears only misdemeanors, the felony cases being heard by the supreme or county court of general jurisdiction. The trend is to recommend a statewide system in which the juvenile court is part of the court of general trial jurisdiction, a structure recommended by the standards. Questions of appointment or election of judges, judicial qualification, rotation of judges and other court personnel, the relationship of probation to the judiciary or executive branches of government, and procedures for appeals and collateral review also are covered by the standards, in the effort to bring order out of the existing chaos and confusion as to the structure and organization of the juvenile courts among the various states and localities.

Another complex administrative issue concerns records and information. Access to juvenile records by third parties, sealing and expungement of data, and other questions of privacy and confidentiality of records frequently are confused with the issue of closed or open hearings and public accountability. Although juvenile records traditionally are regarded as confidential and not available to the public, at present the harmful effects of contact with the juvenile justice system are widespread because of subsequent disclosure to potential employers, the armed forces, professional schools, and governmental agencies, as well as law enforcement officials. Access is obtained in many ways— through the exercise of the court's broad discretionary powers, through police records and social agency case files, and through other gaps in the confidentiality of court records. The practice of closing hearings to the public also was designed to protect the privacy of juveniles and their families and to reduce the stigmatizing effect of court involvement. However, in many states this concern for secrecy has encouraged court personnel to act autocratically, arbitrarily denying admission to juvenile proceedings to lawyers, concerned civic organizations attempting to monitor the court, and news personnel. At other times, court officials have "choreographed" television coverage, setting up situations to create a desired impression. Such selective and ungovernable actions, together with occasional planned leaks of participants' identity, have made confidential recordkeeping and closed hearings a deliberate cover for secrecy and lack of accountability. The standards propose guidelines to prescribe consistent procedures for recordkeeping, with safeguards against improper disclosure. They also revise the rules on closed hearings.

A further problem related to recordkeeping is the incompatibility of most state, local, and federal systems for comparable, reliable data collection. Available statistics on the incidence of juvenile crime, child abuse, and neglect are virtually useless because every locality follows its own rules on the information retained, the period covered, the definitions of persons or offenses included, and the inclusiveness of the agencies reporting. The results are uncoordinated, overlapping, and inadequate delivery of services; imprecise or nonexistent planning and monitoring; lack of accountability to the community, the legislature, and the executive branch; and easy manipulation by the news media and the agencies of the fears or complacency of the public concerning delinquency, child abuse, and neglect. Simple regulations are recommended in the standards for data systems, planning, and monitoring for the police, courts, agencies, and other resources of the juvenile justice system.

Procedures affecting the juveniles and families involved with the juvenile justice system also are unpredictable. A degree of order has been imposed on the adjudicatory or fact-finding stage by Supreme Court decisions requiring the juvenile courts to provide certain due process safeguards at that stage, although even the Supreme Court has not been entirely consistent in its rulings. But the other stages of the process—apprehension, intake screening, detention, investigation, disposition, probation, and parole—and the role of referral agencies differ greatly according to the locality. Such matters as rules pertaining to detention, including duration and purpose, the facilities permitted to be used, the services required to be provided, the type and degree of testing allowed, disciplinary and grievance mechanisms, and the full range of questions related to institutionalization, although supposedly temporary and short-term, are being challenged in many jurisdictions. Guidelines for minimum standards are seriously deficient in most states, but states with detailed regulations are also vulnerable to charges of improper regard for the presumptive innocence of most of their detainees. However, the inconsistencies among the states create an injustice to juveniles unable to choose the locality in which they are to be apprehended.

For example, a juvenile whose case might be screened out or "adjusted" during the intake stage in New York could be obliged to submit to six months of probation "services" prior to an adjudication on the merits of the case in California, referred to the prosecutor in Texas, or to the court without screening in a number of other states. Furthermore, the criteria for any intake decision are generally so imprecise as to make the outcome in a case almost capricious. Studies have shown that the intake decision is more dependent on the policies applied by the individual intake worker than the facts in the particular case.

But the area of greatest significance in the juvenile justice field and, unfortunately, in greatest disarray, is the dispositional or sentencing stage. The process of applying the various declared juvenile justice goals—treatment, rehabilitation, deterrence, protection of society, serving the best interests of the child, preserving the family—need not be mutually self-defeating, but an understanding of purposes and a recognition of consequences is lacking. Most states purport to be helping the child when they may in fact be hurting him or her, solving family conflicts when they may be exacerbating them, rehabilitating transgressors and preventing future criminality when they may be creating career criminals. Treatment or services can co-exist with sanctions in correctional programs. However, the state must first consider what it is doing and why—and whether the conduct or condition to which the court is responding justifies the degree of intervention into the private lives of the citizens affected, adult and juvenile. The standards project has taken bold steps to explore this dilemma and to propose solutions.

To appreciate the controversial nature of positions adopted in the standards on the "sanctions versus treatment" issue in juvenile court dispositions, we should examine four brief extracts:

Edwin M. Schur, in *Radical Nonintervention: Rethinking the Delinquency Problem* (1973), said:

> Somehow, good intentions notwithstanding, the special mechanisms developed for dealing with young offenders on an individual basis and in a nonpunitive way have backfired. Most acute observers now express considerable disenchantment with nonadversary procedures of the traditional juvenile court, the specialized and rehabilitation-oriented "treatment institutions," and the allegedly nonstigmatizing terminology of delinquency policies. *Id.* at 3.

But "Children in Custody: A Report on the Juvenile Detention and Correctional Facility Census of 1971," published by the National Criminal Justice Information and Statistics Service of the U.S. Department of Justice, stated:

> Since the traditional goal of the juvenile court is, ideally, the care and reformation of the young offender rather than his punishment, both the juvenile court itself and the correctional system which serves it tend to be more flexible and less dependent on the use of highly codified law and procedures than the judicial and correctional institutions that handle adults. *Id.* at 3.

The National Assessment of Juvenile Corrections study on juvenile delinquency referred to earlier expresses a contrary view: ". . . attempts to pursue rehabilitative and punishment goals simultaneously often become self defeating." *Id.* at 4.

One of the peculiar consequences of pursuing a treatment-rehabilitation model of juvenile court to its logical conclusion is demonstrated in § 29 (b) of the provisions of the Uniform Juvenile Court Act of 1968, with respect to disposition after a finding that a juvenile committed a felony, as follows:

> In the absence of evidence to the contrary, evidence of the commission of acts which constitute a felony is sufficient to sustain a finding that a child is in need of treatment or rehabilitation. If the court finds that that child is not in need of treatment or rehabilitation, it shall dismiss the proceeding and discharge the child from any detention or other restitution theretofore ordered.

Recently there has been an outcry against the release of juvenile felons, with several state legislatures adopting special provisions for mandatory sanctions for serious crimes, labeling such juveniles "habitual offenders," "violent juveniles," and similar special classifications to remove them from traditional juvenile court dispositional policies. However, juveniles at the opposite end of the spectrum have not aroused equivalent public outrage. Juveniles who commit trivial offenses or who are found to be dependent or neglected can be incarcerated. In the language of the Uniform Juvenile Court Act, "If the court finds...that the child is *deprived* or that he is in need of treatment or rehabilitation *as a delinquent or unruly child,* the court shall proceed...to make a proper disposition of the case." (Emphasis added.) And as "Children in Custody" observes, "...circumstances unrelated to juvenile delinquency may precipitate commitment as a dependent or neglected child when no other arrangements can be made for appropriate care." *Id.* at 3.

This anomalous situation with respect to sentencing has not escaped the attention of the standards project, which has adopted a comprehensive set of guidelines in its volumes on dispositions, sanctions, child abuse and neglect, and noncriminal misbehavior.

It is difficult to separate the formulation of uniform standards for juvenile justice from the resolution of conflicts over the basic concepts and goals of the system. As the members of the IJA-ABA Joint Commission discovered, achieving uniformity and consistency in the standards compelled a rigorous and painful reexamination of conventional wisdom. They soon found that the price of their movement toward reform of the system was intense opposition, controversy, and even calumny from those seeking to preserve the system as it is. Many juvenile court judges, probation workers, corrections officers, social agency personnel, and other participants in the system recoiled at the new concepts imposing criteria on actions taken, curtailing the exercise of official discretion, requiring written reasons for decisions, and generally opening the judicial process to greater scrutiny and review. That the effort to produce uniform standards also resulted in a challenge to the conceptual foundations of the system was an unexpected and often unwelcome consequence.

## 1.4 Failure of Coordination Within the System.

The second goal of developing a uniform set of standards is to ensure the effective operation of the system. Such an overview should result in a clear definition of the roles of those involved in the system, identification of the resources needed, and recognition of the mechanisms necessary for the proper allocation and coordination of those resources—whether personnel, services, or facilities—in order to fulfill the legitimate purposes of the system. The word "system" presupposes an organized whole, arranged in a rational order. The dictionary defines it as "an assemblage of objects united by some form of regular interaction or interdependence." Yet every critique of the juvenile justice system singles out lack of coordination; defects in delivery of services; confusion of the roles and responsibilities of judges, social workers, counsel, public and voluntary service agencies, child protective agencies, police and correction officers, and state, local, and federal officials; and failure to achieve its dual objective of protecting society and helping children and their families.

The Commission was able to perform its task successfully by reaching an understanding of what a juvenile justice system and its component parts can and must do. The confusion and overreach implicit in the expectation that a court is capable of devising dispositions "in the best interest of the child" in the absence of guidelines, of reliable predictive measures of future criminal behavior, or of models for effective rehabilitation or treatment programs, punctured the myth of the medical model of juvenile justice at the outset. With treatment and services regarded in the standards as a secondary goal of the system (except for voluntary programs), justice for juveniles, their families, and the community emerged as the focal point; traditional issues of justifiable intervention became the major concern of the project. It was conceded that the system existed as a system of *justice* to deal with the situations in which there was a need for intervention. Therefore the Commission had to consider the questions of what was needed, who should prescribe it, under what constraints the providers should operate, and how the whole operation should be conducted.

To set standards for issues connected with determining situations and behavior justifying intervention, the volumes defining the jurisdiction of the court were assigned to Committee I, Intervention in the Lives of Children. The protection to be afforded juveniles and adults before the court are covered by the standards from Committee II, Court Roles and Procedures. The nature and degree of the intervention are described by Committee III, Treatment and Corrections. And the methodology for planning, monitoring, and governing the system was developed by Committee IV, Administration. Not all of the functions of the juvenile justice system devolve on the court. Separate volumes on police, youth service agencies, schools and education, architecture of facilities, probation intake and investigation, and correctional administration were an important part of the project's effort to pull together all elements in the community outside the courts whose activities focus on juveniles. They too are an essential element of the juvenile justice system and its operation. The integration of standards for the juvenile court process with standards for the providers of community services and for pre- and post-judicial action affecting juveniles is a major accomplishment of the project.

## 1.5 Need to Review Basic Premises.

The third purpose stated for adopting standards is the reexamination of the concepts and premises underlying the current laws governing the system. As indicated above, that process turned out to be the most painful yet crucial assignment for the Commission, drafting committees, reporters, and others connected with the standards project. Contrary to the usual experience of projects of this sort, many participants found their views changed as they reconsidered the validity of their assumptions. They found some of their most cherished ideas challenged and ultimately vanquished by exposure to unexpected formulations and findings concerning the performance and goals of the juvenile justice system. Agreement on principles was the primary concern, although once basic positions were adopted, the Commission was exhaustively conscientious in hammering out the precise language to be adopted in the individual standards.

One serious problem that is expected to be encountered in seeking state by state adoption is resistance to change. But equally serious is the possibility that legislatures may fail to recognize the inseparability of some of the concepts from those that can be rejected or approved without destroying the standards as a whole. For example, whether seventeen or eighteen is the maximum age for the court's jurisdiction is important but not integral to the standards. The same applies to the minimum age for delinquency or the maximum term for confinement. Although these figures were selected with care, after extensive study and deliberation, the standards on juvenile delinquency and sanctions would not collapse if they were changed. However, if the concept of proportionality in sanctions (which would require the severity of a disposition to be related to the seriousness of the offense, with *maximum* penalties prescribed accordingly) were to be adopted only with respect to serious criminal acts and rejected for trivial offenses or noncriminal misconduct, the concept would be meaningless. The entire fabric of the Commission's position on dispositions is inextricably woven from theories of fairness, justifiable intervention, proportionality to the state's adult penal sanctions, determinacy, and objectivity in decision making. Therefore, if the criminal act were to determine the sanction for serious felonies, while subjective judgments governed the decision as to whether a status offender or misdemeanant should be subjected to removal to a correctional facility in his or her best interests, the basic principles on which the standards are premised would be abrogated. Unfortunately, there is a trend in the states to do exactly that. Pursuing a media-induced, fear-ridden double standard, legislatures are creating a new classification, such as "violent juvenile," for juveniles who commit certain serious crimes, with mandatory incarceration for a fixed term of years. Simultaneously, these legislatures are refusing to revise their juvenile codes' statements of purpose, clinging to their initial endorsement of individualized dispositions based on the child's circumstances, best interests, and rehabilitative needs. This anomaly gives the court officials the best of all worlds and the juveniles the worst—absolute discretion to impose any disposition on virtually any juvenile, since status offense definitions could include anyone, and mandatory sanctions without having to prove need for a single class of juvenile offenders.

Every effort will be made by proponents of the standards to impress upon the legislatures, courts, lawyers, and other influential persons the importance of conforming to consistent principles in revising the juvenile law. It is difficult to discourage piecemeal adoption of the standards, because any adoption seems like a victory when a bill passes. For example, some states are moving toward determinate sentences. But without well-developed policies on parole and release practices, aftercare, and procedures for modification of sentences, a state imposing a fixed sentence will find itself lacking a coherent body of law. The discretionary and disciplinary powers of the correctional authorities, the inmate's ability to earn time off for good behavior, the continuing jurisdiction of the court after a disposition has been imposed, and related issues also must be resolved if determinate sentences are to be enforced rationally.

The conclusion that must be drawn is that one of the functions of recommending a comprehensive set of standards to the states and other jurisdictions—the revision or reaffirmation of underlying principles as part of a total review of the system—will not be within the control of the project after the text of the standards and commentary has been released to the public. As will be seen, that fear has begun to be confirmed by the actions of the state legislatures. Efforts addressed to responsible dissemination of the standards are discussed in Part VIII, on Future Impact, but it must be observed here that the risk exists of misconceived, partial, and illogical responses to so voluminous an outpouring of complex materials. If the various jurisdictions can be influenced to take a fresh look at the totality of their juvenile justice system, that in itself will be progress. But that is a long way from a complete overhaul. Conventional wisdom is not easily abandoned.

## 1.6 Producing a Model Act.

Finally, the fourth goal of formulating standards is the codification of the recommended body of law to produce a model act or uniform codes for adoption by the states, localities, and federal government. The standards have been drafted in a style designed to be easily transformed into statutory form. Not all the reporters observed the instruction that the bold-face standards without commentary be in simple, concise language, but neither do most legislators. The adaptation of the standards into a juvenile code generally should be a routine task.

Some difficulties are unavoidable. The language in each code would have to conform to similar usages throughout the jurisdiction's laws. For example, a juvenile court might be a part, a division, a branch, a section, or other terminology to describe its relationship to the court of general trial jurisdiction. Also, the subject matter of the volumes would not necessarily all belong in the respective juvenile court acts.

Several model acts might be drafted—a family court and a juvenile corrections law, or a combination similar to the California Welfare and Institutions Code, with model amendments to the education law and health and safety laws, and possibly an amendment to the traffic law and the adult penal code to cover juvenile offenders. The best approach, if the standards could be consolidated without becoming indigestible, would be a single juvenile code with subdivisions covering the normal statutory divisions indicated above: family court, institutions for juvenile delinquents, institutions for child care, youth service agencies, education (student rights and obligations), and civil rights of minors.

In addition, the administrative law of the jurisdictions would require substantial changes. The current regulations issued by the Departments of Justice and of Health and Human Services with respect to social service and "Safe Streets" funding, child protective services, definitions of child abuse, neglect, noncriminal juvenile offenses, institutional care, delinquency prevention, and a vast array of conditions and definitions designed to encourage pre-delinquency intervention, broad mandatory reporting of suspected cases of neglect and abuse, and other departures from the standards would have to be revised to conform the federal law to the standards.

The task of bringing the standards down from Mount Olympus into the state consolidated laws, local administrative codes, Congressional acts, and executive orders is awesome. But a growing awareness of the inadequacies and unfairness in the current system is expected to precipitate an army of scholars, practicing lawyers, legislators, and civic reformers to enlist in the cause of producing a total reform of the juvenile justice system. One does not have to be immersed in the works of John Rawls to understand that justice is fairness. The current juvenile justice system lacks fairness, from its dedication to the cause of identifying pre-delinquents to its long-range surveillance of former juvenile offenders—that is, from pre-start to post-finish. Advocates of justice may be expected to join the cause once the standards have been studied and accepted as a model for a reformed juvenile justice system.

# PART II: THE PROCESS AND THE PRODUCT

## 2.1 Scope of the Summary Volume.

This book is designed to be more than a compilation of the standards for juvenile justice contained in the twenty-three volumes in this series. It is an attempt to synthesize the disparate parts and analyze them, tracking common elements, reconciling divergence, and explaining apparent inconsistencies. Portions that were adopted after extensive consideration will be identified. The reasons for their adoption will be presented, as well as the rationale for rejecting alternative positions.

Therefore, both a process and a product are summarized here. The product, a comprehensive new juvenile justice system, and the process of creating the product are completed now, after ten years of work. There were hundreds of participants in the work over the years—reporters, editors, drafting committees, Commission members, affected practitioners, and consultants. Their contributions also are discussed.

The Institute of Judicial Administration initiated the project in 1971 and was joined by the American Bar Association in 1973 as co-sponsor. Several organizations have provided funding or otherwise cooperated in advancing the work of the project. Some organizations have steadfastly opposed it. Their views also will be part of the discussion where they had or are expected to have an impact on the standards.

In addition, this volume describes the intricate procedures followed in the course of preparing, reviewing, revising, and approving the proposed standards.

The many factors constituting the process and the product will be considered within the context of the history of the juvenile justice system. The background and genesis of the separate juvenile court and the current status of the juvenile justice system will be examined.

By thus following the steps in the work of the project, the methods followed, the roles of the participants, the reasons for the positions adopted, and the responses of concerned agencies, organizations, and individuals, within the framework of the past and present system, we hope to give meaning to the myriad proposals contained in the standards. If it is possible to discern and illuminate a logical pattern in twenty-three separately prepared volumes, that is the aim of this book.

To the extent possible, this volume will avoid dwelling on the sensationalism and exploitation of the public's fear of young people, especially minority youngsters, that characterize media coverage of juvenile crime. However, such phenomena as youth gangs, riots, campus uprisings, and other headline-producing events cannot be totally ignored in their impact on trends in juvenile law. Isolated but well publicized instances of child abuse or custody battles between foster parents and natural parents have had significant impact on the law. They also have produced enormous reallocation of limited child care funds and even created new bureaucracies to concentrate on the popular issues of the day, such as the federal, state, and local child protective service and reporting network financed by the Department of Health and Human Services (HHS) and burgeoning delinquency prevention programs funded by the Law Enforcement Assistance Administration of the Department of Justice (LEAA). At present the political impetus is to dismantle social service, advocacy, and research programs. LEAA is being phased out and funding for the Office of Juvenile Justice and Delinquency Prevention was omitted from the 1982 federal budget submitted by the Office of Management and Budget. Appropriations to subsidize adoptions and foster care also have been cut drastically.

The trend toward mandatory terms for so-called violent juveniles or habitual offenders was alluded to earlier. The ebb and flow of teenage gang activities also produce dramatic shifts in attention from the government, based not so much on increases in crime incidence as on media attention.

In drafting the standards, the project has attemped to be scrupulous in not responding to the inflamed issues of the moment, but to deal with the problems from a measured, long-range perspective of juveniles and their families in their relationships with social institutions and the surrounding community. Whether the prominent issue of the day is mugging, arson, drugs, vandalism, student strikes, deserting fathers, or juvenile prostitution, the standards have clung to an overview proposing definitions of justifiable grounds for state intervention, dispositional choices, rights and obligations of juveniles, parents, and institutions, and guidelines for planning and monitoring programs. The project has not been unaware of current developments but has responded to them only as they appear to advance the range of possibilities for improvement within the juvenile justice system. Similarly, recent trends will be referred to in this summary volume if they illuminate the reasoning behind adoption of a particular standard or account for opposition to it within the Commission or from outside sources. But the standards still must be viable after the newspaper headlines are forgotten.

## 2.2 The Process.

A brief description of the lengthy and frequently tedious procedures followed in the course of designing, drafting, revising, and approving the standards volumes and of the persons involved in those procedures might be useful as a background to the standards ultimately adopted.

The Juvenile Justice Standards Project was established by the Institute of Judicial Administration as a successor to the American Bar Association Project on Minimum Standards for Criminal Justice in order to deal with the special issues peculiar to the juvenile justice system that were left unresolved by the adult standards. A planning committee met in October 1971. Six subcommittees were formed (on Nonjudicial Handling, Structure and Jurisdiction of Court, Pretrial Procedure, Hearings, Corrections, and Administration) to identify and analyze issues. Preliminary working papers and reports were prepared by specialists in the field and distributed to the members of the planning committee and the subcommittees; topics for the volumes were chosen and divided among four newly formed drafting committees; reporters were selected to draft the volumes under the supervision of drafting committees; and work on the volumes commenced. In February 1973, the American Bar Association became co-sponsor of the project and the IJA-ABA Joint Commission on Juvenile Justice Standards supplanted the planning committee as the executive body. IJA continued to serve as the secretariat.

Over two hundred juvenile justice experts have been actively engaged in preparing the standards. Approximately thirty-five people serve on the Commission, half of whom are distinguished lawyers and judges and half recognized specialists in such related fields as social work, psychology, education, sociology, psychiatry, corrections, law enforcement, and health care. The four drafting committees have had over one hundred members reviewing the standards as they were developing. More than thirty reporters, mostly law school or university faculty members, drafted the volumes. On occasion, special consultants have been called upon to contribute to the work of the project.

Each drafting committee and small working groups within each committee met with the reporters to discuss the positions to be taken on the various issues affecting their volumes. Critical issues were referred to the Commission for its deliberation. As drafts were completed, they were circulated among members of the committees, although in some committees the practice was more scrupulously followed than in others. Questions of cross-volume and cross-committee conflicts on positions frequently were addressed to the project staff, whose editors and directors concerned themselves not only with style and form but with consistency of content as well. In a few cases the drafts were sent to outside experts for their advice and reactions.

After a volume was certified by the drafting committee chairperson as ready for Commission review, copies were sent to all members of the Commission and the volume was placed on the agenda of the next regularly scheduled full Commission meeting. The responsible committee chairpersons and reporters presented the volumes to the Commission, outlining the salient features and indicating innovations and areas of controversy or conflict. The Commission members voted on every standard, revising some at the meeting and stipulating other changes to be made as a condition to their approval. Changes in the commentary accompanying the standards also were specified. During the last year of the drafting phase, standards as revised at the Commission meeting were approved in principle, subject to final review of the volume after the manuscript was completed under the guidance of three- or four-member editorial committees appointed by the Commission from its membership and chaired by the drafting committee chairperson responsible for the volume. After the final draft of the volume was certified by the editorial committee as completed, it was made available to the members of the Commission for final review to confirm that the revisions complied with the Commission's directives prior to transmittal to the publisher. In some instances, volumes or individual standards were reviewed by the Commission several times before receiving approval.

It can be seen that ample opportunity was provided for the standards to be challenged, defended, and reevaluated over the life of the project. Nevertheless, there was some dissent both within and outside the project. Although most standards were adopted unanimously or by a clear majority, there was a predictable division on issues related to the single most significant conflict among juvenile justice specialists—between proponents of the justice or due process model of the juvenile court and of the rehabilitative, treatment, or medical model. As will be apparent when the standards are presented, the Commission adopted a justice model, prescribing rigorous procedural safeguards, nonwaivable representation by counsel at every crucial stage of the proceeding, and severe restrictions on the discretionary powers of the court. At the same time, the Commission stressed the importance of voluntary services, referrals to community youth service agencies, reduced court jurisdiction, and the rights of minors to health care. Thus services, treatment, and rehabilitation programs were supported, but not as the basis of the court's jurisdiction nor as a coerced dispositional alternative.

The project's publication phase was concluded in 1977. After the volumes were distributed to the appropriate ABA sections and reviewed by them, the standards were submitted to the ABA House of Delegates for adoption. Through ABA participation on the Commission (three former ABA presidents and other representatives have been active members of the Commission) and in drafting committees, through several meetings attended by project staff, Commission members, and ABA section leaders, and through materials provided by the project to the section representatives, there had been some preparation for the reception of the volumes, but the prospect for the ABA sections seemed overwhelming nonetheless. The concepts of twenty-three volumes of standards and commentary were not easily assimilated.

Because no single ABA juvenile justice section existed, volumes were circulated among a dozen sections, divisions, and special committees, with the Sections of Criminal Justice and Family Law usually, but not always, taking the lead. At times, the Young Lawyers Division, Judicial Administration Division, Special Court Judges Committee, or Sections of Individual Rights and Responsibilities, General Practice, or others expressed influential opinions. This broad review ensured that the ABA would consider the divergent views of the various sections before approving the standards.

After all salient comments from the ABA and other important professional groups were studied by the executive committee of the IJA-ABA Joint Commission (to which the decision-making authority of the Joint Commission had been delegated at its last meeting in 1976), the executive committee met in 1977, 1978, and 1979 and reviewed the tentative drafts of the volumes. The basic thrust of the volumes was not changed, but a number of standards were revised and the commentary was expanded to reflect the views of the commentators. The decisions of the executive committee were set forth in minutes issued after the meetings, copies of which were provided to the ABA to assist the House of Delegates in its deliberations. The House first considered the standards at its midyear meeting in 1979. Before that meeting began, some groups within the ABA mounted a campaign to defeat the standards through the classic device of delay. But, after a long and spirited debate, highlighted by statements from the many ABA sections that supported the standards, the House approved seventeen volumes. The proponents of the standards overcame renewed opposition at the following midyear meeting. A motion for reconsideration and revision of the previously approved volumes was soundly defeated and the House approved three more volumes. None of the remaining three volumes was rejected, but the *Noncriminal Misbehavior* volume was tabled because the proposal to eliminate juvenile court jurisdiction over status offenders provoked intense controversy among the delegates. The *Schools and Education* volume was not submitted to the House of Delegates on the ground that it was too specialized and the *Abuse and Neglect* volume was revised too extensively for the final approved draft to be completed before the project disbanded. These three volumes are published as the product of the IJA-ABA Joint Commission.

The specific revisions in the standards and commentary in each volume are described in the Appendix. In addition, they are referred to in Parts IV through VII and as part of the overall discussion of the proposed new juvenile justice system.

## 2.3 The Product.

The actual writing of the standards volumes was assigned to reporters, most of whom are law school professors. Other reporters are professors of sociology, criminal justice, urban studies, and architecture, and the rest are law practitioners. The planned volumes were distributed according to subject matter to fall within the purview of the appropriate drafting committees.

Drafting Committee I was responsible for statements on Intervention in the Lives of Children. The volumes prepared by Committee I deal with permissible grounds for the court's jurisdiction, defining juvenile offenses and acts constituting child abuse and neglect. Thus they also set limits on state intervention, propose alternatives to court involvement for matters deemed inappropriate to judicial proceedings, and offer guidelines for police handling of juvenile problems. The committee also recommended standards defining the legal rights and obligations of minors in civil matters unrelated to criminal behavior or status offenses, such as contract rights, employment, medical care, and education. The volumes drafted under the aegis of Committee I are:

*Abuse and Neglect, Juvenile Delinquency and Sanctions, Noncriminal Misbehavior, Police Handling of Juvenile Problems, Rights of Minors, Schools and Education, Youth Service Agencies.*

Drafting Committee II, Court Roles and Procedures, prescribed standards for the organization and operation of the family court. Drawing on the experience and knowledge of those practicing in juvenile and family courts, the committee formulated an entirely new family court, with a new structure and new duties for the prosecutors, public juvenile defenders and private counsel, probation workers, and judges. Procedures and limitations concerning the various stages of the court process also include transfer from family court to criminal court and appeals or collateral review of family court decisions. The volumes submitted to the Commission by Committee II are:

*Adjudication, Appeals and Collateral Review, Counsel for Private Parties, Court Organization and Administration, The Juvenile Probation Function: Intake and Predisposition Investigative Services, Pretrial Court Proceedings, Prosecution, Transfer Between Courts.*

Drafting Committee III was labeled Treatment and Corrections, but "treatment" rarely is mentioned in the standards. Concerned principally with the facilities and programs in which juveniles are placed before, during, and after adjudication and disposition, "Services and Sanctions" would seem a more appropriate title. Standards for detention and correctional institutions, their structure, administration, available services, grievance, disciplinary, and modification procedures are provided, as well as detailed guidelines for dispositional choices following delinquency adjudications. The volumes released by Committee III are as follows:

*Architecture of Facilities, Correctional Administration, Dispositional Procedures, Dispositions, Interim Status: The Release, Control, and Detention of Accused Juvenile Offenders Between Arrest and Disposition.*

Drafting Committee IV, Administration, attempts to pull together the various component parts of the juvenile justice system to devise methods for coordinating its activities and resources in a rational and responsible manner. Standards governing juvenile court and agency records and information practices, planning juvenile justice programs, and monitoring their operation were adopted by this committee. The volumes issued by Committee IV are:

*Juvenile Records and Information Systems, Monitoring, Planning for Juvenile Justice.*

In addition to the volumes in the series on juvenile justice standards, the project also has sponsored the publication of several monographs, pamphlets, and studies. Special volumes on migrant children, sex discrimination, race discrimination, and Indian children, focusing on the effect of minority status on juvenile issues, were commissioned by the project.

There can be no doubt that it has been an ambitious project, striving to deal responsibly and judiciously with the widest possible range of issues pertaining to juveniles' rights and duties in our society. Difficult problems have not been avoided, nor have novel approaches been ignored. Research, experimentation, study, discussion, drafting, and redrafting have produced a massive and bold formulation for a reformed juvenile justice system. The intricate details of the system can only be comprehended through a careful reading of the volumes themselves. In this summary volume we can try to suggest the outlines.

## 2.4 Basic Principles.

The titles of the four drafting committees indicate the major concerns of the project. But such divisions are necessarily artificial and arbitrary in a project of this magnitude. Clearly, intervention in the lives of children is the subject of all the volumes, just as consideration of court roles and procedures, treatment and corrections, and administration affects the choices made in adopting positions throughout all the standards. A reading of the volumes discloses a pattern of preferences that might be described as a philosophy or at least a consistent point of view underlying the proposed juvenile justice system. In Parts IV, V, VI, and VII, the standards will be traced among the volumes and distinctions will be clarified. Here the object is to begin to specify the fundamental positions adopted by the Commission.

In December 1975, the staff prepared an Information Packet to distribute to ABA section representatives in preparation for a discussion prior to the January 1976 Commission meeting. The packet consisted of a background paper on the juvenile justice system and the standards approved as of that date, an information paper with cross-volume references concerning the principal positions adopted, and summaries of each of the thirteen volumes approved prior to the January 1976 Commission meeting. The thirteen volumes covered by the papers were: *Juvenile Delinquency and Sanctions, Noncriminal Misbehavior, Youth Service Agencies, Appeals and Collateral Review, Adjudication, Counsel for Private Parties, Court Organization and Administration, Pretrial Court Proceedings, Prosecution, Transfer Between Courts, Dispositional Procedures, Dispositions,* and *Interim Status: The Release, Control, and Detention of Accused Juvenile Offenders Between Arrest and Disposition.*

Ten underlying principles were capsulized in the background papers as follows:

1. Proportionality in sanctions for juvenile offenders based on the seriousness of the offense committed, and not merely the court's view of the juvenile's needs, should replace vague and subjective criteria.

2. Sentences or dispositions should be determinate. The practice of indeterminate sentencing, allowing correctional authorities to act

arbitrarily to release or confine juveniles as the convenience of their programs dictates, should be abolished. Such sentences permit wide disparity in the punishment received for the same misconduct and create a potential for abuse that the public is helpless to prevent.

3. The least restrictive alternative should be the choice of decision makers for intervention in the lives of juveniles and their families. If a decision maker, such as a judge or an intake officer, imposes a restrictive disposition, he or she must state in writing the reasons for finding less drastic remedies inappropriate or inadequate to further the purposes of the juvenile justice system.

4. Noncriminal misbehavior (status offenses, PINS) and private offenses (victimless crimes)* should be removed from juvenile court jurisdiction. Possession of narcotic drugs, however, has been retained as a basis for court jurisdiction. Juvenile court intervention in these areas has proven ineffective, if not socially harmful, damaging a significant number of children and frequently turning unruly juveniles into criminals. Voluntary community services to deal with these problems, such as crisis intervention programs, mediation for parent-child disputes, and alternative residences or "crash-pads" for runaways, are proposed as more suitable responses to noncriminal misconduct. School disciplinary proceedings, alternate programs, peer counseling, and other remedies within the educational system are suggested for truants. Neglect or abuse petitions would be filed where children are found living in dangerous conditions.

5. Visibility and accountability of decision making should replace closed proceedings and unrestrained official discretion.

6. There should be a right to counsel for all affected interests at all crucial stages of the proceedings.

7. Juveniles should have the right to decide on actions affecting their lives and freedom, unless they are found incapable of making reasoned decisions.

8. The role of parents in juvenile proceedings should be redefined with particular attention to possible conflicts between the interests of parent and child.

9. Limitations should be imposed on detention, treatment, or other intervention prior to adjudication and disposition.

10. Strict criteria should be established for waiver of juvenile court jurisdiction to regulate transfer of juveniles to adult criminal court.

*Decriminalization of victimless crimes, although consistent with the concepts underlying the standards, should be deleted from the ten principles because the revised *Juvenile Delinquency and Sanctions* standards no longer include it, on the ground that the states' penal codes must define crimes for the delinquency jurisdiction.

The first four underlying principles might be seen as part of a logical sequence of positions with respect to dispositions—the sanction can be no more severe than the seriousness of the offense merits (proportionality); it must be imposed with specificity and certainty by the judge at the dispositional hearing and not be modified without a subsequent judicial hearing (determinate sentences); it must be the least intrusive disposition appropriate to the case (least restrictive alternative); and the court can prescribe no disposition for juveniles accused of misconduct not punishable for adults (removal of court jurisdiction over status offenses).

The unarticulated but fundamental premise of all of these principles relating to dispositions is genuinely shattering with regard to the function of juvenile court—that the prescribing of treatment or services by the court is not inherently beneficial to the juvenile or other respondent and should be restrained. Heretofore the court's intervention was assumed to be in the best interests of the child, designed to help the child to overcome difficulties in conforming to society's expectations because of his or her deficient home environment or psychological problems. Interviews, social investigations, and testing were expected to identify the cause of the problem with scientific precision and the court would attempt to remove the symptoms by placing the child in a program or setting selected to cure the problem that caused the unacceptable behavior, i.e., to rehabilitate the juvenile offender. Therefore, the major decision of the project was to reject the medical or rehabilitative model of the juvenile court.

The second cluster of principles violates another sacred concept of juvenile court—that secrecy, closed proceedings, and non-adversarial informal proceedings advance the child's interest by (1) protecting privacy and (2) creating an unthreatening, relaxed atmosphere in which the court officers can develop a relationship of trust and confidence, and become acquainted with the child and his or her background in order to choose a disposition suited to the child's needs. The project supports the principle of confidentiality of records and has adopted rigorous standards to limit access to juvenile records and information systems. However, closed hearings and unregulated procedures have resulted in arbitrary decision making and unjustifiable disparity in outcomes. Cultural biases, discrimination because of race or sex, subjective attitudes, and excessive moral or religious zeal frequently influenced decisions that fell within the wide range of official discretion. The Commission adopted the view that the best way to protect juveniles was to ensure fair proceedings through procedural safeguards, representation by counsel, fixed criteria to guide official action, written decisions subject to judicial review, and full participation by juveniles in consultations with counsel and their parents if the parents' interests are not adverse to the juveniles'. By thus holding court officers accountable for their actions, the standards did not eliminate discretion, but merely subjected it to responsible scrutiny.

Dedication to the presumption of innocence and preference for the dispositional choices available in juvenile court after adjudication are the foundation of the last two apparently unrelated principles restricting both predispositional intervention and transfer to adult courts. The Commission strongly supported juvenile court handling for serious or habitual juvenile offenders, considering it the responsibility of the system to devise appropriate and effective dispositions for all such juveniles. Therefore, it chose to impose rigid restraints on removal of juveniles to criminal courts. The Commission also was concerned that no inferences be drawn from the fact that the court had transferred a juvenile. As a minimal protection, the standards require a probable cause hearing prior to transfer. In any case, treatment, unnecessary or extended detention, or other interference in the lives of juveniles is rigidly proscribed by the standards prior to a judicial finding that the juvenile committed the delinquent acts alleged and a full dispositional hearing to select the program or other disposition most suitable, after consideration of the offense committed, the age of the juvenile, culpability, and other relevant factors.

Subsequent to the formulation of the ten principles enumerated in the background paper, the Commission approved ten more volumes of standards and commentary at its final meetings in January and May 1976. These volumes were less directly focused on juvenile offenses and court procedures, extending the project's scope to consideration of such diverse matters as education, planning, monitoring, police, probation, corrections administration, abuse and neglect, architecture of facilities, rights of minors, and records and information. With certain obvious adjustments for the new agencies, institutions, and areas of the law affected by the additional volumes, the ten principles enunciated are essentially the basis for the last ten standards volumes too.

For example, the *Schools and Education* volume calls for nonjudicial handling of student disciplinary problems. But principles of proportionality, least restrictive alternative, open hearings with procedural safeguards, and written decisions setting forth reasons for the rulings, determinate dispositions ("sanctions"), full participation by the juvenile, recognition of possible conflicts with parental interests, and limited intervention prior to a final determination of the matter can be seen as the foundation of the standards for the prescribed school administrative disciplinary proceedings. Standards for grievance and disciplinary proceedings in the *Corrections Administration* volume also closely follow these principles.

Similarly, standards governing police intervention and the exercise of discretion in pre-court police practices for juveniles accused or suspected of misconduct or in situations of suspected neglect or abuse reflect the same points of view held by the Commission in adopting the standards in the *Police Handling of Juvenile Problems* volume.

Restraints on the exercise of discretion are especially significant in *The Juvenile Probation Function: Predisposition, Intake, and Investigative Services* volume, where criteria are specified in precise detail as guidelines for decisions by intake workers.

Every volume breaks new ground in some areas. The principle of family autonomy is essential to the *Rights of Minors* volume, providing that intra-familial matters should not be grounds for judicial or other state intervention except in specific instances where the juvenile's interests are not adequately protected without court involvement, such as the right to sue for support.

The *Abuse and Neglect* volume also adopts family autonomy as a standard and strictly limits official intervention in families to cases of specific harm, requiring a clear showing that a child is or may be endangered before coercive action is authorized.

Finally, the volumes on planning and monitoring the juvenile justice system, on architecture of facilities, and on juvenile records and information systems concern themselves with setting up mechanisms and specific criteria to ensure the effective functioning of the system within the guidelines required by the underlying principles set forth above. The records and information standards maintain a fine balance between preserving confidentiality, by limiting access to records to persons or agencies with legitimate interests, and imposing sanctions for improper use, and making necessary data available for research, evaluation, and public accountability. Standards for preservation of records and for sealing or expunging information are established.

The standards are remarkably consistent throughout the twenty-three volumes, with precise definitions, explicit procedures, freshly conceived roles for the participants, specific criteria for decisions, a calibrated scale of maximum sanctions according to the seriousness of offenses as codified in each state's penal laws, clarification of dispositional goals and encouragement of innovation in programming, specifications for the size, type, and location of facilities clearly articulated, balancing of the rights and obligations of juveniles, their families, and the community, and detailed descriptions of every significant feature of the juvenile justice system proposed.

After tracing the historical background and evolution of the juvenile justice system, this summary volume will attempt to delineate the broad outlines and essential features of each of the volumes as they were planned, drafted, revised, reviewed, and approved in final form by the JJSP staff, reporters, drafting committees, the IJA-ABA Joint Commission on Juvenile Justice Standards, and the ABA House of Delegates. The rare instances of conflict within the standards will be identified and discussed, if not resolved.

The changes adopted by the executive committee of the Joint Commission in response to the comments received from the ABA sections and divisions and other concerned groups will be discussed in the analysis of specific standards in Parts IV through VII of this volume. They also appear in detail in the Appendix.

# PART III: THE HISTORICAL DEVELOPMENT OF THE JUVENILE JUSTICE SYSTEM

## 3.1 Significant Events.

The development of the current juvenile justice system, often heralded as a courageous and innovative reform movement, is permeated with confused concepts, grandiose goals, and unrealized dreams. The system has failed in many ways. Yet it really is wonderful in many ways, too—a social institution that cares, a separate court to deal exclusively with juvenile and family problems, a blending of public and voluntary programs, a body of law focused on the best interests of the child, and a correctional authority organized for the rehabilitation of offenders. The system's inability to achieve its noble ideals can be understood best by examining its history.

The most significant fact about the history of juvenile justice is that it evolved simultaneously with the child welfare system. Most of its defects and its virtues derive from that fact.

Prior to the nineteenth century, children who committed crimes were handled by the same institutions as adults. Children under seven were considered incapable of possessing criminal intent and therefore were deemed not responsible for criminal acts. For children between the ages of seven and fourteen, the presumption was rebuttable. Otherwise, juveniles were tried by criminal courts and confined in adult jails and prisons. Children who were inadequately cared for by their families were assisted with relative informality by their local communities or churches as charity cases. Thus, poverty and crime were treated separately before the rise of a formal child welfare system. Describing the historical development of social welfare in Great Britain, Walter A. Friedlander states in *Introduction to Social Welfare:* "The *Poor Law of 1601* set the pattern of public relief.... It established the principle that the local community—the parish—had to organize and finance poor relief for its residents, provide sustenance to the unemployable and children, and work to the ablebodied." *Id.* at 18. Then, hailing the arrival of the British social security system and its national assistance programs, he writes: "Voluntary agencies are

**29**

now able to concentrate on their real task, on the difficult, intangible problems of bringing aid to human beings in need of understanding and encouragement, and, especially, on the prevention of juvenile delinquency." *Id.* at 58.

That blending of the welfare function with a sense of social responsibility to intervene in the lives of poor families to prevent delinquency, categorizing victims of deprivation as incipient predators, expresses succinctly the prevailing fallacy governing the juvenile justice system today. Perhaps if the behavioral sciences had fulfilled their expectations by providing the capability of reliably identifying predelinquents and devising effective methods for rehabilitating them, the issue of justifiable coercive intervention might have taken another form. The proven failure of science to do either eliminates the possibility of any such justification.

According to Sanford J. Fox's construction of juvenile justice reform in "Juvenile Justice Reform: An Historical Perspective," 22 *Stan. L. Rev.* 1187 (1970), three events have received the accolade of a "major reform in the means of dealing with juvenile deviants." They are the opening of the New York House of Refuge in 1825, the establishment of the Illinois juvenile court in 1899, and *In re Gault* in 1967. Fox's "historical perspective" of the events has been described as revisionist, which also is reflected in his 1972 casebook, *Cases and Materials on Modern Juvenile Justice.* Fox and the other revisionists rejected many of the altruistic interpretations of the accomplishments attributed to the nineteenth century reformers.

The innovative trend in the nineteenth century was to create "shelters" for dependent, neglected, or abandoned children. As child welfare became a more formal public concern, a moralistic "child saving" tone intruded. For example, a report by the Society for the Prevention of Pauperism in the City of New York in 1823 referred to parents as "too poor or too degenerate," whose children were "obliged to beg, and even encouraged to acts of dishonesty, to satisfy the wants induced by the indolence of their parents...." The report urged a "Christian community" to try to rescue these children from "sinking still deeper in corruption." The formula was clear: poverty and indolence yield corruption and delinquency. Or is it vice versa?

In either case, the next step for society was clear and it followed in 1825 when the New York House of Refuge was established under a charter granted to the Society for the Reformation of Juvenile Delinquents, the successor to the organization that issued the 1823 report on pauperism. It authorized the admission of "children as shall be taken up or committed as vagrants, or convicted of criminal offenses...as may...be proper objects." According to Fox, the "emphasis on minor offenses, belief in the innocence of the children despite their wrongs and summary commitment procedures were all central features of the predelinquency campaign." *Id.* at 18.

The *parens patriae* concept to support confinement in a House of Refuge was cited by a Pennsylvania court in *Ex parte Crouse,* 4 Whart. 9 (Pa. 1838). In that case, the statute authorized the House to admit children whose parents had shown them to be "incorrigible." The juvenile's mother had brought the charge and her father sought her release on a writ of habeas corpus on the grounds that the juvenile had been denied a trial by jury. As cited by Fox, the court held as follows:

> The object of the charity is reformation, by training its inhabitants to industry; by imbuing their minds with principles of morality and religion; by furnishing them with means to earn a living; and above all, by separating them from the corrupting influence of improper associates. To this end, may not the natural parents, when unequal to the task of education, or unworthy of it, be superseded by the parens patriae, or common guardian of the community? *Id.* at 27.

Fox calls the *Crouse* case the leading authority for the state's right "to make coercive predictions about deviant children."

The next major event was the passage of the Illinois Juvenile Court Act in 1899. Leading commentators attach different meanings to the Act but its importance is undisputed. In an excellent article delineating some of the more extreme criticisms of the Illinois Act presented by Fox and by Anthony M. Platt in his 1969 study, *The Child Savers: The Invention of Delinquency,* Larry Schultz (original codirector of the Juvenile Justice Standards Project) redresses the revisionist imbalance in "The Cycle of Juvenile Court History," 19 *Crime & Delinq.* 457 (1973).

It may be impossible to discuss the first juvenile court act without the intrusion of personal value judgments upon objective analysis, and this presentation is probably no exception. The Illinois Juvenile Court Act can be said to have made the following contributions to the development of the juvenile justice system:

1. It established a separate court for cases involving juveniles under sixteen alleged to be delinquent, dependent, or neglected.

2. It defined a delinquent as a child under sixteen "who violates any law of this state or any city or village ordinance."

3. It introduced special procedures governing the hearing and disposition of juveniles' cases.

4. It required separation of children from adults when placed in the same institution.

5. It barred detention of a child under twelve in a jail or police station.

6. It provided for probation officers to investigate cases, represent the child's interest, or supervise children on probation.

7. Its purpose clause directed that "the care, custody, and discipline of a child shall approximate as nearly as may be that which should be given by its parents, and in all cases where it can properly be done the child be placed in an improved family home and become a member of the family by legal adoption or otherwise."

Some of the controversy over the significance of the Act was related to whether its provisions actually were innovations. The probation concept had been adopted from Massachusetts and the new procedures and preferences for home-like treatment were part of the prevailing social welfare thrust in juvenile penology, as manifested in the House of Refuge provisions and increased emphasis on foster home placements. Fox and Platt claimed the Act was conservative, not progressive, pointing to the religious, middle class biases inherent in the provision requiring placement with custodians (persons or institutions) who had the same religious beliefs as the child's parents, thus ensuring continued public subsidizing of private sectarian agencies. They also criticized its reliance on coercive predictions for crime prevention.

Three questions are implicit in this controversy: are the informal summary proceedings prescribed in the Act desirable; should middle class values be imposed coercively on errant lower class juveniles, or can voluntary programs be entrusted with delinquency prevention; and is rehabilitation through involuntary treatment programs achievable (if that is assumed to be the justification for the court's jurisdiction)?

Although not stressed in these analyses, it could be argued that the most reprehensible feature of the Illinois contribution to juvenile justice is the continued erosion of distinctions between juveniles who commit criminal acts, thereby demonstrating objectively that they are a present threat to community safety, and those who are themselves victims as abused, neglected, or dependent children.

Fox notwithstanding, there were a number of important events in the years between the Illinois Act and *Gault*, especially the expanding jurisdiction of juvenile courts and the burgeoning network of states passing juvenile court legislation. In 1901, noncriminal misbehavior was added to the definition of delinquency in the Illinois Act. However, punishment for such misconduct was an ancient tradition, with examples recorded in colonial times.

By 1917, juvenile courts had been established in all but three states. The juvenile court was considered part of the total child welfare system, removing juveniles from the criminal law process and substituting a network of special programs for delinquent, dependent, and neglected children. These programs were supposed to solve problems through scientific methods, if appropriate after removing the children from their blighted urban homes and inadequate families. A professional class of modern criminologists, sociologists, and social workers began to emerge to deal with the phenomena of delinquency and predelinquency, in pursuit of the rehabilitative ideal. According to Platt, the emphasis was on studies of the socialization or treatment of delinquency and other deviant behavior, with the law seen as essentially irrelevant to those concerned about the causes and cures of delinquency.

The next major event took place in the revised New York Family Court Act in 1962, which not only combined its Children's Court and Girl's Term and other juvenile divisions in a single family court, but also created a new separate classification for noncriminal misconduct. The new label was PINS—Person in Need of Supervision. This label was supposed to be less stigmatizing than delinquent, which had been supposed to be less stigmatizing than criminal. It also was designed to represent an expectation that innovative treatment programs would be devised to meet the needs and circumstances of such children. Other states followed New York's example, rapidly adopting their own labels—CINS, CHINS, MINS, JINS. Some referred to them as "unruly minors." The misbehavior formerly included in the delinquency statutes in most states covered truancy, running away, disobedience, undesirable companions, staying out late, disruptiveness, sexual activity, and the catch-all, incorrigibility—all acts or conduct for which adults would not be punishable.

The two objectives of creating the special PINS category, sometimes known as status offenders—the elimination of the delinquency stigma and the development of appropriate dispositional choices for such children—were not effectuated. The PINS label, connoting court contact, became almost as troublesome to the affected juveniles. Child care specialists and corrections officials were eager to proclaim their enlightened view that all of the labels were meaningless. A 1973 report of the Council of Voluntary Child Care Agencies, representing over one hundred member agencies in New York, gave the results of a survey of its membership in which the overwhelming majority opinion was that children in foster care had the most severe behavior problems of any children in residential care, regardless of the original reason for their placement. Similarly, the New York State Division For Youth (DFY), responsible for administering all state juvenile correctional facilities, officially adopted the position that distinctions between the problems they found in PINS and delinquent DFY residents were insignificant and did not necessitate separate programs. As first adopted, the New York Family Court Act provision on dispositions excluded placement of PINS in a training school. Within a year, the law was amended to authorize such placement.

Currently, the trend, as mandated by the Juvenile Justice and Delinquency Prevention Act of 1974, is to bar confinement in secure facilities for juveniles charged with noncriminal misbehavior. But juvenile correctional authorities and other rehabilitation specialists have yet to demonstrate the ability to deal effectively with traditional adolescent behavior problems in coercive treatment programs, whether in a secure or a nonsecure facility. Their few successes are more than balanced by the regularity with which juveniles removed involuntarily from their homes to court-ordered placements reinforce the antisocial label affixed to them by society.

A more significant development in the law is indicated by the decisions of several states (e.g., Maine and Washington) to remove status offenses from court jurisdiction. Equally significant, but less promising, is the shift to harsher dispositions in other jurisdictions, including New York, Colorado, and Washington, D.C.

Perhaps it is not surprising that after many years of relying on the informal procedures and rehabilitative goals of the juvenile court, there was a reaction against the patent failure of the system to protect society or to help the children subject to its jurisdiction. It also was becoming impossible to ignore the fact that the broad discretionary powers the court officials had been granted were resulting in flagrant discrimination against girls in some cases, boys in others, racial and ethnic minorities, and poor families. Selective interventions screened out white, middle- and upper-class delinquents, who were returned to their home environments, with prescriptions for private treatment, regardless of the seriousness of the crimes. In most localities the juvenile court had become the place to prevent or punish crime from the ghetto as severely as possible and to enforce standards of social morality as informally as possible, with the juvenile court judges and probation workers charged with the duty to make these subtle, sometimes unfathomable, distinctions.

In 1966 and 1967, three events dramatized a growing concern about juvenile justice: the decision in *Kent v. United States*, 383 U.S. 541 (1966), requiring procedural regularity for a valid transfer from juvenile to adult court; the *Task Force Report: Juvenile Delinquency and Youth Crime* issued by the President's Commission on Law Enforcement and Administration of Justice in 1967, expressing grave doubts about many of the premises of the system, its effectiveness and its lack of procedural safeguards, favoring voluntary services, and skeptical about the validity of the status offense category; and *In re*

*Gault,* 387 U.S. 1 (1967), which held that juveniles accused of crimes are entitled to due process of law in the adjudicatory stage of the proceedings.

The *Gault* case required such minimal protection at the fact-finding hearing as notice of charges, right to counsel, confrontation and cross-examination of witnesses, and the privilege against self-incrimination. Subsequent Supreme Court decisions have expanded those rights in some cases and contracted them in others. *In re Winship,* 397 U.S. 385 (1970), compelled proof beyond a reasonable doubt for juveniles charged with criminal offenses in a juvenile proceeding, but *McKeiver v. Pennsylvania,* 403 U.S. 528 (1971), rejected a plea for trial by jury.

The members of the Court have published many memorable statements about juvenile justice. In *Kent,* Mr. Justice Fortas noted that the juvenile appeared to be receiving the worst of both worlds: "...he gets neither the protections accorded to adults nor the solicitous care and regenerative treatment postulated for children." 383 U.S. at 556. In *Gault,* he stated: "Due process of law is the primary and indispensable foundation of individual freedom. It is the basic and essential term in the social compact which defines the rights of the individual and delimits the powers which the State may exercise." 387 U.S. at 20.

But in *McKeiver,* Mr. Justice Blackmun spoke approvingly of "every aspect of fairness, of concern, of sympathy, and of paternal attention that the juvenile court system contemplates." 403 U.S. at 550. He considered those traits in juvenile court officials an adequate substitute for a jury trial, suggesting that there would be "little need" for a separate juvenile court if all the formalities of criminal trials were required.

The net result is total confusion as to the rationale for the unique character of juvenile court, compounded by frequent references to lack of resources and other transient imperfections as the basis for "disillusionment" with the court, rather than the court's denial of inherent rights. The social compact theory of juvenile courts—that juveniles have traded off some of the formalities of due process for the benevolent purposes of the juvenile court—is distinguished from criminal justice and the malevolent punitive goals of adult court.

If the "due process" line of cases has failed to clarify the juvenile justice concept, the "right to treatment" line of cases may cause a total breakdown. Demanding that the courts, executive branch, and legislatures fulfill the noble promises of the juvenile court acts, the parties asserting a right to treatment argue that if the institutions and programs in which juveniles are placed do not provide appropriate treatment for the purposes for which the dispositions were rendered, the juveniles are being deprived of their constitutional rights under the fourteenth amendment. Courts in such cases as *Morales v. Turman,* 535 F.2d 864 (5th Cir. 1976), 383 F. Supp. 53 (E.D. Tex. 1973), and *Martarella v. Kelley,* 349 F. Supp. 575 (S.D.N.Y. 1972), have attempted to specify the minimum conditions the institutions must meet to qualify as proper environments in which to detain or confine a juvenile for treatment.

These cases have served admirably to challenge the practices and policies of the juvenile custodial authorities in maintaining inadequate and inhumane facilities under the guise of administering rehabilitative treatment programs. The cases rely also on eighth amendment arguments against cruel and unusual punishment in accusing the institutions of failing to provide confined juveniles with reasonable opportunities for normal growth and development. They have resulted in improved conditions in correctional facilities and in heightened awareness of the issues created by the incarceration of juveniles.

But the problem presented by the right to treatment line of cases is that it requires an implied concession that coerced treatment is a legitimate societal intervention in response to juvenile offenses; a tacit acceptance of the premise that causes of juvenile misbehavior or criminality can be diagnosed and treated; and acquiescence in the theory that such treatment for a juvenile offense will prevent future criminal behavior. The most critical issue raised by right to treatment is whether a court or a system of justice is the proper locus for diagnosing and treating behavior problems. The question that has not been resolved in juvenile law is whether a court is capable of providing more than a forum for a fair hearing of the facts, a fair adjudication of innocence or guilt, and a fair penalty for the transgression of society's rules of acceptable behavior.

An approach that may prove more fruitful than right to treatment theories is the argument that the doctrine of least restrictive alternative requires not only the examination of existing facilities, but the duty to provide alternative facilities. In *Pennhurst v. Halderman,* 49 U.S.L.W. 4363 (April 20, 1981), *rev'g* 612 F.2d 84 (3d Cir. 1979) the United States Supreme Court ruled that the "bill of rights for the retarded" in the Developmental Disabilities Act of 1975 did not impose a statutory obligation on the states to provide appropriate facilities. Nevertheless, in *Youngberg v. Romeo,* No. 80-1429, *cert. granted* 49 U.S.L.W. 3851 (May 19, 1981), the Court has agreed to consider the constitutional rights of patients in institutions to the least intrusive treatment available in another case involving the Pennhurst State School in Pennsylvania.

Similarly, in *Parham v. J.R.*, 442 U.S. 584 (1979), the Court allowed the commitment of juveniles to mental hospitals by their parents or the state and held that a nonadversarial independent professional review satisfied due process requirements. However, the Court appeared to apply the doctrine of less drastic means to commitment proceedings by relying heavily on the fact that the state first attempted to treat the children in the community prior to the hospital referral. By extension to all involuntary placements of juveniles, a declaration by the Supreme Court that there is a constitutional right to the least restrictive alternative necessary to achieve the purpose intended could be a most advantageous development for juveniles.

Thus we have traced the significant events that have culminated in the current juvenile justice system and suggested some of the issues they have raised. It is important to see an event whole in its context to appreciate its impact. For example, if Gerald Gault had not been the victim of so flagrant an imbalance in the disposition to which he was liable as compared to an adult, would the same decision have been reached? Gault was committed to an institution for a maximum six-year term for an offense (making a lewd or indecent telephone call) for which an adult could have been punished by a fine of $5 to $50 or imprisonment for not more than two months. If the potential penalties for adults and juveniles had been more nearly comparable in the case, one wonders whether the court would have been moved to challenge the cherished myth of a benign, paternalistic, nonadversary proceeding designed to bring help to troubled children. And if the decision had not followed the President's Task Force Report, and if juvenile crime and recidivism rates were not so high. . . .

History, community biases and ideals, scientific advances, technological changes, and the other factors that influence the evolution of social institutions have shaped the juvenile justice system. A closer look at the issues and the system as it functions today will complete the background information provided as a preparation for our examination of the standards adopted by the IJA-ABA Joint Commission.

### 3.2 The Emerging Issues.

The issues arising from the way in which the juvenile justice system developed historically were touched on lightly but by no means inclusively in the preceding section. However, isolating the issues into tidy classifications is difficult because they have a way of dissolving into each other. Most striking is how little the issues have changed, in fact, how little progress has been made since the first juvenile court act in 1899. The standards are long overdue.

Although chronology will be observed if it can be done without torturing the concepts involved, the organizing framework to be followed here will approximate the drafting committee headings under which the standards were prepared: intervention in the lives of children, court roles and procedures, treatment and corrections, and administration. The characteristics of the juvenile justice system— confusion in concepts and roles, euphemistic blurring of purposes, abuses of discretion, lack of accountability, ineffectiveness in programs and personnel—as well as the admirable features worth preserving might become apparent under any rubric. But for convenience and symmetry, we will follow the structure of the project in classifying the issues.

### 3.3 Issues in Coercive Intervention.

### 3.3.1 Equation of poverty and predelinquency.

The unfortunate historical fact is that the juvenile justice system, developed in tandem with the child welfare system, began with the right observation and the wrong conclusion. Manifestly, poor people are more likely to beg, steal, and commit certain other crimes related to their social and economic status than affluent people. Although socially unacceptable, crime could be seen as a response to poverty. It was a way to get money. The preferred solutions—jobs, vocational training, financial assistance for the unemployable—required a constructive community attitude toward the disadvantaged. But a combination of Calvinism, prejudice, and social Darwinism confused cause and effect—idleness, inferiority, and criminality were seen as causing poverty, rather than the reverse. Therefore progressive elements in the community, the social reformers, felt justified in saving impoverished children from the inexorable path of crime by investigating their homes and families, attempting to imbue them with principles of Christian morality, and, if unsuccessful, removing them to a better environment.

Cultural, ethnic, economic, and class bias combined to blind the zealous ladies bountiful and their male counterparts to the injustice of their cause. They convinced themselves that they were helping the children by putting them in shelters and foster homes. Of course, that was pre-Freud, and now we understand the motivation for such "good works," or one would have thought so if not exposed to the literature of the 1981 child savers—juvenile court judges, social workers, legislators, child care agencies, etc. They still, like their nineteenth-century forebears, espouse the view that today's neglected and abused children are tomorrow's criminals and therefore should be placed in shelters and foster homes, after child protective service agencies have investigated their families and "provided services"; that status offenders often have more serious behavior problems than delinquents and therefore should be kept in "treatment programs" for longer periods of time than delinquents, until they are cured of their status offenses by becoming adults.

Therefore, many issues have emerged from the equation of poverty and predelinquency:

1. jurisdiction based on status alone;
2. jurisdiction based on age alone;
3. indiscriminate removal from home;
4. institutionalization for social protection masked as "best interests of the child";
5. discriminatory selective enforcement;
6. indeterminate sentences disproportionate to objective factors;
7. "treatment" unrelated to any diagnosed illness, arising from the therapeutic model of the juvenile justice system;
8. intrusive investigations of families.

Demonstrably, the mental set of the society that established a House of Refuge in 1825 and other shelters for dependent, neglected, and "mildly delinquent" but salvageable juveniles is not so different from the attitude of the juvenile justice establishment today.

### 3.3.2 Parents with adverse interests.

Traditionally, parents are the protectors and custodians of their children, a relationship that gives them virtual control over the children's personal and property rights. Consent, waiver, voluntary placements in foster care, voluntary commitment to institutions, transfer of property—the volition comes from the parents and obedient acquiescence from the children, or they become "children in trouble." But the assumption on which the parent's power is premised is a relationship of natural love and concern. Mutuality of interests and the children's presumed incapacity to protect themselves provide the grounds for the parents to act on their children's behalf.

That identity of interest usually is not questioned. Yet we saw in the *Crouse* case that the child's mother was the active party in placing her in the Philadelphia House of Refuge. Nor should adversity of interests be presumed. It was the child's father who sought the writ of habeas corpus to get his daugher released. In a juvenile justice system, the fairest approach would seem to be to give parents every opportunity to protect their children's legitimate interests, in the absence of a clear showing of antagonism. But if conflict is proved, the parents should lose their power to act on behalf of their children. Yet the law has not progressed that far. The issue in *Bartley v. Kremens*, U.S. app. pndg., 423 U.S. 1028 (1976), 426 U.S. 945 (1977), 402 F. Supp. 1039 (E.D. Pa. 1975), *vacated as moot* 431 U.S. 119 (1977), was whether a juvenile committed to a mental institution by his or her parents could be admitted under voluntary procedures, regardless of the juvenile's denial of consent. *Crouse* was in 1838, *Bartley v. Kremens* in 1977. We had not come a very long way in one hundred thirty-nine years. Two years later, in *Parham v. J.R.*, 442 U.S. 584, the Court slid back a few notches by holding that such "voluntary" commitments satisfied due process without an adversary proceeding, right to counsel, or other safeguards, except an independent medical evaluation of the child's need for confinement.

### 3.4 Issues in a Separate Juvenile Court: Roles and Procedures.

#### 3.4.1 Preservation and reform of the court.

Despite all the defects found by its critics and the overstatement of accomplishments claimed by its champions, the Illinois Juvenile Court Act of 1899 stands as a magnificent achievement. It revolutionized the judicial system by establishing a court that removed children from the cruel and punitive atmosphere of criminal court. It barred detention of juveniles in adult jails and required that they be separated from adults if unavoidably confined in the same institutions. It was premised upon the fact that children are different from adults and must be treated differently: "that the care, custody, and discipline of a child shall approximate as nearly as may be that which should be given by its parents...." Toward that end, it authorized probation services to investigate, represent, and supervise children and placements in foster homes, private agencies, or institutions designed for children. Even more incredible, the concept spread, so that separate juvenile courts replaced criminal court for children within less than thirty years.

The establishment of the juvenile court stands as a momentous event. Today, the court and the system of which it is the centerpiece need to be refurbished, rearranged, reformed. They need a new structure, new concepts, new definitions, new procedures. The court's jurisdiction must be expanded in some ways, reduced in others. Self-righteousness and omnipotence must be replaced by fairness, openness, and an admission of fallibility. The juvenile court is unique; it also must be just. The task of the project is to propose standards to make it possible for the court to do effectively what it is rightfully charged to do.

The seeds of future problems were planted in the first Act. Informal procedures and summary trials can produce a Star Chamber. Judges who are playing the stern father and probation workers who both investigate and represent children have tough, potentially contradictory roles to play. Without more precise guidelines, total discretion can lead to autocratic and arbitrary decisions. The provision of the Illinois Act requiring sectarian placement not only created an imbalance in available resources in favor of some religions, but subsidized private voluntary agencies to the detriment of public programs.

The principal defect was not created by the court, but it was perpetuated in the blurring of distinctions between the responsibility of the court to dependent and neglected children and the duty owed society by delinquent children. There is nothing incompatible about a court serving both the best interests of the child and the protection of society if the court pursues those objectives appropriately. The problem was exacerbated by amendments expanding the definition of delinquency to noncriminal misbehavior. The broad sweep of some of the language ("growing up in idleness") and the vagueness of the rest ("incorrigibility") could bring any child within the court's jurisdiction.

### 3.4.2 The participants' roles.

There are several problems that have arisen concerning the roles of participants in the juvenile justice system, which were inevitable results of the way in which the system evolved. Consider those involved: police, judges, probation workers, juveniles, parents, counsel, social agencies, correctional authorities, schools, doctors, mental health agencies, other service providers. The list is open-ended. So the first, most obvious problem is that too many people and organizations are involved and no one is coordinating their activities. Resource allocation, delivery of services, identification of needs, avoidance of gaps and overlapping services, encouragement of responsible experimentation, performance evaluation—all of the essential aspects of planning and monitoring a complex system are in disarray. This subject will be discussed more fully in the section on administration, but it is an important facet of the overall inability of the participants to achieve a clear understanding of their respective roles. The absence of a supervisory authority over the parts of the system has contributed to its inefficiency, waste, and impotence and to the participants' confusion about their duties.

Second, the presumed incapacity of the central figures in the system—the juveniles—to make decisions for themselves introduces a second party, the parents, to act on their behalf. Two dilemmas immediately arise: (1) if juveniles are held responsible for their actions and behavior, why are they not presumed capable of making choices; and (2) if the juvenile's presence in court is considered at least partly the result of parental inadequacy, why is the parent considered a qualified spokesperson for the juvenile's interests? The contradictions could be posed in many other ways. For example, what is the parent's role with respect to consents and waivers when the parent is the petitioner, the respondent, or the state's witness? On the other hand, from the juveniles' point of view, how effective can proceedings in which they have been passive observers, denied a true participant's role, be in gaining their respect, understanding, or cooperation?

The court has attempted to deal with some of these questions by adding two more to the cast of characters: a guardian *ad litem* and a public defender. But for a court that is supposedly in the business of treating adolescent problems it has been remarkably inept at identifying criteria for developmental stages and the levels of maturity at which a juvenile might be presumed competent—or as competent as an adult—to participate in the decisions that will affect his or her life and liberty without the protection of a parent or a guardian.

The roles of counsel in the juvenile courts are singularly muddy. The prosecutors, who are a recent addition to the system, are uncertain as to whether they are expected to aim for a conviction or for an outcome in the best interests of the child. The defense counsel usually is more single-minded in seeking release, acquittal, or the least restrictive disposition, preferably diversion to a community program or probation. The active participation of defense counsel at the dispositional stage contrasts with the customary absence of the prosecutor, whose role apparently is assumed by the probation worker, whose job is to recommend an appropriate dispositional choice to the judge. The probation workers, who regard themselves as the children's helpers or as impartial participants, resent the more openly adversarial role forced upon them by the unequivocally partisan recommendations of defense counsel.

The probation workers' role has been mired in conflict from its inception. It is incongruous to expect that the same worker or workers in the same probation department will be unaffected by their close relationship to the state in investigating a complaint. Even with the most constructive attitude toward the juveniles and their families, they are motivated by training and inclination to intervene. To a social worker, nonintervention is an abdication of professional duty. To a juvenile, in most cases, unconditional release is the preferred outcome.

Voluntary services are not under discussion here, since court-ordered service necessarily is coerced treatment.

Two other important actors in this drama are the police and the judge. Both have been granted almost unlimited discretion to retain, divert, or release juveniles, but whereas the police have expressed a desire to be governed by guidelines in their decisions, judges appear hostile to any restraint on their actions. It should be noted that the principle in the standards that all decisions affecting substantial rights be regulated by specific criteria, be in writing, be subject to judicial review, and include reasons for not adopting a less restrictive alternative, is objectionable to the National Council of Juvenile and Family Court Judges, as are the positions on proportionality and determinate sentences. All are construed as antithetical to the individualized justice that the National Council considers the foundation of the juvenile justice system. It also should be noted that although the police agree that guidelines are needed for their decisions on apprehension, release, diversion, and referral to court of juveniles, they want to be active participants in the development of the guidelines, a position in which the project concurs for the police and all other decision makers in the system.

Equally involved in the juvenile justice system, but structurally independent, are the agencies that provide the services and programs for juveniles referred by the court throughout the various stages of the process. The predictable balance of arguments between publicly and privately sponsored programs applies here. Private or voluntary programs are less constrained by civil service, budgetary, political, and other restrictions, are freer to experiment and develop innovative programs, have multiple sources of funding, and have the involvement of private citizens. On the other hand, the dispersal of public funds to private sources depletes the money available for public programs, avoids certain regulations designed to protect residents, users, or others, and sets up a screen between the public and its programs. Private or voluntary agencies are not subjected to equivalent scrutiny or personnel control and cannot be compelled to accept cases they find difficult, disruptive, unprofitable, or otherwise undesirable. Lack of public accountability for privately run programs is a common complaint. There also have been charges of religious and racial discrimination, as in *Wilder v. Sugarman,* 385 F. Supp. 1013 (S.D.N.Y. 1974) and *Wilder v. Bernstein,* 499 F. Supp. 980 (S.D.N.Y. 1980), in which minority juveniles charged over one hundred public and private agencies with bias in denying them the more desirable placements concentrated in voluntary sectarian agencies, relegating them to state facilities because there were insufficient openings for predominantly black Protestant children in need of residential care. In some jurisdictions, enormous sums of public money are spent for programs that fail to meet the most serious needs of the community and the juvenile justice system. Empty beds for young children and no vacancies for adolescents frequently can be seen, yet the public and the courts lament the inadequacy of resources to no avail. However, public programs also can be unresponsive, refusing to take a chance on placing youngsters in innovative or nonsecure facilities. The lack of rational coordination between the providers and consumers of services predominates in the public and private sectors. The quality of services often is superior in voluntary programs, but such services may not be available to the juveniles who need them the most.

Other agencies that consider themselves outside the system, such as schools, mental health departments, and hospitals are in fact essential parts of the system with mutual concerns that demand planning, periodic consultation, and cooperative efforts. The unwillingness of these agencies to work with the juvenile courts and child care agencies to help solve problems affecting all agencies that come into contact with children, to make their resources available, and to draw on the experience and skills of the specialists working with the courts has resulted in a fragmented and ineffective system, to the detriment of all.

The correctional authority administering the public institutional facilities, secure and nonsecure, is another part of the juvenile justice system that prefers to be autonomous. Issues connected with this participant in the juvenile justice system will be covered in section 3.5 on treatment and corrections.

### 3.4.3 Court procedures.

The informal procedures considered so integral a part of juvenile court were designed to facilitate a prompt, personalized response to juvenile and family problems. In practice the courts have become as backlogged and over-loaded as the most formal system. A lack of formality, when translated into insufficient rules and regulations, does not produce a smoothly running operation. A relaxed atmosphere needs time and a pleasant environment, neither of which can be found in family court. Instead, the result of informal procedures has been uncertainty of consequences because of the wide disparity in outcomes, abuse of discretion, discrimination, absence of accountability, and a general sense of manipulative behavior, hypocrisy, and unfairness. Further, there is a loss of dignity in having the privacy of the family invaded and made part of a social history containing data that may be in no way related to the subject of the proceedings nor to the potential disposition. And because the officials generally are middle class mainstream or assimilated citizens and the respondents are lower class members of minority groups and strangers to the system, there is a feeling of oppression in the waiting room of a juvenile court. There are no peers trying facts in juvenile court.

Much has been made of the due process revolution following *Kent* and *Gault* and it certainly has had an impact. There are more lawyers to protect juvenile and parental interests, more frequent appeals, and a bit more formality. But *Gault* only affected the adjudicatory stage and *Kent* only pertained to a narrow transfer statute. Procedural safeguards in a court empowered to act in the undefined best interests of children and simultaneously charged to protect society are not enough to eliminate inequitable results.

Procedures do keep hearings orderly. There is a better chance that everyone will be heard in a matter and that the facts will be evaluated fairly. But to what end? If a child can be charged with being unruly, how can a prosecutor fail to prove the case? What child is not unruly at some time? If a boy is found to have committed a serious felony and the investigator's report indicates that he is contrite, his home is clean, and his parents are concerned, what treatment is recommended? In other words, the confused concepts of juvenile justice and of official dispositions unrelated to the grounds for judicial intervention are not clarified or corrected by formal procedures. The outcome of particular conduct is still unpredictable. Individualized justice continues to reign and it is as singular, perverse, and ungovernable as the individual decision maker. Studies have shown that variations in dispositions at intake and after adjudication are determined as much by the identity of the official as by the facts of the case. The single most significant variable is the attitude or demeanor of the respondent. Discretionary justice, formal or informal, will be subjective, arbitrary, and capable of infinite rationalization in the absence of reasonable guidelines.

However, one should not denigrate the advantages of a fair factfinding, with a right to adequate notice of charges, representation by counsel, confrontation of witnesses, the privilege against selfincrimination (somewhat less than complete in a system that makes the respondent an accomplice in providing incriminating information for dispositions), and the state's burden of proof beyond a reasonable doubt. At least innocent parties should be protected—if there is a way to be innocent of incorrigibility when a mother or teacher says a child is incorrigible.

The general approach of the standards to court roles and procedures is to limit discretion; recommend guidelines for decisions at every stage of the proceeding; prescribe open procedures with full representation by counsel, nonwaivable for juveniles; require appointment of guardians *ad litem* for juveniles incapable of making customary client decisions with their counsel; acknowledge the adversary nature of delinquency, neglect, and abuse cases and provide for fair and balanced hearings with full participation of prosecution, defense, juveniles, and parents and disclosure to the affected parties of information considered by the court after adjudication; prohibit treatment or other intervention during interim status except for emergency care; and provide a right to appeal all final orders.

The structure of the court itself is spelled out in one volume of the standards, elevating its status to that of a division of the court of general trial jurisdiction, with rotation of judges among the divisions. Nonjudicial personnel are not permitted to perform judicial functions, although certain clearly defined proceedings are diverted to referees. Other standards in the court roles and procedures volumes will be discussed in the chapter covering the work of Drafting Committee II.

### 3.5 Issues in Treatment and Corrections.

Many of the issues concerning treatment and corrections have been mentioned previously because they are so closely related to the subject of intervention in the lives of juveniles. Treatment and corrections as discussed here are the product of juvenile court intervention. Treatment programs entered into voluntarily are covered in the *Youth Service Agencies* volume.

Aside from cases that are adjusted or dismissed, treatment or corrections is the dispositional choice for the court after adjudication. It could be argued that that statement is more theoretical than real. Treatment often is provided at the intake level if a worker helps a family resolve its problems without going on to court, or at the police level in some jurisdictions that attempt to bring services to a juvenile or family before pressing charges. Diversion is a hybrid of voluntary and involuntary predispositional treatment if the alternative is a court referral—as voluntary as a choice between "your money or your life," if not as drastic. Furthermore, detention frequently is indistinguishable from corrections, in duration, punitive aspects, and other conditions of confinement. Also, many jurisdictions administer treatment programs during the detention period, called "interim status" or predisposition in the standards.

The issues that arise concerning juvenile treatment and corrections are simply expressed but difficult to resolve. The first, most fundamental question is the proper function of the court's disposition: treatment, incapacitation, or punishment. The second question is the permissible range of dispositions in response to criminal or noncriminal misbehavior. The traditional juvenile court principles are that the needs of the individual child as determined by the court's observation, professional diagnosis of behavioral scientists, social histories, other relevant data, and the juvenile and family attitudes and ability to handle the problem through independent means are all evaluated to produce the appropriate disposition in the individual case. The judge has about twelve minutes to perform this miracle of wisdom on a slow day, assisted by the recommendation of the probation officer and frequently today by defense counsel. But even this swift exercise of the judgment of Solomon can be frustrated by the unavailability of the resource chosen. Juveniles spend many days and weeks in detention waiting for a placement to open up. The same "scientific" process applies to both delinquents and status offenders and in modified form, to neglected and abused children. The trend to prohibit placement in secure facilities for status offenders has produced anomalies. Runaways placed in nonsecure facilities run away. Having violated the court's dispositional order, they qualify as delinquents in many states. But a common result is that they are placed on probation rather than in a secure facility, which is puzzling to some logicians but conforms to the official view that children in need of supervision may require more treatment and care than delinquents.

Another issue is whether dispositions really should depend primarily on the court's perception of the child's needs. Needs and treatment are difficult to relate to criminal behavior. What illness is being treated and by what methods, even if antisocial behavior is deemed *per se* deviant?

But the worst effect of the current system is the juveniles' notion that if they are smart enough, they can manipulate the system and get away with anything. "Turnstile" or "revolving door" justice is the term used.

The standards opt for proportionality in sanctions, relating the *maximum* disposition in duration and severity to the seriousness of the crime. Noncriminal misbehavior would not subject a juvenile to any sanction. Objective factors, such as age, previous record, and culpability enter into the disposition, as do the juvenile's needs, in choosing among programs. Although juveniles under the standards generally cannot be compelled to accept treatment or services, the state has an affirmative duty to provide appropriate services needed for the normal growth and development of residents in corrections facilities.

The dispositional standard that is a companion to the concept of proportionality is determinacy, which would require the court to set a fixed term at the conclusion of the dispositional hearing in place of the prevailing practice of indeterminate dispositions. Indeterminate sentences permit the correctional agencies to discharge juveniles at their discretion. This practice has resulted in longer confinement periods for docile juveniles than for troublemakers. Release decisions are determined more by population flow in the facility and administrative convenience than the readiness of the juvenile for return to the community or the nature of the offense committed.

Correctional authorities are accustomed to exercising a great deal of discretion to preserve order and for the safety and security of the residents, staff, and surrounding community. Discipline and grievance mechanisms, if any, are principally within the control of the administrators. Home visit, release, discharge, and parole decisions also rest with the institution, although in some jurisdictions parole has been delegated to citizen boards. Even then, membership of parole boards is drawn largely from present and past corrections personnel and persons of similar backgrounds.

Other problems in correctional institutions are the inadequacy and inappropriateness of the services and programs available, the inhumane living conditions, the stifling of normal adolescent developmental needs, and the tacit acceptance of inmate brutality against weaker juveniles. All of the charges usually leveled at adult prisons plus those provoked by the unrealized promise of therapeutic goals have been applied to juvenile correctional facilities. Some of the factors to consider if there is to be a possibility of preparing the residents to reenter the community, or "normalization" as it is termed in the standards on architecture, are the size and location of facilities, the training of the staff, the services to be provided, the guidelines for disciplinary and grievance procedures, and many other details pertaining to corrections administration.

Much stress has been placed on the issue of secure versus nonsecure facilities. Yet a locked door is far less important than the environment and size of an institution. In a small facility, security precautions can be minimal regardless of whether it has a lock or a fence. Contact with concerned adults, opportunities to communicate with other juveniles in a relaxed atmosphere, improved vocational and reading programs, maintenance of neighborhood and family ties, aid in developing social and business skills, and nurturing of normal developmental needs can be accomplished with or without a locked door. Thus, the standards on detention, dispositions, corrections, and architecture focus on facilities, voluntary services, and administration as the keynote to treatment issues of juveniles within the jurisdiction of the system before and after disposition.

## 3.6 Issues in Administration.

Three volumes deal exclusively with the problems of administering the juvenile justice system through recordkeeping, planning, and monitoring. The need for confidentiality of juvenile records often conflicts with research, evaluation, planning, and monitoring of programs. Without an accessible information system it is impossible to determine the number and types of programs, the dispositions following adjudication for particular offenses, recidivism rates, resource allocation, vacancies and overcrowding in facilities, intake effectiveness in adjusting cases, and the rest of the data needed to coordinate the system. The problem is not difficult to solve if identifying information is excluded and access is restricted to responsible persons or agencies with legitimate purposes, with sanctions for misuse or abuse of the privilege of obtaining such data. But monitoring must be conducted by persons outside the system as well as those inside to provide public accountability.

Planning and monitoring can be useless endeavors if they are not comprehensive. Gaps in information and selective or self-monitoring could continue the isolation, fragmentation, and lack of accountability that characterize the system today. The system's needs and resources must be pulled together if it is to succeed. The standards for that purpose will be reviewed in the chapter covering the three administration volumes.

## 3.7 The Standards and the Issues.

The historical development of the juvenile justice system has produced a magnificent monster. The time has come to face the issues and propose solutions within the framework of a total, integrated system. In its early planning days between 1971 and 1973, the project had each of its six subcommittees prepare a survey of issues that it believed should be considered in the drafting phase of the project. Then a report was prepared discussing the following with respect to each issue: (1) existing practices; (2) known innovations or experiments; (3) needed new research; and (4) an analysis of the problems presented. This analysis might include basic assumptions and alternative policies, as well as pertinent values and present knowledge.

Priorities were assigned to each group of issues. The reports were distributed to committee members and reporters and subcommittee meetings were held in the winter of 1971. This painstaking process of thorough analysis, discussion, and selection of key issues moved slowly. By 1973 only six "guidelines for action" had been adopted on jurisdiction, procedural rights, sanctions, abuse and neglect protection, control of official discretion, and right to voluntary services and programs. These guidelines were "not sufficient at the moment to establish a coherent system of justice for children."

More papers were distributed, research conducted, meetings held, standards approved. This "inductive" approach continued—gathering data and defining problems before making final decisions and drafting principles. Standards were submitted, reviewed, revised, and adopted. Finally, the Commission met for its last full meeting in May 1976 and approved in principle the last five of its twenty-three volumes of standards and commentary. The design for a coherent system of justice for children was completed. Some of the details were modified by subsequent review of the published tentative drafts, but the basic concepts and structure were unchanged. A discussion and summary of the standards follow.

# PART IV: INTERVENTION IN THE LIVES OF CHILDREN

## 4.1 Jurisdiction of Juvenile Courts and Agencies.

Intervention can be voluntary or involuntary. In ordinary parlance, intervention means the act of coming into a situation. At law, an intervenor is a third person not originally a party to an action or other legal proceeding who enters the case for the protection of an interest allegedly at stake in the proceeding. Intervention in the life of an individual may be active or passive, official or unofficial. An intervenor can be a policeman who arrests or rescues you; a doctor who treats you or reports you; a therapist you visit or to whom you are referred; an agency that places your child in a foster home; a judge, teacher, social worker, lawyer, relative, or friend.

The crucial factor is not the intent of the intervenor—the most cruelly intended intervention could benefit its subject and a benevolently motivated intervention could destroy the person—which is difficult to evaluate objectively in any case. Instead, the factors to be isolated in examining the standards for intervention in the lives of juveniles are the following:

1. *The grounds for intervention.* We will scrutinize the definitions of behavior, action, and condition or status that give rise to intervention in the lives of children.

2. *The sources of the intervention.* The moving party, initiator, petitioner, or actor will be identified. This can include voluntary intervention, in which the person who is the subject is also the initiator, or involuntary, when a second or third party can have invoked the intervention. A victim, a party to a contract, a parent, or a neighbor directly affected could report an incident to the police, probation department, or prosecutor or commence an action by filing a petition or complaint in the court. The intervenor could be a court, public or private agency, school, or an officer or employee of any social institution dealing with children or families.

3. *The nature of the intervention.* The type, duration, and extent of the intervention can be determined by the matter giving rise to it, the

person who sought it, the intervening force, the outside force that imposed it, or a body of law, rules, or regulations adopted by society to define the boundaries of intervention. For example, parties to a contract are limited by considerations of public policy as to what are enforceable rights and obligations, including the duration of a term, as in a real estate agreement that can suspend vesting of title only for a specified period of lives in being. Compulsory education laws are limited by the age of the juvenile, as the age at which a child commits a crime determines whether he or she will be tried by a juvenile or an adult court.

Similarly, abuse of a child by a parent may constitute child abuse and fall within the purview of a juvenile court, but if a non-relative assaults a child, the matter goes before a criminal court. Unexcused absence from school may or may not be within the jurisdiction of a juvenile court, depending on the laws of the state. The same is true for divorce, separation, adoption, support, custody, and other matrimonial matters that variously are handled by courts of general trial jurisdiction, probate or surrogate courts, or juvenile courts as courts of original or concurrent jurisdiction.

Even if it has been determined that the juvenile court can intervene in a matter, enacted rules, guidelines, or statements of policy may restrict the nature of the intervention. Prescribed prerequisites will compel certain findings of fact prior to action. Procedural safeguards are provided to prevent unjustified interference with the juvenile's or parent's freedom before and after adjudication. Limits are placed on interrogation, treatment, detention, investigation, and other intrusions.

After the presumption of innocence has been overcome, whether in a court hearing or a disciplinary proceeding in a school or other institution, limits also are prescribed as to the sanctions, treatment, services, placements, transfers, or other remedial dispositions available to the dispositional authority.

Equally significant are limits placed on treatment, commitment placement, or other restraints or remedies which can be prescribed for persons voluntarily seeking intervention.

As a whole, the three factors indicated could be seen as constituting the single issue of jurisdiction, which fixes the power or authority of an entity to control an individual. That generally is the subject covered in this part, which deals with the standards adopted by Drafting Committee I, Intervention in the Lives of Children. The volumes planned and prepared by that committee are:

*Abuse and Neglect, Juvenile Delinquency and Sanctions, Noncriminal Misbehavior, Police Handling of Juvenile Problems, Rights of Minors, Schools and Education, Youth Service Agencies.*

*Juvenile Delinquency and Sanctions* will be discussed both here and in the part on treatment and corrections. The volume originally was drafted under Committee I's auspices, but the need to coordinate its principles and design for sanctions with the *Dispositions* volume became apparent at a Commission meeting in October 1975 and resulted in the appointment of a single editorial committee to complete the two volumes, under the supervision of the chairperson of the committee on treatment and corrections. Therefore, final certification came from Drafting Committee III, even though the bulk of work was done with Committee I.

As discussed in the Introduction and in Part II, the tentative drafts that aroused the greatest concern were *Abuse and Neglect, Noncriminal Misbehavior,* and *Schools and Education.* Not surprisingly, all three were the product of Drafting Committee I, the group with the most sensitive task: to define the boundaries of justifiable state intervention in the lives of families and children. That task was fundamental to the project; in a sense, everything else was mere detail. It was inevitable that protests would be heard when practitioners in the field recognized that the IJA-ABA Joint Commission had adopted the basic assumption that intervention, however benevolently intended, could be harmful and must be limited strictly to actions warranting official state coercion. The dismay of professionals accustomed to exercising broad discretionary power was not restricted to juvenile court judges and prosecutors, but was expressed by police and probation officers, educators, correctional administrators, psychiatrists, and others. Nevertheless, most professionals supported the standards, agreeing that guidelines for decision-making were long overdue, that treatment models were not proving effective, and that limited resources were being squandered on inappropriate or unobtainable objectives.

The unresolved controversy over these volumes led the executive committee of the Joint Commission to conclude that the standards defining the court's jurisdiction flowed inevitably from principles essential to the proposed new scheme for a reformed juvenile justice system. Experimenting with slightly expanded grounds for court intervention in cases of incorrigibility, child endangerment, and school-related problems or other efforts at rapprochement between inherently irreconcilable positions would not be faithful either to the basic premises of the project or to the traditional concepts espoused by the dissidents. Therefore, the three volumes were tabled by the executive committee and not submitted for further consideration by the ABA House of Delegates. They continue to be distributed as the product of the Joint Commission. *Noncriminal Misbehavior* and *Schools and Education* were not revised at all and *Abuse and Neglect* was revised to make it more consistent with the other volumes in the series.

Underlying principles, specific standards, and analysis of the reasons for similarities and distinctions among the volumes released by Drafting Committee I will be covered under the categories enumerated above: the grounds, sources, and nature of intervention.

**4.2 Grounds for Intervention by the Court: Delinquency, Abuse, and Neglect.**

As a result of major decisions made by Drafting Committee I and ratified by the Commission, the volumes prepared by Drafting Committees II, III, and IV deal almost exclusively with delinquency, with only passing reference to abused and neglected children, and almost none to status offenders. There are two distinct reasons, one of which is major and conceptually clear and the other minor, if slightly muddled.

The first reason is that the Commission voted to remove status offenders from the jurisdiction of juvenile court. Therefore, only juveniles who committed acts that would be crimes if committed by adults would be handled as juvenile offenders and continue to be labeled juvenile delinquents. A motion to call them juvenile criminals was defeated. Practical and theoretical arguments mingled: developmental differences of children must be recognized in dealing with juvenile crime; abandonment of the term "delinquency" would be too abrupt and politically unpalatable, jeopardizing acceptability of the standards; and a "juvenile criminal" label could produce a more rigid, punitive community response to youthful crime.

The second reason for stressing delinquency issues, and not the other family court areas, may be related to the genesis of the project, which was established to fill in the gaps left after the adult criminal justice standards were adopted.

With status offenses out of the courts, the volumes on court roles and procedures, treatment and corrections, and administration concentrated primarily on delinquents. Although the *Court Organization and Administration* volume provided for original jurisdiction of the juvenile court over adoption, termination of parental rights, offenses against children, and divorce, as well as juvenile law violations and neglected and abused children, the stress of the standards is on delinquency. The *Abuse and Neglect* volume attempts to be self-contained with regard to relevant proceedings and remedies, as are the *Youth Service Agencies* and *Schools and Education* volumes, but divorce, separation, adoption, and other specialized family matters involving adults apparently were seen as raising issues beyond the purview of juvenile justice experts. However, the decision to expand the jurisdiction of juvenile court to a family court to include all family matters would seem to call for a reaching out to matrimonial and family law practitioners for a volume covering this area. But twenty-three volumes may be enough for any series and more than can be digested with sufficient ease by the community.

The standards defining juvenile delinquency, endangerment (abuse and neglect), and the elimination of status offenses from juvenile court jurisdiction follow.

*Juvenile Delinquency and Sanctions* Standard 2.1 gives the juvenile court exclusive original jurisdiction in cases of conduct constituting delinquency if alleged to have been committed by a person not less than ten and not more than seventeen years of age at the time the offense is alleged to have been committed and not more than twenty years of age at the time delinquency proceedings are initiated. Delinquency jurisdiction in Standard 2.2 is defined as follows:

**A. The delinquency jurisdiction of the juvenile court should include only those offenses which are:**

**1. punishable by incarceration in a prison, jail, or other place of detention, and**

**2. except as qualified by these standards, in violation of an applicable federal, state, or local criminal statute or ordinance, or**

**3. in violation of an applicable state or local statute or ordinance defining a major traffic offense.**

**B. For purposes of this standard, major traffic offense should include:**

**1. any driving offense by a juvenile less than thirteen years of age at the time the offense is alleged to have been committed, and**

**2. any traffic offense involving reckless driving; driving while under the influence of alcohol, narcotics, or dangerous drugs; leaving the scene of an accident; and such other offenses as the enacting jurisdiction may deem sufficiently serious to warrant the attention of the juvenile court.**

**C. Any offense excluded by this standard from juvenile court jurisdiction should be cognizable in the court having jurisdiction over adults for such offenses, notwithstanding that the alleged offender's age is within the limits prescribed by Standard 2.1** *supra.*

The standards originally excluded victimless crimes, pursuant to former Standard 2.4, Elimination of Private Offenses, but that standard was deleted by the executive committee as contrary to Standard 2.2, which defines delinquency according to the state's criminal code.

The delinquency standards also permit discretionary dismissal if the court finds, under Standard 1.3, the following:

**A. the person or persons whose personal or property interests were threatened or harmed by the conduct charged to constitute the offense were members of the juvenile's family, and the juvenile's conduct may be more appropriately dealt with by parental authority than by resort to delinquency sanctions; or**
**B. the conduct charged to constitute the offense**
**1. did not actually cause or threaten the harm or evil sought to be prevented by the law defining the offense or did so only to a trivial extent, or**
**2. presents such other extenuations that it cannot reasonably be regarded as within the contemplation of the legislature in forbidding the conduct.**

With respect to sexual offenses, the standards had attempted to make distinctions based on the respective ages of the assenting juvenile and the person to whom assent is given to determine whether consent to sexual intercourse could constitute consensual sexual behavior and exclude criminal liability. That provision, Standard 4.1, was eliminated for the same reasons that former Standard 2.4 was deleted, i.e., that the state's criminal code would determine the statutory grounds for culpability.

Other defenses to criminal liability are lack of *mens rea*, the effect of parental authority, and absence of capacity to understand or avoid criminality, set forth in Standards 3.1 through 3.5.

**3.1 *Mens rea*—lack of *mens rea* an affirmative defense.**
**Where an applicable criminal statute or ordinance does not require proof of some culpable mental state, it should be an affirmative defense to delinquency liability that the juvenile:**
**A. was neither negligent nor reckless with respect to any material element of an offense penalizing the unintended consequence of risk-creating conduct; or**
**B. acted without knowledge or intention with respect to any material element of an offense penalizing conduct or the circumstances or consequences of such conduct.**

3.2 *Mens rea*—reasonableness defense.

Where an applicable criminal statute or ordinance penalizes risk-creating conduct, it should be a defense to juvenile delinquency liability that the juvenile's conduct conformed to the standard of care that a reasonable person of the juvenile's age, maturity, and mental capacity would observe in the juvenile's situation.

3.3 Consent.

A. Where delinquency liability is defeated or diminished by consent to the conduct charged to constitute the offense, such consent should not be deemed ineffective solely on the ground that it was given by a person who, by reason of youth, was legally incompetent to authorize the conduct.

B. Effective consent by a juvenile should be a defense to juvenile delinquency liability based on conduct that causes or threatens bodily harm where:

    1. the bodily harm caused or threatened by the conduct consented to is not serious; or

    2. the conduct and the harm are reasonably foreseeable hazards of participation in a contest, sport, game, or play.

C. Consent by the person whose interest was infringed by conduct charged to constitute an offense should be implied in juvenile delinquency proceedings when such conduct was, within a customary license or tolerance, neither expressly forbidden by such person nor inconsistent with the purpose of the law defining the offense.

3.4 Parental authority.

A. A juvenile should not be adjudicated delinquent for complicity in an offense committed by another if he or she terminated his or her involvement in such offense prior to its commission and

    1. gave timely warning to law enforcement authorities or to a parent, legal guardian, or custodian, or to an adult otherwise entrusted with the care or supervision of the juvenile; or

    2. otherwise made a reasonable effort to prevent the commission of the offense.

B. It should be a defense to a delinquency liability that a juvenile engaged in conduct charged to constitute an offense because a parent, legal guardian, or custodian, or an adult otherwise entrusted with the care or supervision of the juvenile, used or threatened to use force or disciplinary measures against him or her or another which a person of reasonable firmness in the juvenile's situation would have been unable to resist.

**3.5 Responsibility.**
Juvenile delinquency liability should not be imposed if, at the time of the conduct charged to constitute the offense, as a result of mental disease or defect, the juvenile lacked substantial capacity to appreciate the criminality of his or her conduct or to conform his or her conduct to the requirements of the law.

Standard 2.3 excludes conduct that would not be designated a crime if committed by an adult. This is consistent with the first standard in *Noncriminal Misbehavior,* Standard 1.1, which provides as follows:

A juvenile's acts of misbehavior, ungovernability, or unruliness which do not violate the criminal law should not constitute a ground for asserting juvenile court jurisdiction over the juvenile committing them.

*Abuse and Neglect* standards present the most complex and difficult-to-apply definitions of grounds for court intervention, the exact text of which follows. Standard 2.1 was amended to authorize court intervention for sexual abuse by a person outside the household if parents fail to take action. Standard 2.2 substituted "To justify intervention" for "In order to assume jurisdiction."

**2.1 Statutory grounds for intervention.**
Courts should be authorized to assume jurisdiction in order to condition continued parental custody upon the parents' accepting supervision or to remove a child from his/her home only when a child is endangered in a manner specified in subsections A.-F.:
A. a child has suffered, or there is a substantial risk that a child will imminently suffer, a physical harm, inflicted nonaccidentally upon him/her by his/her parents, which causes, or creates a substantial risk of causing disfigurement, impairment of bodily functioning, or other serious physical injury;
B. A child has suffered, or there is a substantial risk that the child will imminently suffer, physical harm causing disfigurement, impairment of bodily functioning, or other serious physical injury as a result of conditions created by his/her parents or by the failure of the parents to adequately supervise or protect him/her;

C. a child is suffering serious emotional damage, evidenced by severe anxiety, depression, or withdrawal, or untoward aggressive behavior toward self or others, and the child's parents are not willing to provide treatment for him/her;

D. a child has been sexually abused by his/her parent or a member of his/her household or by another person where the parent knew or should have known and failed to take appropriate action (alternative: a child has been sexually abused by his/her parent or a member of his/her household, and is seriously harmed physically or emotionally thereby);

E. a child is in need of medical treatment to cure, alleviate, or prevent him/her from suffering serious physical harm which may result in death, disfigurement, or substantial impairment of bodily functions, and his/her parents are unwilling to provide or consent to the medical treatment;

F. a child is committing delinquent acts as a result of parental encouragement, guidance, or approval.

2.2 Need for intervention in specific case.

The fact that a child is endangered in a manner specified in Standard 2.1 A.-F. should be a necessary but not sufficient condition for a court to intervene. To justify intervention a court should also have to find that intervention is necessary to protect the child from being endangered in the future. This decision should be made in accordance with the standards proposed in Part VI.

Although the *Abuse and Neglect* standards on emergency temporary custody refer initially to nonjudicial intervention, they lead to court review and further judicial involvement. Therefore, they are covered here to permit inclusiveness concerning the grounds for court intervention, but they should also be considered part of the sections on grounds for agency intervention and on sources and nature of intervention. Standard 4.3 was revised to reflect changes in new Part V and provision for a court-approved plan of investigation prior to filing a petition was deleted.

4.1 Authorized emergency custody of endangered child.

A. Any physician, police or law enforcement official, or agent or employee of an agency designated pursuant to Standard 4.1 C. should be authorized to take physical custody of a child, notwithstanding the wishes of the child's parent(s) or other such caretaker(s), if the physician, official, or agent or employee has probable cause to believe such custody is necessary to prevent the child's imminent death or serious bodily injury and that the child's parent(s) or other such caretaker(s) is unable or unwilling to protect the child from such imminent death or injury; provided that where risk to the child appears created solely because the child has been left unattended at home, such physician, official, or agent or employee should be authorized only to provide an emergency caretaker to attend the child at home until the child's parent returns or sufficient time elapses to indicate that the parent does not intend to return home; and provided further that no such physician, official, or agent or employee is authorized to take physical custody of a child without prior approval by a court pursuant to Standard 4.3 unless risk to the child is so imminent that there is no time to secure such court approval. Any physician or police or law enforcement official who takes custody of a child pursuant to this standard should immediately contact an agency designated pursuant to Standard 4.1 C., which should thereupon take custody of the child for such disposition as indicated in Standard 4.2.

B. Any physician, police or law enforcement official, or agent or employee of an agency who takes custody or care of a child pursuant to Standard 4.1 A. should be immune from any civil or criminal liability as a consequence of such action, provided that such person was acting in good faith in such action. In any proceeding regarding such liability, good faith should be presumed.

C. The state department of social services (or equivalent state agency) should be required to designate at least one agency within each geographic locality within the state, of those agencies listed as qualified report recipient agencies pursuant to Standard 3.2, whose agents or employees would be authorized to take custody of children pursuant to Standard 4.1. To qualify for such designation, an agency must demonstrate to the satisfaction of the state department that it has adequate capacity to safeguard the physical and emotional well-being of children requiring emergency temporary custody pursuant to this Part. The state department should be required to promulgate regulations specifying standards for personnel qualification, custodial facilities, and other aspects of temporary custodial care which an agency must provide, or have access to, regarding children subject to this Part. Each agency designated should thereafter be required to demonstrate, in conjunction with review proceedings pursuant to Standard 3.2 C., that it continues to meet the requirements for designation pursuant to this standard, in view of its efficacy in safeguarding the well-being of children subject to this Part.

4.2 Agency disposition of children in emergency temporary custody.

A. An agency taking custody of a child pursuant to Standard 4.1 should place the child in a nonsecure setting which will adequately safeguard his/her physical and emotional well-being. Such agency should be authorized to provide immediately, or secure the provision of, emergency medical care if necessary to prevent the child's imminent death or serious bodily injury, notwithstanding the wishes of the child's parent(s) or other such person(s). The agency should ensure that the child's parent(s) or other such caretaker(s) has opportunity to visit with the child, at least every day for the duration of custody pursuant to this Part (including without limitation the provision of transportation for the parents(s) or other such person(s)) unless such visits, even if supervised, would be seriously harmful to the child (due account being given, among other considerations, to the child's wishes regarding visits).

B. No later than the first business day after taking custody of a child pursuant to Standard 4.1, the agency should be required to report such action to the court authorized to conduct proceedings by Part V and to explain the specific circumstances justifying the taking of custody and the specific measures implemented to safeguard the physical and emotional well-being of the child. The agency should, at the same time, submit a petition without prior screening by the intake processing agency, under Standard 5.1 B., except that if the agency decides against such submission, it should immediately return the child to the custody of his/her parent(s) or other such caretaker(s).

4.3. Court review regarding children in emergency temporary custody.

A. Immediately upon receipt of a petition submitted pursuant to Standard 4.2, the court should direct notification pursuant to Standard 5.1 C., appointment of counsel for the child pursuant to Standard 5.1 D., and referral of the petition for prosecution pursuant to Standard 5.1 B. On the same business day if at all practicable, and no later than the next business day, the court should convene a hearing to determine whether emergency temporary custody of the child should be continued.

**B. The court should be authorized to continue emergency temporary custody of the child, pursuant to Standard 4.1, if it determines:**

1. custody of the child with his/her parent(s) or other such caretaker(s) named in the petition would create an imminent substantial risk of death or serious bodily injury to the child, and no provision of services or other arrangement is available which would adequately safeguard the child in such custody against such risk;

2. the conditions of custody away from the child's parent(s) or other such caretaker(s) are adequate to safeguard his/her physical and emotional well-being (including without limitation direction by the court to provide emergency medical care to the child if necessary to prevent the risk found pursuant to subsection 1.); and

3. the child's parent(s) or other such person(s) named in the petition would be provided opportunity to visit with the child at least every day for the duration of custody pursuant to this Part (including without limitation the provision of transportation for the parent(s) or other such caretaker(s)) unless such visits, even if supervised, would be seriously harmful to the child (due account being given, among other considerations, to the child's wishes regarding visits).

**4.4 Custody during pendency of proceeding.**

Upon motion of any party to a proceeding pursuant to Part V, at any time during the pendency of the proceeding, the court may, following a hearing, authorize emergency temporary custody of a child with an agency designated pursuant to Standard 4.1 C., if the court determines such custody is justified pursuant to the criteria specified in Standard 4.3 B.

*Abuse and Neglect* Standards 8.1 to 8.3 originally permitted termination of parental rights at the dispositional hearing after a finding of endangerment and as a possible disposition at every review hearing thereafter. Therefore termination of parental rights is discussed as a disposition or remedy in section 4.5.2 rather than as a basis for court jurisdiction, although the revised standards now provide a separate course of action for such termination.

Aside from special arrangements, such as one prescribed in *Schools and Education* in which the court can be petitioned to preside over a conference between school officials and juveniles with their families to devise a plan for school attendance with no sanctions for noncompliance, the standards spell out in detail no other specific definitions of the grounds for juvenile or family court jurisdiction. Other examples of incompletely developed proceedings are the procedure for court approval of an alternative placement described in the *Noncriminal Misbehavior* standards and the hearing to modify a disposition because of a subsequent change of circumstances in the *Dispositions* standards. Perhaps it was expected that some of the procedural volumes would fill in the gaps by providing further information concerning the special proceedings, but that does not appear to have happened. The court roles and procedures volumes assumed traditional delinquency, child abuse, and neglect jurisdiction, focusing on delinquency cases and proceedings at the preadjudication, adjudication, disposition, and postdisposition stages.

The balance of this summary volume proceeds on the premise, not explicitly stated in the other volumes in the series, that the standards cover the juvenile court part of the proposed family court. Presumably, standards for matrimonial actions, family offenses, adoption, support, and other cases within the jurisdiction of a court handling all family matters will be promulgated by a project in the future.

The above refers to juvenile court jurisdiction only. Intervention in the lives of juveniles through other parts of the juvenile justice system or combined with a special kind of court involvement warrant a separate section.

## 4.3 Grounds for Intervention by the Agencies.

### 4.3.1 Schools and discipline in an institution.

The courts are not the only institution empowered to intervene in the lives of children. Parents, schools, health care facilities, social agencies, and police can exercise authority over juveniles in many situations. The standards have attempted to delimit the areas and scope of intervention through definitions of rights and responsibilities, as in the *Schools and Education* volume, in which the grounds and procedures for school regulatory power, disciplinary proceedings, and the available sanctions are prescribed, as well as the boundaries of students' right to an education, rights of expression and privacy, and other protections within the special institutions called schools.

Since we are using intervention in the involuntary sense only, the method provided for handling truancy is an excellent example of noncoercive procedures. Standard 1.10 requires juveniles to attend public school or to receive equivalent instruction elsewhere if they are between the ages specified by the state statute, but no older than sixteen. The circumscribed action prescribed by Standards 1.11 and 1.12 for recurrent or extended unexcused absences is as follows:

**1.11 If a juvenile fails to attend school without valid justification recurrently or for an extended period of time, the school:**
A. should so inform the parent by a notice in writing (in English and, if different, in the parent's primary language) and by other means reasonably necessary to achieve notice in fact;
B. should schedule a conference (and separate conferences, if appropriate) for the parent and juvenile at a time and place reasonably convenient for all persons involved for the purpose of analyzing the causes of the juvenile's absences;
C. should take steps
1. to eliminate or reduce those absences (including, if appropriate, adjustments in the student's school program or school or course assignment); and
2. to assist the parent or student to obtain supplementary services that might eliminate or ameliorate the cause or causes for the absence from school; and
D. in the event action taken pursuant to provisions A., B., and C. is not successful in reducing the student's absences, may petition the court for the sole purpose of developing, with the participation of student and parent, a supervised plan for the student's attendance.

**1.12 A.** Neither school officials nor police officers (nor other officials) should have any power to take a juvenile into custody, with or without a warrant, by reason of the fact alone that a juvenile is absent from school without valid justification.
**B.** A duly authorized school official may return a student to school if the student is found away from home, is absent from school without a valid justification, and agrees to accompany the official back to school.

Standard 1.13 bars action against parents for failure to cause the juvenile to attend school, but such evidence is admissible in a neglect proceeding brought on the basis of other evidence.
The grounds for official school intervention are discussed in the standards in Part III of the volume, on the school regulatory power. School authorities are permitted to regulate student conduct or status

reasonably and properly related to educating school students and only in furtherance of: (1) their education *per se* function of educating students; and (2) their host function of protecting both the persons or property for which the school is responsible and the integrity of the educational process. But schools may exercise their educational *per se* function *only* when the educational interest involved clearly outweighs applicable countervailing factors, and their host function when such conduct or status substantially involves significant interests beyond that of the schools *only* if there is a clear and imminent threat of harm that cannot otherwise be eliminated by reasonable means.

School regulations do not pertain to students only. For example, Standard 3.8 also permits the schools to restrict access to school premises by persons other than students or school personnel. Standard 3.9 permits a person serving as a school counselor to disclose or be compelled by legal process or in a proceeding to disclose information from a student only if:

**1. such disclosure is required to be made to the student's parent pursuant to any other of these standards; or**

**2. the privilege of nondisclosure is waived by the student or parent pursuant to Standard 2.2 hereof; or**

**3. the information or communication was made to the counselor for the express purpose of being further communicated or being made public; or**

**4. the counselor believes that disclosure is necessary to prevent substantial property destruction or to protect the student involved or other persons from a serious threat to their physical or mental health.**

**For purposes of this and the following standard a person is deemed to be serving as a school counselor if such person has been designated by the appropriate school authorities to act specially as a counselor for students, regardless of whether such person has been specially certified as a counselor or such person is expected to perform administrative or teaching duties in addition to counseling students.**

In addition, Standard 3.9 requires disclosure by teachers or school administrators of confidential communications from a student: (1) in situations 2-4 above; or (2) if such disclosure is compelled by legal process issued by a court, or by an agency authorized to issue process to compel testimony or production of documents.

It also should be noted that the student's right to an education, as defined in Standards 1.1 to 1.5 and 1.9, can invoke intervention in assignment to special programs or to a particular school to which the student may object. The right to an education is defined as follows:

**1.1 Every juvenile who is living within the state and is between the ages of six and twenty-one (or younger or older if so specified by state law) and not a graduate of high school (or higher level specified by state law) should have the right to an education provided at state expense; and education should be so provided by the local school district (or other unit of government specified by state law).**

**1.2 Without regard to age, the right to at least a high school education (as specified in Standard 1.1) may be acquired in a continuous period or two or more separate periods of attendance.**

**1.3 The right to education established by Standard 1.1 includes the right to an education that is appropriate for each individual student.**

**1.4 In the absence of special circumstances affecting or identifying a student's educational needs or educational development, every student should have the right to an education that is:**
**    A. substantially similar in kind to that which is provided other students in the school district; and**
**    B. provided through a substantially equal allocation of educational resources on a statewide basis.**

**1.5 In the absence of special circumstances affecting or identifying a student's educational needs or educational development, every student should have equal opportunity to select among alternative schools, programs, or courses when such alternatives are provided, subject to minimal restrictions reasonably necessary for efficient administration.**

**1.9 If any student is lacking fluency in the language primarily used for instruction in the school of attendance, that student should receive special instruction to the extent necessary to offset any educational disadvantage resulting from the student's particular language development.**

Standards for a grievance mechanism to challenge or correct improper assignments are covered in Standards 1.6 to 1.8, as follows:

**1.6** All students are presumed to be similarly stituated for educational purposes in the absence of a particularized determination of special circumstances affecting or identifying a particular student's educational needs or development.

**1.7** A student's race, sex, nationality, or ethnic identity should never be the basis of a determination that a student should be assigned to a particular school, program, or course because that student has unique educational needs or educational development.

**1.8 A.** A student may be assigned to a particular school, program, or course, or denied access to a particular school, program, or course on the basis of that student's educational needs or educational development.

B. A student assigned or denied access to a particular school, program, or course by reason of the student's educational needs or educational development is entitled to receive, at the student's request, an explanation (in writing, if requested) of the basis for the assignment or denial and a conference to discuss the assignment or denial.

C. If the student believes the explanation of the assignment or denial is based on erroneous factual information, the student should be given a hearing with respect to the claimed factual error or errors consistent with the hearing specified in Part V, subject to the following qualifications:

1. the student should have the burden of establishing that there is reasonable ground to believe that a factual error in assignment or denial has been made;

2. the school should thereafter have the burden of rebutting evidence of factual error or of establishing the existence of educational needs or educational development making the assignment or denial appropriate notwithstanding the factual error;

3. the standard of proof under Standard 1.8 C.1. and 2. should be the preponderance of the evidence.

D. Without regard to a request for an explanation under Standard 1.8 B. or belief of factual error under Standard 1.8 C., the student should be given a hearing consistent with the hearing specified in Part V, if the assignment or denial involves either:

1. assignment or denial of access to a particular school; or
2. both
   a. an assignment or denial of access to a particular program or course; and
   b. an assignment or denial entailing segregation from other students, not having the same educational needs or educational development, for more than 30 percent of the average school day.

E. The school should have the burden of proving that one or more decisions involving an assignment or denial under Standard 1.8 D. would be appropriate on the basis of special circumstances affecting or identifying the student's educational needs or educational development.

Finally, the student's right of expression is not absolute. Schools may intervene if student expression exceeds prescribed limits, as set forth in Standards 4.1 to 4.6.

4.1 Subject to the limitations and elaborations set forth in the succeeding standards, a student's right of expression is not affected by the fact of student status or presence on school premises, except where:

A. particular facts and circumstances make it reasonably likely that the expression will cause substantial and material disruption of, or interference with, school activities, which disruption or interference cannot be prevented by reasonably available less restrictive means; or

B. where such expression unduly impinges upon the rights of others.

4.2 Schools should not restrict student expression based on the content of the expression except as stated in Standard 4.1 and except for student expression that:

A. is obscene; libelous; or

B. is violative of another person's right of privacy by publicly exposing private details of such person's life, the exposure of which would be offensive and objectionable to a reasonable person of ordinary sensibilities; or

C. advocates racial, religious, or ethnic prejudice or discrimination or seriously disparages particular racial, religious, or ethnic groups.

4.3 Where one or more students are provided by the school with expression privileges not equally shared by all students, with resources not provided to all students, or with special access to fellow students, such expression is subject to the same rights and restrictions as other types of student expression except that schools:

A. should take all necessary action to insure that the student expression does not advocate racial, religious, or ethnic prejudice or discrimination, or seriously disparage particular racial, religious, or ethnic groups; and

B. should take all necessary action to insure that the student privilege, resource, or access do not become vehicles for the consistent expression of only one point of view to the exclusion of others; and

C. if not able to insure the prohibition of subsection A. hereof or the equal access of subsection B. consistent with the continued existence of the student expression involved, may curtail or prohibit the continued existence of such student expression.

4.4 Schools should provide reasonable bulletin board space for the posting of student notices or comments. Where such space is provided, schools may not regulate access based on the content of material to be posted, except in accordance with these standards. School authorities may also enforce reasonable regulations regarding the size and duration of posted student notices or comments.

4.5 School authorities may adopt and enforce reasonable regulations as to the time, place, and manner of distribution or circulation of printed matter on school grounds and may require prior authorization for the distribution or circulation of substantial quantities of printed matter in school and/or for the posting in school of printed matter provided that:

A. school authorities should not deny such authorization except in writing and except on grounds set forth in these standards; and

B. school authorities have set forth clearly in writing standards for such prior authorization which specify to whom and how printed matter may be distributed, a definite, brief period

70 STANDARDS FOR JUVENILE JUSTICE

of time within which a review of submitted printed matter will be completed, the criteria for denial of such authorization, and the available appeal procedures.

4.6 Student conduct that violates otherwise valid regulations that have not been adopted or invoked for the purpose of inhibiting expression and that are designed to achieve substantial interests that cannot reasonably be achieved by alternatives that limit expression substantially less than other alternatives may be subjected to school sanctions even though a student has committed such violation for purposes of expression or incidental to expression.

The procedures for disciplinary action, including safeguards, and the sanctions available will be discussed below in section 4.5 on the sources and nature of intervention.

It should be noted here that provisions for administrative disciplinary and grievance procedures for juveniles confined in correctional institutions are included in the *Corrections Administration* volume, but these will be discussed in the chapter covering the volumes prepared by Drafting Committee III, Treatment and Corrections.

### 4.3.2 Limited intervention for noncriminal behavior problems.

Most innovative are the proposals in the *Noncriminal Misbehavior* volume for limited custody for juveniles found in dangerous circumstances and for runaways, and for a hearing for alternative residential placements for juveniles in family conflict. The volume also includes standards for emergency psychiatric and medical services, but these standards are relatively conventional.

With the decision to eliminate court jurisdiction over status offenders, the drafting committee, the Commission, and the reporter were left with the problem of devising a feasible system of providing services to children and families with difficulties that did not constitute delinquency, neglect, or abuse. The most favored solution was to make available all appropriate social, health, educational, and vocational services, as expressed in Standard 4.1 *et seq.*: "A broad spectrum of services should be provided which are reasonably designed to assist a juvenile in conflict with his or her family to resolve their conflicts." These would include both crisis intervention and continuing service components. Such services clearly are designed to meet the needs of

families who otherwise might have filed petitions alleging incorrigibility, unruliness, late hours, disobedience, and other problems of
"parenting," as well as the usual kind of family or juvenile counseling
problems that do not lead to a court contact at the juvenile stage but
might forestall serious adjustment problems surfacing in later years.
That role for a community agency will be discussed in the section
covering the *Youth Service Agencies* volume.

It was recognized that many juveniles with problems requiring
counseling or other services might not seek help voluntarily or that
their families might not cooperate. In the absence of a valid basis for
invoking the court's jurisdiction, other methods for bringing help to
endangered juveniles were developed, creating something of a hybrid
between voluntary and short-term involuntary treatment for children
with noncriminal problems. This reflected the reluctance of the
committees and Commission to abandon certain intransigent situations to strictly noncoercive community remedies.

Limited custody for juveniles in circumstances endangering safety
is set forth in Standards 2.1 through 2.4 of the *Noncriminal Misbehavior* volume as follows:

## 2.1 Limited custody.

Any law enforcement officer who reasonably determines that
a juvenile is in circumstances which constitute a substantial and
immediate danger to the juvenile's physical safety may, if the
juvenile's physical safety requires such action, take the juvenile
into limited custody subject to the limitations of this part. If the
juvenile consents, the law enforcement officer should transport
the juvenile to his or her home or other appropriate residence,
or arrange for such transportation, pursuant to Standard 2.2. If
the juvenile does not so consent, the law enforcement officer
should transport the juvenile to a designated temporary nonsecure residential facility pursuant to Standard 2.3. In no event
should limited custody extend more than six hours from the time
of initial contact by the law enforcement officer.

## 2.2 Notice to parent; release; responsibility of persons taking
juvenile from limited custody.

A. The officer taking a juvenile into limited custody should
inform the juvenile of the reasons for such custody and should
contact the juvenile's parent, custodian, relative, or other responsible person as soon as practicable. The officer or official
should inform the parent, custodian, relative, or other respon-

sible person of the reasons for taking the juvenile into limited custody and should, if the juvenile consents, release the juvenile to the parent, custodian, relative, or other responsible person as soon as practicable.

B. The officer so releasing a juvenile from limited custody should, if he or she believes further services may be needed, inform the juvenile and the person to whom the juvenile is released of the nature and location of appropriate services and should, if requested, assist in establishing contact between the family and the service agency.

C. Where a parent or custodian could not be reached and release was made to a relative or other responsible person, the officer should notify the parent or custodian as soon as practicable of the fact and circumstances of the limited custody, the release of the juvenile, and any information given respecting further services, unless there are compelling circumstances why the parent or custodian should not be so notified.

D. Where a juvenile is released from limited custody to a person other than a parent or custodian, such person should reasonably establish that he or she is willing and able to be responsible for the safety of the juvenile. Any such person so taking the juvenile from limited custody should sign a promise to safeguard the juvenile and to procure such medical or other services as may immediately be needed.

2.3 Inability to contact parents; use of temporary nonsecure residential facility; options open to the juvenile; time limits.

A. If the law enforcement officer is unable by all reasonable efforts to contact a parent, custodian, relative, or other responsible person; or if the person contacted lives at an unreasonable distance; or if the juvenile refuses to be taken to his or her home or other appropriate residence; or if the officer is otherwise unable despite all reasonable efforts to make arrangements for the safe release of the juvenile taken into limited custody, the law enforcement officer should take the juvenile to a designated temporary nonsecure residential facility licensed by the state for such purpose. The staff of such facility should promptly explain to the juvenile his or her legal rights and the options of service or other assistance available to the juvenile and should in no event hold the juvenile for a period longer than six hours from the time of the juvenile's initial contact with the law enforcement officer.

B. If the juvenile taken into limited custody and taken to such facility refuses to return home, and the safe release of the juvenile cannot be effected within six hours from the time of the juvenile's initial contact with the law enforcement officer, the provisions of Part III of these standards should apply and the case should be handled pursuant thereto, whether the juvenile was initially absent from home with or without the consent of his or her parent or custodian.

**2.4 Immunity for officer acting in good faith pursuant to standards.**

A law enforcement officer acting reasonably and in good faith pursuant to these standards in releasing a juvenile to a person other than a parent or custodian of such juvenile shall be immune from civil or criminal liability for such action.

The troublesome problem of runaway juveniles is handled in similar fashion in Standard 3.1

**3.1 Use of limited custody where possible; nonsecure detention time limits; notification of parent.**

A. If a juvenile is found by a law enforcement officer to be absent from home without the consent of his or her parent or custodian, and it is impracticable to secure the juvenile's return by taking limited custody pursuant to Part II of these standards, the juvenile should be taken to a temporary nonsecure residential facility licensed by the state for such purpose.

B. As soon as practicable, the staff of the facility should reasonably attempt to notify the juvenile's parent or custodian of his or her whereabouts, physical and emotional condition, and the circumstances surrounding his or her placement, unless there are compelling circumstances why the parent or custodian should not be notified.

C. Upon such juvenile's admission to the temporary facility, the staff of the facility should undertake to make arrangements for the juvenile's return home as soon as practicable. The juvenile may remain in the facility for a period not to exceed twenty-one days from his or her date of admission to the facility without the filing of a neglect petition, in order that arrangements be made for the juvenile's return home or for alternative residential placement pursuant to Part V of these standards. If the juvenile and the parent or custodian agree, in writing, the juvenile may remain longer than twenty-one days in the temporary facility without the filing of a neglect petition. In any case, the staff of the temporary facility should seek to effect the juvenile's return home or alternative living arrangements agreeable to the juvenile and the parent or custodian as soon as practicable.

A further departure from the principle of noncoercive intervention is available under Standard 5.1, which permits an alternative residential placement in a relative's home, foster or group home, or other family setting with the mutual consent of the juvenile and family, but further provides as follows:

No alternatve residential placement should be arranged over the objection of a juvenile or of his or her parent or custodian, except that if they cannot agree as to an alternative residential placement and a juvenile not emancipated refuses to return home, the juvenile court may approve an alternative residential placement upon motion pursuant to this part.

Finally, the standards permit a juvenile to be taken into custody for emergency psychiatric or medical evaluation and treatment, for which the juvenile may be admitted and detained at an appropriate facility for a period not to exceed seventy-two hours. If care beyond seventy-two hours appears necessary because the juvenile is suicidal, seriously assaultive or seriously destructive, or otherwise evidences need for care, application should be made pursuant to the mental health laws of the jurisdiction. The basic standard for emergency services, Standard 6.1, reads as follows:

When any juvenile, as a result of mental or emotional disorder, or intoxication by alcohol or other drug, is suicidal, seriously assaultive or seriously destructive toward others, or otherwise similarly evidences an immediate need for emergency psychiatric or medical evaluation and possible care, any law enforcement officer, member of the attending staff of an evaluation psychiatric or medical facility designated by the county (state, city, etc.) or other professional person designated by the county (state, city, etc.) may upon reasonable cause take, or cause to be taken, such juvenile into emergency custody and take him or her to a psychiatric or medical facility designated by the county (state, city, etc.) and approved by the state department of health (or other appropriate agency) as a facility for emergency evaluation and emergency treatment.

A semantic problem arose concerning Standard 6.7 on voluntary application for medical or mental health services. The standard states:

**Nothing in these standards should be construed as limiting in any way the right otherwise given by law of any juvenile, or of the parent, guardian, or custodian of any juvenile, to make voluntary application at any time to any public or private agency or practitioner for medical or mental health services, on an inpatient or outpatient basis, whether by direct application in person or by referral from any private or public agency or practitioner.**

One of the members of the Commission, Patricia M. Wald, requested inclusion of a footnote to Standard 6.7, which stated:

**Commissioner Patricia M. Wald registers her interpretation that this standard in no way suggests that parents, over juveniles' objections, may "volunteer" children into mental hospitals without the opportunity for a due process hearing. See *Bartley v. Kremens*, U.S. app. pndg., 423 U.S. 1028 (1976), 426 U.S. 945 (1977), 402 F. Supp. 1039 (E.D. Pa. 1975).**

It should be noted that *Bartley v. Kremens* was vacated as moot in 431 U.S. 119 (1977), but the issue was considered in *Parham v. J.R.*, 442 U.S. 584 (1979).

### 4.3.3 Police intervention.

Other volumes permitting limited intervention in the lives of juveniles outside the juvenile court are *Police Handling of Juvenile Problems* and *Youth Service Agencies.* The police standards are exceptionally careful to distinguish between formal intervention for acts requiring court referral and problems not involving serious misconduct but calling for some form of crisis intervention or other police assistance. Standards 2.2 and 2.3 express the underlying point of view of the volume with respect to records and referrals; Standard 2.4 enumerates less serious criminal conduct that may require police intervention and sets forth the choices police must make among courses of action ranging from deliberate nonintervention to mandatory referral for treatment. Standard 2.2 was amended to add a cross-reference to the *Juvenile Records and Information Systems* standards. The text of these standards is:

**2.2 Police departments should retain juvenile records only**

when necessary for investigations or formal referrals to the juvenile or criminal justice systems. Police officers should avoid the stigmatizing effect of juvenile records by retaining only minimal records necessary for investigation and referral, in accordance with *Juvenile Records and Information Systems* standards for retention of police records.

2.3 Since other volumes in the Juvenile Justice Standards Project conclude that serious harm can be done to juveniles simply by their being referred into the formal juvenile justice process, police should not make such referrals unless:

A. serious or repeated criminal conduct is involved; or

B. less serious criminal conduct is involved and lesser restrictive alternatives such as those described in Standard 2.4 are not appropriate under the circumstances.

2.4 For juvenile matters involving nuisance, mischievous behavior, minor criminal conduct (e.g., being intoxicated, engaging in minor thefts), or parental misconduct (such as neglect) not involving apparent criminal behavior, police should select the least restrictive alternative from the following courses of action, depending upon the circumstances:

A. nonintervention;

B. temporary assistance to those seeking or obviously needing such assistance (incuding situations in which the potential of serious physical harm is apparent);

C. short-term mediation and crisis intervention (e.g., resolution of family conflicts);

D. voluntary referral to appropriate community agencies; or

E. mandatory temporary referral to mental or public health agencies under statutory authorization to make such referrals (e.g., to detoxification program).

In dealing with juvenile problems, police agencies should not attempt to initiate their own deterrence or treatment programs (such as informal probation), but rather should limit their services to short-term intervention and referral.

Guidelines for police departments to follow in formulating policies for handling juvenile problems are proposed in Standard 2.5.

2.5 In order to stimulate police handling of juvenile problems (both criminal and noncriminal) in ways that are consistent with previous and subsequent standards, the following steps should be taken:

A. Juvenile codes should narrowly limit police authority to utilize the formal juvenile justice process.

B. Juvenile codes should clarify the authority and immunity from civil liability of police to intervene in problems involving juveniles in ways other than through use of their arrest power in dealing with matters in which the juvenile or criminal courts are to be involved. This means authority and emphasis should be given to the use of summons in lieu of arrest. For matters in which police must act to assist a juvenile in need against his or her will, authority to take a juvenile into protective custody or to make a mandatory temporary referral should be specified and should be properly limited. It should also be specified that a juvenile cannot be detained, even temporarily, in adult detention facilities.

C. Police agencies should formulate administrative policies structuring the discretion of and providing guidance to individual officers in the handling of juvenile problems, particularly those that do not involve serious criminal matters. Such policies should stress:

1. avoiding the formal juvenile justice process unless clearly indicated and unless alternatives do not exist;

2. using the least restrictive alternative in attempting to resolve juvenile problems; and

3. dealing with all classes and races of juveniles in an even-handed manner.

D. Police training programs should give high priority, in both recruit and inservice training, to available and desirable alternatives for handling juvenile problems.

E. Police administrators should work collaboratively with both public and private agencies in ensuring that adequate services are available in various neighborhoods and districts so that referrals can be made to such services, and ensuring that joint policies and common understandings are reached whenever necessary. In addition, police administrators, because of their knowledge of deficiencies in this area, should focus attention on gaps in public and private resources that must be filled in order to meet the needs of juveniles and their families, and on the unwillingness or inability of existing agencies and institutions to respond to the needs.

Part III covers the authority of the police to handle delinquency cases. In such matters, the standards hew fairly closely to police policies for adult criminals, with some recognition of a need to experiment with special innovative methods more appropriate to juveniles. Standard 3.4 was amended to substitute "action" for "interest." Standard 3.5 on constitutional restrictions on police investigations was deleted, but the text was added to the commentary to Standard 3.2.

**3.1 Serious juvenile crimes require the concern and priority attention of police as well as other agencies within the criminal and juvenile justice systems and the public at large. Police work in handling such cases should follow patterns similar to those used in the investigation of serious crimes committed by adults.**

**3.2 Police investigation into criminal matters should be similar whether the suspect is an adult or a juvenile. Juveniles, therefore, should receive at least the same safeguards available to adults in the criminal justice system. This should apply to:**
   **A. preliminary investigations (e.g., stop and frisk);**
   **B. the arrest process;**
   **C. search and seizure;**
   **D. questioning;**
   **E. pretrial identification; and**
   **F. prehearing detention and release.**
   **For some investigative procedures, greater constitutional safeguards are needed because of the vulnerability of juveniles. Juveniles should not be permitted to waive constitutional rights on their own. In certain investigative areas not governed by constitutional guidelines, guidance to police officers should be provided either legislatively or administratively by court rules or through police agency policies.**

**3.3 Even if a juvenile is taken into custody under authority other than the arrest power (see Standard 2.5), police should be subject to the same investigative restrictions set forth above in the handling of the juvenile.**

**3.4 The action by a police officer in filing a complaint against a juvenile either in a juvenile or in a criminal court should be subject to review by a prosecutor (to determine legal sufficiency) and by probation or intake staff (to determine if formal action is appropriate under the surrounding circumstances).**

### 4.3.4 Youth service agencies.

The *Youth Service Agencies* volume is a linchpin of the standards series, establishing the principles governing the voluntary service sector of the juvenile justice system. In an early project statement of six "guidelines for action" developed to assist the reporters and committees in drafting the standards, the following position was enunciated:

> *Right to Voluntary Services and Programs.* Official coercion, so far as possible, should be avoided in favor of offering children voluntary services and programs. Existing rights will be more sharply defined and perhaps new legal rights—such as the right to education and to psychiatric and medical help—need formulation. Those children in institutions should enjoy the same right to voluntary services enjoyed by those in the community at large.

Actually, the last concept was expanded in the *Dispositions* volume, which requires institutions to provide all necessary and appropriate services, not limited by the services available in the community at large, thus imposing a higher obligation upon institutions in which juveniles are involuntarily confined by the correctional authorities.

The function of the youth service agency is defined as ensuring the delivery of needed services to youth in the community and their families, including youth diverted to the agency from the court. The agency must develop: (1) a listing of available services; (2) a self-referral system for youth and families in need of service; (3) a comprehensive service system to diagnose needs and ensure delivery of services through existing resources; and (4) a monitoring system.

Juveniles may avail themselves of the agency's services informally through self-referrals, parental referrals, citizen, agency, and school referrals, and formal referrals by police and courts. These will be discussed further in the section on sources of intervention.

Since our subject in this section is the ground for intervention, it should first be noted that service or treatment is an intervention. The main issue is whether the intervention is coerced or voluntary. For our purposes, the criterion applied is one of consequences or effect: if the alternative to admission to a program is a risk of deprivation of liberty—i.e., court referral, placement in a more restrictive facility or program, detention or continuation in a facility or program from which the youth wishes to be released, a fine or other penalty—the decision to seek treatment or services is not deemed voluntary. The only acceptable reason for a truly volitional choice is the juvenile's own sense of a need for the service, regardless of who may have suggested it originally.

Therefore, the standards construe involuntary participation in a youth service agency program as that stemming from formal referrals. For example, the voluntary aspect of an informal referral by a citizen, agency, or school is protected by a request to the referring source to sign a waiver of complaint to ensure the juvenile's voluntary participation, unhampered by an implied threat that nonparticipation will result in a complaint being filed. Further, police may *not* formally refer a juvenile for noncriminal misbehavior or for other conduct that would previously have resulted in release with a warning. The standards for formal police referral to a youth service agency are:

**4.5 Police diversion standards.**

**Police diversion should be made pursuant to guidelines in order to avoid discrimination based on race, color, religion, national origin, sex, or income. At a minimum, the following standards should be observed:**

**A. No juvenile who comes to the attention of the police [or court] should be formally referred to the youth service agency if, prior to the existence of the diversionary alternative, that juvenile would have been released with a warning. Such juveniles should, however, be informed of the existence of the program, the services available, and their eligibility for such services through a voluntary self-referral.**

**B. In keeping with Standard 1.1 of the** *Noncriminal Misbehavior* **volume eliminating the jurisdiction of the juvenile court over juveniles for acts of misbehavior, ungovernability, or unruliness that do not violate the criminal law, such juveniles should not be formally referred to the youth service agency.**

**C. All juveniles accused of class four or five offenses (as defined in Standard 5.2\* of the** *Juvenile Delinquency and Sanctions* **volume) who have no prior convictions or formal referrals should be formally referred to the youth service agency rather than to the juvenile court.**

**D. All other juveniles accused of class four or five offenses who have been free of involvement with the juvenile court for**

---

\*Former Standard 5.2 of the *Juvenile Delinquency and Sanctions* volume was renumbered to 4.2 subsequent to the publication of the revised *Youth Service Agencies* volume.

the preceding twelve months should be formally referred to the youth service agency rather than to the juvenile court.

E. Serious consideration should be given to the formal diversion of all other apprehended juveniles, taking into account the following factors:

1. prosecution toward conviction might cause serious harm to the juvenile or exacerbate the social problems that led to his or her criminal acts;

2. services to meet the juvenile's needs and problems may be unavailable within the court system or may be provided more effectively by the youth service agency;

3. the nature of the alleged offense;

4. the age and circumstances of the alleged offender;

5. the alleged offender's record, if any;

6. recommendations for diversion made by the complainant or victim.

The standards for court referrals are:

**4.7 Court referrals.**

No juvenile should be petitioned to the court without an independent determination by the court intake official that diversion is not appropriate, pursuant to the guidelines of Standard 4.8. Every decision to petition should be accompanied by a written statement of the intake official as to why the juvenile is not diverted.

**4.8 Court diversion guidelines.**

Court intake guidelines, at a minimum, should contain the same diversion standards set forth in Standard 4.5 above. If it is determined that the apprehended juvenile is an active participant in a youth service agency program, the decision on whether to petition may be deferred up to twenty-four hours beyond the normal time limit in order to obtain a report from the youth service agency on the juvenile's progress in the program.

Class four and five juvenile offenses are crimes that would be misdemeanors if committed by adults (respectively, crimes punishable for adults by imprisonment for over six months up to one year and imprisonment for six months or less). Therefore, Standard 4.5 C. provides for *mandatory* diversion for those charged with misdemeanors if they have no previous convictions or formal referrals.

The scope of the juvenile's obligation to participate in the programs will be discussed in the section on the nature of the intervention.

## 4.4 Rights of Minors to Prevent Intervention.

A different type of intervention in the lives of children is the subject of the *Rights of Minors* volume. As the title suggests, these standards could be seen as concerning the other side of the coin, guidelines for the invoking of intervening powers by the juvenile. The tension is between principles of family autonomy, safeguarding the family from outside intrusion with respect to its private concerns, and the juvenile's right to be free of family or legal constraints related to age or maturation. Thus, the standards deal in sequence with the age of majority, emancipation, support obligations, medical care, youth employment, minors' contracts, and first amendment rights. The fundamental question is the extent to which a minor should be treated as an adult or, to use juvenile rights terminology, standards for the right of a juvenile to act independently in a reasonable and proper manner without legal or social disability on the grounds of age and presumed incapacity.

However, the terminology of nonintervention also applies to the principle of family autonomy, the distinction resting on the unit to be protected. If the family unit is the principal object of concern, intervention in the process by which families resolve disputes is condemned, as in the Introduction, which states: "to the maximum extent possible courts should not interfere with family decision-making unless the parents' behavior falls below a legislatively mandated minimum standard of parental care as established in the juvenile court's neglect jurisdiction." But since the juvenile is the main focus of attention in the standards, family autonomy frequently must yield to the rights of minors.

The most obvious ground for denying a juvenile's right to act is age. Under the standards, eighteen is the age of majority. The twenty-sixth amendment to the Constitution adopted in 1971 established the minimum voting age of majority as eighteen. But some states still maintain higher age limits for other citizenship rights. And for some purposes, lower age limits bestow limited powers. As with the age of criminal liability, set at ten in *Juvenile Delinquency and Sanctions,* age alone is necessarily an arbitrary measure with objectivity and predictability its principal virtues. The presumption of possessing sufficient maturity to vote at eighteen is not rebuttable, but other age limits permit more flexibility, especially when combined with concepts of the mature minor and emancipation.

Emancipation as a concept developed to ameliorate the rigidity of fixed age demarcations for removal of the disabilities of minority. The volume introduces "a new approach to emancipation" in Standard 2.1.

A. The legal issues traditionally resolved by reference to the emancipation doctrine should be resolved legislatively as aspects of the substantive doctrines which govern legal relationships between child and parent, between parent and parent, between child and nonmembers of the family, and between parents and nonmembers of the family.

B. Legislatively created, narrowly drawn doctrines which obviate the need for relying upon the vague criteria of the traditional emancipation doctrine should include the following principles:

1. a parent should not be permitted to recover from the child's employer wages due or paid by the employer to the child;

2. a child should be permitted to sue his or her parent and the parent should be permitted to sue the child for damages arising from intentional or negligent tortious behavior so long as the behavior is not related to the exercise of family functions.

C. Because legal disputes concerning the activities and needs of children will inevitably arise—between child and parent, between parent and parent, between child and nonmembers of the family, and between parents and nonmembers of the family—and the disputes will arise in contexts and present legal issues which cannot be forecast legislatively, the legislature should also enact an emancipation doctrine of general applicability.

1. The doctrine should not permit emancipation by judicial decree.

2. The doctrine should be explicitly limited to issues not addressed by other standards of this volume and should authorize a finding of emancipation when a child, prior to the age of majority, has established a residence separate from that of his or her family, whether or not with parental consent or consent of a person responsible for his or her care, and is managing his or her own financial affairs.

Although there was some disagreement on the Commission with respect to the standard barring emancipation by judicial decree, there was general assent to the criteria for a finding of emancipation: the child's (1) establishment of a resident separate from his or her family regardless of parental consent and (2) management of his or her own financial affairs.

The right of a juvenile to sue persons legally obligated to support the juvenile would seem justified on its face, but it was the subject of a hard fought battle at the last Commission meeting. The conflict was resolved against pure family autonomy (support enforceable only by a parent in divorce or separation, by a third party suing for the value of goods or services, or by a non-parent who has custody) in favor of the juvenile's right to bring an action for support against a parent even in an on-going family unit. Standard 3.1 provides for a broad parental support obligation, extending to any parent, regardless of marital or adoptive status.

**3.1 Who is obligated to support.**

**A child entitled to support is entitled to support from each of his or her parents, natural or adopted, whether or not they are married.**

Part IV of *Rights of Minors* specifies the circumstances in which medical services may be provided to a juvenile without prior parental consent in Standards 4.4 to 4.9. Standard 4.4 was amended to insert "emancipated" before "minor." Standard 4.6 was amended by bracketing "sixteen" and adding a reference to Standard 4.2 B. Standards 4.7 and 4.8 were amended by changing "physician" to "person or agency."

**4.4 Emancipated minor.**

**A. An emancipated minor who is living separate and apart from his or her parent and who is managing his or her own financial affairs may consent to medical treatment on the same terms and conditions as an adult. Accordingly, parental consent should not be required, nor should there be subsequent notification of the parent, or financial liability.**

**1. If a physician treats a minor who is not actually emancipated, it should be a defense to a suit basing liability on lack of parental consent, that he or she relied in good faith on the minor's representations of emancipation.**

**4.5 Emergency treatment.**

**A. Under emergency circumstances, a minor may receive medical services or treatment without prior parental consent.**

**1. Emergency circumstances exist when delaying treatment to first secure parental consent would endanger the life or health of the minor.**

2. It should be a defense to an action basing liability on lack of parental consent, that the medical services were provided under emergency circumstances.

B. Where medical services or treatment are provided under emergency circumstances, the parent should be notified as promptly as possible, and his or her consent should be obtained for further treatment.

C. A parent should be financially liable to persons providing emergency medical treatment.

D. Where the emergency medical services are for treatment of chemical dependency (Standard 4.7); venereal disease, contraception, or pregnancy (Standard 4.8); or mental or emotional disorder (Standard 4.9), questions of notification of the parent and financial liability are governed by those provisions and Standards 4.2 B., 4.2 C., and 4.3.

### 4.6 Mature minor.

A. A minor of [sixteen] or older who has sufficient capacity to understand the nature and consequences of a proposed medical treatment for his or her benefit may consent to that treatment on the same terms and conditions as an adult.

B. The treating physician should notify the minor's parent of any medical treatment provided under this standard, subject to the provisions of Standard 4.2 B.

### 4.7 Chemical dependency.

A. A minor of any age may consent to medical services, treatment, or therapy for problems or conditions related to alcohol or drug abuse or addiction.

B. If the minor objects to notification of the parent, the person or agency providing treatment under this standard should notify the parent of such treatment only if he or she concludes that failing to inform the parent would seriously jeopardize the health of the minor, and complies with the provisions of Standard 4.2.

### 4.8 Venereal disease, contraception, and pregnancy.

A. A minor of any age may consent to medical services, therapy, or counseling for:

1. treatment of venereal disease;

2. family planning, contraception, or birth control other than a procedure which results in sterilization; or

3. treatment related to pregnancy, including abortion.

B. If the minor objects to notification of the parent, the person or agency providing treatment under this standard should notify the parent of such treatment only if he or she concludes that failing to inform the parent would seriously jeopardize the health of the minor, and complies with the provisions of Standard 4.2.

**4.9 Mental or emotional disorder.**

A. A minor of fourteen or older who has or professes to suffer from a mental or emotional disorder may consent to three sessions with a psychotherapist or counselor for diagnosis and consultation.

B. Following three sessions for crisis intervention and/or diagnosis, the provider should notify the parent of such sessions and obtain his or her consent to further treatment.

A juvenile's right to work is limited by age levels and other considerations, such as school attendance requirements, work permits, and special prohibitions based on the hazardous nature of the job activities. The standards on youth employment are as follows:

**5.1 Employment during school.**

A. No minor below the age of sixteen who is required to attend school should be employed during the hours in which he or she is required to be in school, as indicated on the work permit. See Standard 5.4.

　　1. This prohibition should not apply to a minor employed during school hours in a school sanctioned work-study, vocational training, or apprenticeship program.

**5.2 Minimum age of employment.**

A. No minor below twelve years of age should be employed in any occupation, trade, service, or business:

　　1. except that, with the consent of the minor's parent, no minimum age limitations or restrictions should apply to a minor employed:

　　　　a. by his or her parent in nonhazardous occupations, as defined in Standard 5.3; or

　　　　b. by third parties in domestic service, casual labor, or as a youthful performer, provided that such exempt services should not be performed by a minor required to attend school during hours in which the school is in session. See Standard 5.1.

5.3 Employment in hazardous activities.

A. No minor below sixteen years of age should be employed in any occupation determined to be hazardous.

B. The secretary of labor [or state labor commissioner] should promulgate specific standards and regulations defining what occupations are hazardous.

1. The secretary should regularly review and investigate to determine if a particular occupation or employment should be added to or deleted from the list of those which are hazardous.

C. The prohibition on employing minors in hazardous activities does not apply to a minor fourteen or older who is employed in or supervised under a state or federal apprentice training or work-study program in which the minor receives training and supervision.

5.4 Work permit as proof of eligibility for employment.

A. No minor below sixteen years of age should be employed without presenting to an employer or prospective employer a permit to work, which is the sole basis by which eligibility to work should be established.

Finally, *Rights of Minors* sets guidelines for the validity of contracts entered into by minors.

6.1 Minors' contracts.

The validity of contracts of minors, other than those governed by other standards of this volume, should be governed by the following principles:

A. The contract of a minor who is at least twelve years of age should be valid and enforceable by and against the minor, as long as such a contract of an adult would be valid and enforceable, if:

1. the minor's parent or duly constituted guardian consented in writing to the contract; or

2. the minor represented to the other party that he or she was at least eighteen years of age and a reasonable person under the circumstances would have believed the representation; or

3. the minor was a purchaser and is unable to return the goods to the seller in substantially the condition they were in when purchased because the minor lost or caused them to be damaged, the minor consumed them, or the minor gave them away.

Part VII in the tentative draft confirmed juveniles' rights to the same constitutionally protected first amendment freedoms that adults enjoy. However, the executive committee eliminated Part VII from the approved draft of the *Rights of Minors* volume. Students' first amendment rights still are covered in the *Schools and Education* volume.

If it seems strange that constitutional rights should continue to be a cause of contention for citizens of any age, one should reflect on the fact that juveniles have not actually been accorded some of the rights and privileges of citizenship, such as the right to vote and the right to a trial by jury.

## 4.5 Sources and Nature of Intervention.

From the preceding section on grounds for intervention, it should be apparent that the project was determined to limit the circumstances that could provoke official action affecting juveniles and their families. The length of the section, however, indicates the massive range of behavior and situations that would continue to justify intervention by the courts or other agencies that comprise the juvenile justice system. Who commences the action, files the petition or application, or reports the act precipitating the intervention, and how the complaint, charge, petition application, or other means of invoking jurisdiction is handled will be discussed more fully under court roles and procedures, but should be considered here first, because many decisions concerning lives and freedom never reach the courts. And although the chapter on treatment and corrections will cover the kinds of intervention permitted by the system, this section will examine the relationship between the grounds and sources of intervention and the official action that can follow.

### 4.5.1 Delinquency sanctions.

The *Juvenile Delinquency and Sanctions* volume does not specify the persons or procedures for initiating a proceeding, apparently leaving such details to the volumes on court roles and procedures. The only reference is to "the charging authority" in Standard 5.3. However, the standards are comprehensive in covering the types of sanctions, the class of juvenile offenses, and the limitations on type and duration of sanctions, which relate the maximum sanction that can be imposed to the class of the offense the juvenile is found to have committed.

It should be noted that the standards following former Standard 4.1 were renumbered after 4.1 was eliminated from the revised draft. All time frames were bracketed in revised Standards 4.2 and 5.2. The maximum durations for custodial sanctions in revised Standard 5.2 were increased from twenty-four to thirty-six months for class one juvenile offenses and from twelve to eighteen months for class two offenses. In addition, new subdivision C. was added to Standard 5.2 concerning the maximum duration for combined sanctions. Standard 5.3 C. was amended by substituting "committed" for "falling."

**4.1 Types of sanctions.**

The sanctions that a juvenile court may impose upon a juvenile adjudged to have committed a juvenile offense should be of three types, from most to least severe, as follows.

A. Custodial, where the juvenile is ordered

1. to be confined in a secure facility as defined in these standards; or

2. to be placed in a nonsecure facility including a foster home or residence as defined in these standards.

B. Conditional, where the juvenile is ordered

1. periodically to report to probation or other authorities; or

2. to perform or refrain from performing certain acts; or

3. to make restitution to persons harmed by his or her offense or to pay a fine; or

4. to undergo any similar sanction not involving a change in the juvenile's residence or legal custody.

C. Nominal, where the juvenile is reprimanded, warned, or otherwise reproved and unconditionally released.

D. For purposes of this standard,

1. the following institutions or designated portions thereof are secure facilities:

....[to be designated by the enacting jurisdiction]

2. the following types of facilities or designated portions thereof are nonsecure facilities:

....[to be designated by the enacting jurisdiction]

**4.2 Classes of juvenile offenses.**

A. Offenses within the criminal jurisdiction of the juvenile court should be classified as class one through class five juvenile offenses.

B. Where, under a criminal statute or ordinance made applicable to juveniles pursuant to Standard 2.2, the maximum sentence authorized upon conviction for such offense is:

1. death or imprisonment for life or for a term in excess of [twenty] years, it is a class one juvenile offense;

2. imprisonment for a term in excess of [five] but not more than [twenty] years, it is a class two juvenile offense;

3. imprisonment for a term in excess of [one] year but not more than [five] years, it is a class three juvenile offense;

4. imprisonment for a term in excess of [six] months but not more than [one] year, it is a class four juvenile offense;

5. imprisonment for a term of [six] months or less, it is a class five juvenile offense;

6. not prescribed, it is a class five juvenile offense.

5.2 Limitations on type and duration of sanctions.

A. The juvenile court should not impose a sanction more severe than,

1. where the juvenile is found to have committed a class one juvenile offense,

a. confinement in a secure facility or placement in a nonsecure facility or residence for a period of [thirty-six] months, or

b. conditional freedom for a period of [thirty-six] months;

2. where the juvenile is found to have committed a class two juvenile offense,

a. confinement in a secure facility or placement in a nonsecure facility or residence for a period of [eighteen] months, or

b. conditional freedom for a period of [twenty-four] months;

3. where the juvenile is found to have committed a class three juvenile offense,

a. confinement in a secure facility or placement in a nonsecure facility or residence for a period of [six] months, or

b. conditional freedom for a period of [eighteen] months;

4. where the juvenile is found to have committed a class four juvenile offense,

a. confinement in a secure facility for a period of [three] months if the juvenile has a prior record, or

b. placement in a nonsecure facility or residence for a period of [three] months, or

c. conditional freedom for a period of [twelve] months;

5. where the juvenile is found to have committed a class five juvenile offense,

a. placement in a nonsecure facility or residence for a period of [two] months if the juvenile has a prior record, or

b. conditional freedom for a period of [six] months.

B. For purposes of this standard, a juvenile has a "prior record" only when he or she has been formally adjudged previously to have committed:

1. an offense that would amount to a class one, two, or three juvenile offense, as defined in Standard 4.2, within the twenty-four months preceding the commission of the offense subject to sanctioning; or

2. three offenses that would amount to class four or five juvenile offenses, as defined in Standard 4.2, at least one of which was committed within the twelve months preceding the commission of the offense subject to sanctioning.

C. The juvenile court may impose a sanction consisting of confinement or placement for a specified period of time followed by conditional freedom for a specified period of time, provided that the total duration does not exceed the maximum term permissible as a custodial sanction for the offense.

5.3 Multiple juvenile offenses.

A. When a juvenile is found to have committed two or more juvenile offenses during the same transaction or episode, the juvenile court should not impose a sanction more severe than the maximum sanction authorized by Standard 5.2 for the most serious such offense.

B. When, in the same proceeding, a juvenile is found to have committed two or more offenses during separate transactions or episodes, the juvenile court should not impose a sanction

1. more severe in nature than the sanction authorized by Standard 5.2 for the most serious such offense; or

2. longer in duration than a period equal to one and a half times the period authorized by Standard 5.2 for the most serious such offense.

C. When, at the time a juvenile is charged with an offense, the charging authority or its agents have evidence sufficient to warrant charging such juvenile with another juvenile offense, committed within the court's jurisdiction, the failure jointly to charge such offense should thereafter bar the initiation of juvenile court delinquency proceedings based on such offense.

5.4 Termination of orders imposing sanctions.

A juvenile court order imposing sanctions should terminate no later than the [twenty-first] birthday of the juvenile subject to such order.

The *Juvenile Delinquency and Sanctions* standards further require the juvenile court to specify the following details of the sanction in the dispositional order:

**5.1 Orders imposing sanctions.**
**Juvenile court orders imposing sanctions should specify:**
**A. the nature of the sanction; and**
**B. the duration of such sanction; and,**
**C. where such order affects the residence or legal custody of the juvenile, the place of residence or confinement ordered and the person or agency in whom custody is vested; and**
**D. the juvenile court judge's reasons for the sanction imposed, pursuant to** *Dispositions* **Standard 2.1.**

**4.5.2 Agency and court intervention for abuse and neglect.**

The family autonomy concept of nonintervention in family conflicts is articulated in the *Rights of Minors, Juvenile Delinquency and Sanctions,* and *Abuse and Neglect* standards, but in each volume the concept is limited to matters that can be resolved by parental authority without actually causing or threatening substantial harm. A critical question in the *Abuse and Neglect* standards is who or what signals the transgression of the dividing line between nonintervention on the ground of family privacy and intervention based on the risk to a juvenile of imminent harm or deprivation of a significant right or privilege. Jurisdiction for abuse and neglect cases is determined by specific harms caused or threatened by the child's parents or custodian. The responsibility for reporting abused children is equally explicit. Standards 3.1 to 3.3 define mandatory reporters, permissible reporters (any person), the recipients of reports, and the action to be taken by report recipient agencies. Standards 3.4 and 3.5 define the duties and restraints involved in maintaining a central register of child abuse. Standard 3.3 was revised to eliminate a court-approved plan of investigation and to add a requirement of a warrant for agencies seeking to examine, take custody, or interview against the parents' wishes in nonemergency cases. Standard 3.5 was revised to make hearings challenging reports nonpublic.

**3.1 Required reports.**
**A. Any physician, nurse, dentist, optometrist, medical examiner, or coroner, or any other medical or mental health professional, Christian Science practitioner, religious healer, schoolteacher and other pupil personnel, social or public assistance worker, child care worker in any day care center or child**

caring institution, police or law enforcement officer who has reasonable cause to suspect that a child, coming before him/her in his/her official or professional capacity, is an abused child as defined by Standard 3.1 B. should be required to make a report to any report recipient agency listed for that geographic locality pursuant to Standard 3.2.

B. An "abused child," for purposes of Standard 3.1 A., is a child who has suffered physical harm, inflicted nonaccidentally upon him/her by his/her parent(s) or person(s) exercising essentially equivalent custody and control over the child, which injury causes or creates a substantial risk of causing death, disfigurement, impairment of bodily functioning, or other serious physical injury.

C. Any person making a report or participating in any subsequent proceedings regarding such report pursuant to this Part should be immune from any civil or criminal liability as a result of such actions, provided that such person was acting in good faith in such actions. In any proceeding regarding such liability, good faith should be presumed.

D. The privileged character of communication between husband and wife and between any professional person and his/her patient or client, except privilege between attorney and client, should be abrogated regarding matters subject to this Part, and should not justify failure to report or the exclusion of evidence in any proceeding resulting from a report pursuant to this Part.

E. Any person who knowingly fails to make a report required pursuant to this Part should be guilty of a misdemeanor (and/or should be liable, regarding any injuries proximately caused by such failure, for compensatory and/or punitive damages in civil litigation maintained on behalf of the child or his/her estate).

3.2 Recipients and format of report.

A. The state department of social services (or equivalent state agency) should be required to issue a list of qualified report recipient agencies (which may be public or private agencies), and to designate geographic localities within the state within which each such recipient agency would be authorized to receive reports made pursuant to Standard 3.1A. The state department should ensure that there be at least one qualified report recipient agency for every designated geographic locality within the state.

B. An agency should be eligible for listing as a qualified report recipient agency if it demonstrates, to the satisfaction of the state department, that it has adequate capacity to provide, or obtain provision of, protection to children who may be the subject of reports pursuant to this Part. The state department should be required to promulgate regulations setting standards for such adequate capacity which specify requisite staff personnel (which may include, without limitation, pediatric physicians and other medical care personnel, mental health professionals and paraprofessionals, and attorneys and legal paraprofessionals), requisite agency organizational structure, and any other matters relevant to adequate child-protective capacities.

C. The state department should review, at least every two years, whether an agency listed as a qualified report recipient agency continues to meet the requirements for listing pursuant to Standard 3.2 B. For purposes of such review, the state department should examine the agency's disposition of and efficacy in cases reported to it pursuant to this Part. Each agency should maintain records, in a format prescribed by regulations of the state department, to facilitate such review. Such regulations should provide safeguards against any use of such records that would disclose the identity, except where specifically authorized by this Part, or otherwise work to the detriment of persons who have been named in reports made pursuant to this Part.

D. The format of the reports to the report recipient agencies, in satisfaction of the requirements of Standard 3.1 A., should be specified by regulation of the state department. Such regulations should provide that initial reports pursuant to Standard 3.1 A. be made by telephone to a report recipient agency, and that telephonic and any written reports contain such information as the state department may specify.

3.3 Action by report recipient agency.

A. A report recipient agency receiving a report submitted pursuant to Standard 3.1 A. should be required to immediately undertake investigation of the report and to determine *inter alia* whether there is reason to believe the child subject of the report is an abused child, as defined in Standard 3.1 B., and whether protection of the child requires filing of a petition pursuant to Part V, and/or taking emergency temporary custody of the child pursuant to Part IV.

B. 1. If the agency determines, upon initial receipt of the report or at any subsequent time after its initial contact with the child that filing of a petition pursuant to Part V or emergency temporary custody pursuant to Part IV is necessary for the protection of the child, it should promptly take such action, except that the agency has no authority to examine or take custody of the child or to interview the parents or custodians or visit the child's home, against the wishes of the child's parents or custodians named in the report, except as specifically authorized by a court as provided in subsections 2.-5. or as specifically authorized by Part IV regarding emergency temporary custody of the child.

2. If the agency wishes to examine or take custody of the child, to interview the parents or custodians, or to visit the child's home against the wishes of the child's parents or custodians named in the report, it must obtain a warrant to search, duly ordered by the court authorizing the agency to make such investigation. Such an order may be obtained *ex parte.*

3. A warrant should not be granted except upon a finding by the court of probable cause to believe that the child comes within the jurisdiction of the court pursuant to the standards set out in Part II.

4. The warrant should set forth with particularity the places to be investigated, the persons to be interviewed, and the basis for the finding of probable cause. The warrant should state that refusal to allow an investigation may lead to the sanctions provided in subsection 5.

5. a. If the parents or custodians named in the report refuse to allow access to the child after being served with a copy of the warrant ordering such access, the investigating agency may take custody of the child for a time no longer than reasonably necessary for investigative purposes, but in no event should custody of the child be taken for a longer consecutive period than eight hours, nor should custody be maintained between 8:00 P.M. and 8:00 A.M.

b. Where access to other information has been refused after a copy of the warrant ordering such access was served, the court may subject the person having custody of the information to civil contempt penalties until it is provided to the investigating agency.

C. Identifying characteristics in all unsubstantiated reports (including names, addresses, and any other such identifying characteristics of persons named in a report) should be expunged from the files of the report recipient agency immediately following completion of the agency's listing review pursuant to

Standard 3.2 C., within two years of the report's receipt. In any event, identifying characteristics in all reports should be expunged from the files of the report recipient agency within seven years of the report's receipt.

### 3.4 Central register of child abuse.

A. The state department of social services (or equivalent state agency) should be required to maintain a central register of child abuse. Upon receipt of a report made pursuant to Standard 3.1 A., the report recipient agency should immediately notify the central register by telephone and transmit a copy of any written report to the central register for recordation.

B. Within sixty days of its initial notification of a report for recordation, the report recipient agency should be required to indicate its action pursuant to Standard 3.3, and to indicate any subsequent action regarding such report at intervals no later than sixty days thereafter until the agency has terminated contact with the persons named in the report. If at any time the report recipient agency indicates that the report (including names, addresses, and any other such identifying characteristics of persons named in the report) should be expunged, the central register should immediately effect such expungement. In any event, all reports (including names, addresses, and any other such identifying characteristics of persons named in the report) should be expunged from the central register seven years from the date the report was initially received by the report recipient agency.

C. The central register, and any employee or agent thereof, should not make available recordation and any information regarding reports to any person or agency except to the following, upon their request:

1. a report recipient agency within this state, listed pursuant to Standard 3.2, or a child protective agency in another state deemed equivalent, under regulations promulgated by the state department of social services (or equivalent state agency), to such report recipient agency within this state;

2. any person (including both child and parent(s) and alleged abuser [if other than parent(s)]) who is named in a report (or another, such as an attorney, acting in that person's behalf), except that such person should not be informed of the name, address, occupation, or other identifying characteristics of the person who submitted the report to the report recipient agency;

3. a court authorized to conduct proceedings pursuant to Part V;

4. a person engaged in bona fide research, with written permission of the director of the state department (except that no information regarding the names, addresses or any other such identifying characteristics of persons named in the report should be made available to this person). Any person who violates the provisions of this standard by disseminating or knowingly permitting the dissemination of recordation and any information regarding reports in the central register to any other person or agency should be guilty of a misdemeanor (and/or should be liable for compensatory and/or punitive damages in civil litigation by or on behalf of person(s) named in a report).

3.5 Action by central register.

The central register should be required to notify by registered mail, immediately upon recordation of a report, any person (including child and parent(s) and alleged abuser [if other than parent]) who is named in a report recorded in the central register, and to subsequently notify such person of any further recordation or information (including any expungement of the report) regarding such report submitted to the register pursuant to Standard 3.4, except as provided in Standard 3.4 C. 2. Any such person should have the right, and be so informed, to inspect the report and to challenge whether its entire contents, or any part thereof, should be altered or wholly expunged. Proceedings, including nonpublic hearings, except where an interested person can show they should be public, and other procedural matters regarding any such challenge should be governed by the administrative procedures act of this state.

Far more complicated are the authorized forms of intervention that may follow reports of an abused or neglected ("endangered") child. Standard 4.1 authorizes emergency temporary custody of the child by a physician, law enforcement official, or report recipient agency designated by the state department of social services as empowered to take custody of endangered children. Standard 4.2 describes the authority to place the child in a nonsecure facility and provide necessary emergency medical care to forestall imminent death or serious injury, regardless of the wishes of the child's parents or other caretakers. Standard 4.2 B. requires initiation of a report to a court and the filing of a petition (unless custody is relinquished to the parent) by the next business day. These standards are cited in the section on grounds for court intervention.

The usual court procedures prescribed in Standards 4.3 to 4.5 with regard to review of emergency temporary custody, the procedures set forth in Part V on court proceedings "to find a child within the jurisdiction of the court," the requirements pertaining to family supervision, placement, or other intervention, the preadjudication proceedings (hearings, discovery, etc.), and the procedures contained in Part VI on dispositional hearings and reports, might best be considered in the chapter on court roles and procedures, to compare them with delinquency procedural standards. Nevertheless, at the risk of creating confusion over the procedural safeguards the standards generally impose to protect a respondent juvenile, the *Abuse and Neglect* standards on court proceedings are set forth below. Such extraordinary provisions as the admissibility in evidence of the parents' refusal to cooperate in the proceeding can only be explained on the basis of the deep community concern to protect children from harm. Revisions in the procedures in Parts V and VI on preadjudication, adjudication, and dispositional proceedings are so extensive that reference should be made to the Appendix for an enumeration of the specific changes in those standards.

## PART V: COURT PROCEEDINGS

5.1 Complaint and petition.
  A. Submission of complaint.
    1. Any person may submit a complaint to the juvenile court alleging and specifying reasons why the juvenile court should find a child within the jurisdiction of the court, pursuant to the standards set out in Part II. Any complaint that serves as the basis for a filed petition of endangerment should be sworn to and signed by a person who has personal knowledge of the facts or is informed of them and believes that they are true.
    2. Any person submitting a complaint or any person providing information upon which a complaint or petition might be based should be immune from any civil or criminal liability as a result of such action, or as a result of participating in any subsequent proceedings regarding such action, provided that such person was acting in good faith in such action. In any proceeding regarding such liability good faith should be presumed.
  B. Intake review of complaints.
    1. Upon receipt of a complaint, an intake officer of the juvenile probation agency should promptly determine

whether the allegations, on their face, are sufficiently specific and, if proven, would constitute grounds for court jurisdiction pursuant to the standards set out in Part II. If the intake officer determines that the allegations, on their face, are not sufficiently specific, or, if proven, would not constitute grounds for court intervention, the intake officer should dismiss the complaint. If the legal sufficiency of the complaint is unclear, the intake officer should ask the appropriate prosecuting official for a determination of its sufficiency. If the intake officer determines that the complaint is sufficient, the officer should determine a disposition of the complaint. The following are permissible dispositions at intake:

a. Unconditional dismissal of a complaint.

Unconditional dismissal of a complaint is the termination of all proceedings arising out of the complaint.

b. Judicial disposition of a complaint.

Judicial disposition of a complaint is the initiation of formal judicial proceedings through the filing of a petition.

c. Referral to a community agency.

Referral to a community agency is the referral of the child and his/her parents to an agency, including a child protective services agency, for further consideration.

2. In determining a disposition of a complaint at intake, the intake officer should:

a. determine whether coercive intervention appears authorized as provided in Standard 2.1 A.-F.;

b. determine whether judicial intervention appears necessary to protect the child from being endangered in the future, as provided in Standard 2.2; and

c. consider the resources available both within and without the juvenile justice system.

3. The standards for intake procedures set out in Section IV of *The Juvenile Probation Function: Intake and Predisposition Investigative Services* should apply to intake review of complaints of endangerment, except that the privilege against self-incrimination at intake should apply to the parent or other custodian who is the subject of the complaint pursuant to the standards in Part II of this volume, and a right to assistance of counsel should be available to that parent or other adult custodian as a waivable right. The standards incorporated by reference are *Juvenile Probation Function Standards* 2.9 Necessity for and desirability of written guidelines and rules; 2.10 Initiation of intake proceedings and receipt of complaint by intake officer; 2.11 Intake investiga-

tion; 2.12 Juvenile's privilege against self-incrimination at intake; 2.13 Juvenile's right to assistance of counsel at intake; 2.14 Intake interviews and dispositional conferences; and 2.15 Length of intake process. In addition, *Juvenile Probation Function* Standard 2.16, Role of intake officer and prosecutor in filing of petition: right of complainant to file a petition, also should apply to the intake review of complaints of endangerment, except that the references to a petition in those cases in which the conduct charged "would constitute a crime if committed by an adult" should be deemed to refer to a petition of endangerment in this volume.

C. Parties.

The following should be parties to all proceedings regarding a child alleged to be or adjudicated endangered:

1. the child;

2. the child's parents, guardians, and, if relevant, any other adults having substantial ties to the child who have been performing the caretaking role; and

3. the petitioner.

5.2 Preadjudication proceedings.

A. Written petition.

Each jurisdiction should provide by law that the filing of a written petition, sworn to and signed by a person who has personal knowledge of the facts or is informed of them and believes they are true, giving the parents adequate notice of the charges is a requisite for endangerment proceedings to begin. If appropriate challenge is made to the legal sufficiency of the petition, the judge of the juvenile court should rule on that challenge before calling upon the parents to plead.

B. Filing and signing of the petition.

Petitions alleging endangerment should be prepared, filed, and signed by the juvenile prosecutor to certify that he or she has read the petition and that to the best of his or her knowledge, information, and belief there is good ground to support it.

C. Notification of filing, service, and initial appearance.

Upon filing of the petition, the court should issue a summons directing the parties to appear at a specified time and place and serve the summons, with a copy of the petition attached, at least twenty-four hours in advance of the first appearance, upon the parents of the child alleged to be endangered. If, after reasonable effort, personal service is not made, the court should order substituted service. The initial appearance before the court should occur within [one] week of the filing of the petition, except if a child is in emergency temporary custody pursuant to the standards in Part IV, the first appearance should occur on the same business day, if possible, and no later than the next business day. At the first appearance, the court should:

1. notify the parents that such petition has been filed;

2. provide the parents with a copy of such petition, including identification by name of the person submitting such petition;

3. inform the parents of the nature and possible consequences of the proceedings and that they have a right to representation by counsel at all stages of the proceedings regarding such petition;

4. inform the parents that if they are unable to afford counsel, the court will appoint counsel at public expense, provided that, if a conflict of interest appears likely between parents named in the petition, the court may in its discretion appoint separate counsel for each parent; and

5. inform the parents of their right to confront and cross-examine witnesses and to request a probable cause hearing.

D. Appointment of counsel for child.

Upon filing, the court should be required to appoint counsel at public expense to represent the child identified in the petition, as a party to the proceedings. No reimbursement should be sought from the parents or the child for the cost of such counsel, regardless of the parents' or child's financial resources.

E. Attendance at all proceedings.

In all proceedings regarding the petition, the parents of the child should be entitled to attend, except that the proceeding may go forward without such presence if the parents fail to appear after reasonable notification (including without limitation efforts by court-designated persons to contact the parents by telephone and by visitation to the parents' last known address of residence within the jurisdiction of the court). The child identified in such petition should attend such proceedings unless the court finds, on motion of any party, that such attendance would be detrimental to the child. If the parents or custodians named in the petition fail to attend, the court may proceed to the hearing only if the child is represented by counsel. If the parents or custodians named in the petititon were not present at the hearing and appear thereafter and move the court for a rehearing, the court should grant the motion unless it finds that they willfully refused to appear at the hearing or that the rehearing would be unjust because of the lapse of time since the hearing was held.

F. Evidence at all proceedings.

In all proceedings regarding the petition, sworn testimony and other competent and relevant evidence may be admitted pursuant to the principles governing evidence in civil matters in the courts of general jurisdiction in the state. The court may admit testimony by the child who is the subject of the petition or by any other children whose testimony might be relevant regarding the petition if, upon motion of the party wishing to proffer the testimony of such child, the court determines that the child is sufficiently mature to provide competent evidence and that testifying will not be detrimental to the child. In making such determination regarding the child's proffered testimony, the court may direct psychological or other examinations and impose appropriate conditions for taking any testimony to safeguard the child from detriment. However, the court should not have access to any investigational or social history report prior to adjudication unless it has been admitted into evidence. The privileged character of communications between husband and wife and between any professional person and his or her patient or client, except the privilege between attorney and client, should not be a ground for excluding evidence that would otherwise be admissible.

G. Temporary custody.

If the child remains in emergency temporary custody pursuant to Standard 4.3, no later than [two] working days following the filing of the petition, the court should convene a hearing to determine whether emergency temporary custody should be continued.

Once the parents have been informed of the proceeding and counsel has been assigned or retained, the court should hold a second detention hearing upon the request of the parents. At this hearing, the burden should be on the petitioner to show by relevant, material, and competent evidence, subject to cross-examination, that continued emergency temporary custody is necessary, pursuant to the standards set out in Standard 4.3 B.

H. Appointment of independent experts.

Any party to the proceeding may petition the court for appointment of experts, at public expense, for independent evaluation of the matter before the court. The court should grant such petition unless it finds the expert unnecessary.

I. Discovery.

The standards governing disclosure of matters in connection with proceedings to determine whether the petition should be granted, disposition of granted petitions (Part VI), or review proceedings (Part VII) should be the same for the child and the parents as for the respondent in delinquency cases set out in the *Pretrial Court Proceedings* volume.

J. Subpoenas.

Upon request of any party, a subpoena should be issued by the court (or its clerk) commanding the attendance and testimony of any person at any proceeding conducted pursuant to this Part or commanding the production of documents for use in any such proceeding, except that the attendance and testimony of any children (including the child subject of the petition) should be governed by Standard 5.2 E. and F. Failure by any person without adequate excuse to obey a subpoena served upon him/her may be deemed a contempt of the court subject to civil contempt penalties.

K. Interpreters at all proceedings.

The court should appoint an interpreter or otherwise ensure that language barriers do not deprive the parents, child, witnesses, or other participants of the ability to understand and participate effectively in all stages of the proceedings.

5.3 Adjudication proceedings.

A. Proceedings to determine contested petition.

In any proceeding to determine whether the petition should be granted, the following should apply:

1. Upon request of the child or the parents, the sole trier of fact should be a jury whose verdict must be unanimous, and which may consist of as few as six persons. In the absence of such request from either such party, the trier of fact should be the court. Under no circumstances should the trier of fact, or the judge prior to adjudication, have access to any investigational or social history report, unless it has been duly admitted into evidence at the hearing, as provided in Standard 5.2 F.

2. The burden should rest on the prosecutor of the petition to prove by clear and convincing evidence allegations sufficient to support the petition.

3. Proof that access has been refused to sources of or means for obtaining information, or that the parents have refused to attend or to testify without adequate excuse, or regarding conduct of the parents toward another child should be admissible, if the court determines such proof relevant to the allegations in the petition; except that proof of either such

matter, standing alone, should not be sufficient to sustain the granting of the petition.

4. Time for hearing. A hearing regarding a child who has remained in emergency temporary custody should take place no later than [twenty-five] days after the filing of the petition. If, within [twenty-five] days, the petitioner is not ready to go forward with the hearing, the court must order the child returned to his or her parents and dismiss the petition with prejudice unless there is good cause shown for the delay. In the event such cause is shown, the court must continue to find that conditions exist, pursuant to Standard 4.3, justifying the continuation of the child in emergency temporary custody. In no event should a delay beyond [twenty-five] days be authorized for longer than [seven] additional days.

For all other cases under this part, a hearing should be held within [sixty] days of the filing of the petition. If at the end of this time the petition is not ready to proceed, the court should dismiss the petition with prejudice.

B. Uncontested petitions.

If the parents wish to admit to all or any part of the allegations in the petition, sufficient to give the court authority to order a disposition of the proceeding other than dismissal as set out in Part VI, the court should convene a hearing at which testimony should be taken regarding the voluntariness and validity of the parents' decision. The judge should not accept a plea admitting an allegation of the petition without first addressing the parents personally, in language calculated to communicate effectively with them, to:

1. Determine that the parents understand the nature of the allegations;

2. Inform the parents of the right to a hearing at which the petitioner must confront respondent with witnesses and prove the allegations by clear and convincing competent evidence and at which the parents' attorney will be permitted to cross-examine the witnesses called by the petitioner and to call witnesses on the parents' behalf;

3. Inform the parents of the right to remain silent with respect to the allegations of the petition as well as of the right to testify if desired;

4. Inform the parents of the right to appeal from the decision reached in the trial;

5. Inform the parents of the right to a trial by jury;

6. Inform the parents that one gives up those rights by a plea admitting an allegation of the petition;

7. Inform the parents that if the court accepts the plea, the court can enter any final order of disposition set forth in Part VI;

8. Determine that the plea is voluntary; and

9. Determine that parents were given the effective assistance of an attorney, if the parents were represented by counsel.

The court should allow the parents to withdraw a plea admitting an allegation of the petition whenever the parents prove that withdrawal is necessary to correct a manifest injustice. If the court accepts an admission, it should enter an order finding that the child is endangered.

C. Recording proceedings.

1. A verbatim record should be made and preserved of all proceedings, whether or not the allegations in the petition are contested.

2. The record should be preserved and, with any exhibits, kept confidential.

3. The requirement of preservation should be subordinated to any order for expungement of the record and the requirement of confidentiality should be subordinated to court orders on behalf of the parents, child, or petitioner for a verbatim transcript of the record for use in subsequent legal proceedings.

5.4 Findings.

A. The trier of fact should record its findings specifically. Findings of fact and law should be articulated separately on the record. If the trier of fact determines that facts sufficient to sustain the petition have been established, the court should enter an order finding that the child is endangered. If the trier of fact determines that facts sufficient to sustain the petition have not been established, the court should dismiss the petition.

B. Each jurisdiction should provide by law that a finding by juvenile court that a child is endangered should only be used for the purpose of providing the court with the authority to order an appropriate disposition for the child pursuant to Standard 6.3.

5.5 Appeals.

Appeals from a finding that a child is endangered should not be allowed as of right. Interlocutory appeals from such orders may be allowed only in the discretion of the appellate court. Appeals as of right exist only from a final order of disposition. The standards governing appeals from proceedings under this

Part should be the same as those set out in the *Appeals and Collateral Review* standards, except that the parties entitled to take an appeal under *Appeals and Collateral Review* Standard 2.2 also should include the petitioner pursuant to Standard 5.1 C. above.

## PART VI: DISPOSITIONS

6.1 Predisposition investigation and reports.

A. Predisposition investigation.

After the court has entered a finding pursuant to Standard 5.4 F. that a child is endangered, it should authorize an investigation to be conducted by the probation department to supply the necessary information for an order of disposition.

B. Predisposition report.

The predisposition report should include the following information:

1. a description of the specific programs and/or placements, for both the parents and the child, which will be needed in order to prevent further harm to the child, the reasons why such programs and/or placements are likely to be useful, the availability of any proposed services, and the agency's plans for ensuring that the services will be delivered;

2. a statement of the indications (*e.g.,* specific changes in parental behavior) that will be used to determine that the family no longer needs supervision or that placement is no longer necessary;

3. an estimate of the time in which the goals of intervention should be achieved or in which it will be known they cannot be achieved.

4. In any case where removal from parental custody is recommended, the report should contain:

a. a full description of the reasons why the child cannot be adequately protected in the home, including a description of any previous efforts to work with the parents with the child in the home, the "in-home treatment programs," *e.g.,* homemakers, which have been considered and rejected, and the parents' attitude toward placement of the child;

b. a statement of the likely harms the child will suffer as a result of removal (this section should include an exploration of the nature of the parent-child attachment and the anticipated effect of separation and loss to both the parents and the child);

c. a description of the steps that will be taken to minimize harm to the child that may result if separation occurs.

5. If no removal from parental custody is recommended, the report should indicate what services or custodial arrangements, if any, have been offered to and/or accepted by the parents of the child.

C. The investigating agency should be required to provide its report to the court and the court should provide copies of such report to all parties to the proceedings.

**6.2 Proceeding to determine disposition.**

Following a finding pursuant to Standard 5.4 that a child is endangered, the court should, as soon as practicable, but no later than [forty-five] days thereafter, convene a hearing to determine the disposition of the petition. If the child is in emergency temporary custody, the court should be required to convene the hearing no later than [twenty] working days following the finding that the child is endangered. All parties to the proceeding should participate in the hearing, and all matters relevant to the court's determination should be presented in evidence at the hearing. In deciding the appropriate disposition, the court should have available and should consider the dispositional report prepared by the investigating agency pursuant to Standard 6.1 B.

**6.3 Available dispositions.**

A. A court should have at least the following dispositional alternatives and resources:

1. dismissal of the case;
2. wardship with informal supervision;
3. ordering the parents to accept social work supervision;
4. ordering the parents and/or the child to accept individual or family therapy or medical treatment;
5. ordering the state or parents to employ a homemaker in the home;
6. placement of the child in a day care program;
7. placement of the child with a relative, in a foster family or group home, or in a residential treatment center.

B. A court should have authority to order that the parent accept, and that the state provide, any of the above services.

C. It should be the state's responsibility to provide an adequate level of services.

6.4 Standards for choosing a disposition.
   A. General goal.
   The goal of all dispositions should be to protect the child from the harm justifying intervention in the least restrictive manner available to the court.
   B. Dispositions other than removal of the child.
   In ordering a disposition other than removal of the child from his/her home, the court should choose a program designed to alleviate the immediate danger to the child, to mitigate or cure any damage the child has already suffered, and to aid the parents so that the child will not be endangered in the future. In selecting a program, the court should choose those services which least interfere with family autonomy, provided that the services are adequate to protect the child.
   C. Removal.
      1. A child should not be removed from his/her home unless the court finds that:
         a. the child has been physically abused as defined in Standard 2.1 A., and there is a preponderance of evidence that the child cannot be protected from further physical abuse without being removed from his/her home; or
         b. the child has been endangered in one of the other ways specified by statute and there is clear and convincing evidence that the child cannot be protected from further harm of the type justifying intervention unless removed from his/her home.
      2. Even if a court finds subsections 1. a. or b. applicable, before any child is removed from his/her home, the court must find that there is a placement in fact available in which the child will not be endangered.
      3. The court should not be authorized to remove a child when the child is endangered solely due to environmental conditions beyond the control of the parents, which the parents would be willing to remedy if they were able to do so.
      4. Those advocating removal should bear the burden of proof on all these issues.

6.5 Initial plans.
   A. Children left in their own home.
   Whenever a child is left in his/her home, the agency should develop with the parent a specific plan detailing any changes in parental behavior or home conditions that must be made in order for the child not to be endangered. The plan should also

specify the services that will be provided to the parent and/or the child to insure that the child will not be endangered. If there is a dispute regarding any aspect of the plan, final resolution should be by the court.

B. Children removed from their homes.

Before a child is ordered removed from his/her home, the agency charged with his/her care should provide the court with a specific plan as to where the child will be placed, what steps will be taken to return the child home, and what actions the agency will take to maintain parent-child ties. Whenever possible, this plan should be developed in consultation with the parent, who should be encouraged to help in the placement. If there is a dispute regarding any aspect of the plan, final resolution should be by the court.

1. The plan should specify what services the parents will receive in order to enable them to resume custody and what actions the parents must take in order to resume custody.

2. The plan should provide for the maximum parent-child contact possible, unless the court finds that visitation should be limited because it will be seriously detrimental to the child.

3. A child generally should be placed as close to home as possible, preferably in his/her own neighborhood, unless the court finds that placement at a greater distance is necessary to promote the child's well-being. In the absence of good cause to the contrary, preference should be given to a placement with the child's relatives.

6.6 Rights of parents, custodians, and children following removal.

A. All placements are for a temporary period. Every effort should be made to facilitate the return of the child as quickly as possible.

B. When a child is removed from his/her home, his/her parents should retain the right to consent to major medical decisions, to the child's marriage, or to the child's joining the armed services, unless parental consent is not generally required for any of these decisions or the court finds that the parents' refusal to consent would be seriously detrimental to the child.

C. Depending on the child's age and maturity, the agency should also solicit and consider the child's participation in decisions regarding his/her care while in placement.

D. Unless a child is being returned to his/her parents, the child should not be removed from a foster home in which he/she

has resided for at least one year without providing the foster
parents with notice and an opportunity to be heard before a
court. If the foster parents object to the removal and wish to
continue to care for the child, the child should not be removed
when the removal would be detrimental to the child's emotional
well-being.

Equally relevant to intervention in the lives of children and families
is Part VII, Monitoring of Children Under Court Supervision and
Termination of Supervision. Standard 7.1 was amended to allow
grievance officers to request an early court review. Standard 7.5 D.
was amended to substitute a warning of possible termination proceedings for a warning of possible termination at the next review hearing.
And finally, we will consider the ultimate family interventions—
termination of parental rights in Part VIII and voluntary placements
under Part X.

Standard 9.1 provides that parents will be liable for prosecution for
child endangerment only if the court in which the petition is filed
certifies that such prosecution will not unduly harm the child involved.

The provisions in Part VII of the *Abuse and Neglect* standards for
court and agency monitoring of cases under court supervision rely on
the mechanisms of formal court hearings at least every six months;
interim reports to the court by the agencies responsible for providing
services if unable to provide the services ordered; and grievance
officers to receive complaints from parents or children who feel they
are not receiving the court-ordered services.

There clearly are many levels of intervention provided in the
standards, as best exemplified in the standards relating severity of
sanctions or dispositions to classes of juvenile offenses in the *Juvenile
Delinquency and Sanctions* and *Dispositions* volumes. Thus, a nominal
sanction would involve a reprimand and release but no further control
over the juvenile; a more severe sanction would entail conditions such
as probation or assignment to a community program for up to six
months; then placement in a foster home or a nonsecure facility for up
to six months; then placement for six months to a year, for over a year,
and up the scale to three years in a nonsecure placement, or
confinement in a secure facility for any period up to three years. The
severity of some of these sanctions overlaps, but the pattern demonstrates that the least restrictive alternative (nominal disposition)
involves no further intrusion in the juvenile's life, followed by
probation or community agency supervision in a program that permits
the juvenile to remain at home, followed by removal from the home
and placement in a foster home or nonsecure facility, and confinement
in a secure facility. Although the type of facility is a measure of the

severity of the disposition, it can be balanced by the duration of the placement, so that three years in a nonsecure facility would be deemed more restrictive than one year in a secure institution.

In many instances, removal of a child from the home is desired by either or both child and parents. It can be the optimum voluntary solution to an irreconcilable family conflict. It can provide temporary crisis resolution leading to a satisfactory resumption of family life or permanent separation. But in some cases it exacerbates family problems that might have been eliminated by time, maturation, therapy, communication, or changes of circumstances. Sometimes there is no alternative. Governed by a fundamental concern for the preservation of family life, the standards have imposed strict criteria for removal of a juvenile from home, insisting that it be shown that even the worst living arrangements would be improved by the court-ordered placement. Therefore, the final rupture of a family through state intervention, termination of parental rights, is regulated by carefully drafted and explicit safeguards in the *Abuse and Neglect* standards.

These standards were changed radically in the revised Part VIII of the *Abuse and Neglect* volume. Several members of the executive committee preferred that Standard 8.2 provide less formal procedures for voluntary termination and that Standard 8.3 authorize involuntary termination of parental rights after the child has been out of the home for shorter periods of time. They also would have required the parents to demonstrate their readiness for family reunification and would have incorporated a more explicit definition of maintaining contact. In response to the minority views, all the time periods in 8.3 C. and the two-year period for a motion alleging fraud or coercion in 8.2 D. were bracketed and the commentary was expanded to describe the diversity of opinions.

## PART VIII: TERMINATION OF PARENTAL RIGHTS

### 8.1 Court proceedings.

Each jurisdiction should provide by law that the filing of a written petition giving the parents and the child adequate notice of the basis upon which termination of parental rights is sought is a requisite to a proceeding to terminate parental rights.

### 8.2 Voluntary termination (relinquishment).

A. The court may terminate parental rights based on the consent of the parent upon a petition duly presented. The petitioner may be either the parent or an agency that has custody of the child. Such a petition may not be filed until at least seventy-two hours after the child's birth.

B. The court should accept a relinquishment or voluntary consent to termination of parental rights only if:

1. The parent appears personally before the court in a hearing that should be recorded pursuant to Standard 5.3 C. The court should address the parent and determine that the parent's consent to the termination of parental rights is the product of a voluntary decision. The court should address the parent in language calculated to communicate effectively with the parent and determine:

a. that the parent understands that he or she has the right to the custody of the child;

b. that the parent may lose the right to the custody of the child only in accordance with procedures set forth in Standard 8.3;

c. that relinquishment will result in the permanent termination of all legal relationship and control over the child; or

2. If the court finds that the parent is unable to appear in person at the hearing, the court may accept the written consent or relinquishment given before a judge of any court of record, accompanied by the judge's signed findings. These findings should recite that the judge questioned the parent and found that the consent was informed and voluntary.

C. If the court is satisfied that the parent voluntarily wishes to terminate parental rights, the court should enter an interlocutory order of termination. Such order should not become final for at least thirty days, during which time the parent may, for any reason, revoke the consent. After thirty days, the provisions for an interlocutory order for termination of parental rights set forth in Standard 8.5 should apply.

D. Once an order has been made final, it should be reconsidered only upon a motion by or on behalf of the parent alleging that the parent's consent was obtained through fraud or duress. Such a motion should be filed no later than [two] years after a final order terminating parental rights has been issued by the court.

E. Regardless of the provisions of Standard 8.2 B. 1.–2., a court should not be authorized to order termination if any of the exceptions in Standard 8.4 are applicable.

8.3 Involuntary termination.

A. Court proceedings to terminate parental rights involuntarily.

No court should terminate parental rights without the consent of the parents except upon instituting a separate proceeding in juvenile court in accordance with the provisions set forth in this Part.

B. Procedure.

1. Written petition. The grounds for termination should be stated with specificity in the petition in accordance with the standards set forth in subsection C.

2. Petitioner. The following persons are eligible to file a petition under this Part:

a. an agency that has custody of a child;

b. either parent seeking termination with respect to the other parent;

c. a foster parent or guardian who has had continuous custody for at least eighteen months who alleges abandonment pursuant to Standard 8.3 C. 1. c. or a foster parent or guardian who has had continuous custody for at least three years who alleges any other basis for termination;

d. a guardian of the child's person, legal custodian, or the child's guardian *ad litem* appointed in a prior proceeding.

3. Prosecutor. Upon receipt of the petition, the appropriate prosecution official should examine it to determine its legal sufficiency. If the prosecutor determines that the petititon is legally sufficient, it should be filed and signed by a person who has personal knowledge of the facts or is informed of them and believes that they are true. All petitions should be countersigned and filed by the prosecutor. The prosecutor may refuse to file a petition only on the grounds of legal insufficiency.

4. Parties. The following should be parties to all proceedings to terminate parental rights:

a. the child;

b. the child's parents, guardians, custodian, and, if relevant, any other adults having substantial ties to the child who have been assuming the duties of the caretaking role;

c. the petitioner.

5. Service of summons and petition. Upon the filing of a petition, the clerk should issue a summons. The summons should direct the parties to appear before the court at a specified time and place for an initial appearance on the petition. A copy of the petition should be attached to the summons. Service of the summons with the petition should be made promptly upon the parents of the child. The summons should advise the parents of the purpose of the proceedings

and of their right to counsel. Service of the summons and petition, if made personally, should be made at least twenty-four hours in advance of the first appearance. If, after reasonable effort, personal service is not made, the court may make an order providing for substituted service in the manner provided for substituted service in civil courts of record.

6. First appearance. At the first appearance, the court should provide the parents with a copy of the petition, including identification by name and association of the person submitting such petition, and inform the parents on the record of the following:

a. the nature and possible consequences of the proceedings;

b. the parents' and the child's right to representation by counsel at all stages of the proceeding regarding such petition, and their right to appointed counsel at public expense if they are unable to afford counsel;

c. their right to confront and cross-examine witnesses; and

d. their right to remain silent.

7. Appointment of counsel for child. Counsel should also be appointed at public expense to represent the child identified in the petition, as a party to the proceedings. No reimbursement should be sought from the parents or the child for the cost of such counsel, regardless of their financial resources.

8. Attendance at all proceedings. In all proceedings regarding the petition, the presence of the parents should be required, except that the proceedings may go forward without such presence if the parents fail to appear after reasonable notification (including, without limitation, efforts by court-designated persons to contact the parents by telephone and visitation to the parents' last known address within the jurisdiction of the court). The child identified in such petition should attend such proceedings unless the court finds on motion of any party that the attendance of a child under the age of twelve years would be detrimental to the child.

If the parents or custodians named in the petition fail to attend, the court may proceed to the termination hearing. If counsel for the parents has already been assigned by the court or has entered a notice of appearance, he or she should participate in the hearing. If the parents or custodians named in the petition were not present at the hearing and appear thereafter and move the court for a rehearing, the court should grant the motion unless it finds that they willfully refused to appear at the hearing or that the rehearing would be unjust because of the lapse of time since the hearing was held.

9. Interpreters. The court should appoint an interpreter or otherwise ensure that language barriers do not deprive the parents, child, witnesses, or other participants of the ability to understand and participate effectively in all stages of the proceedings.

10. Discovery. General civil rules of procedure, including discovery and pretrial practice, should be applicable to termination proceedings, provided, however, that after the filing of a petition the court may cause any person within its jurisdiction, including the child and the parents, to be examined by a physician, psychiatrist, or psychologist when it appears that such examination will be relevant to a proper determination of the charges. A party's willful and unexcused failure to comply with a lawful discovery order may be dealt with pursuant to the general civil rules of discovery, including the power of contempt. Except as otherwise provided, the standards governing disclosure of matters in connection with proceedings under this Part should be the same for the child and the parents as for the respondent in delinquency cases, as set out in the *Pretrial Court Proceedings* volume.

11. Appointment of independent experts. Any party to the proceeding may petition the court for appointment of experts, at public expense, for independent evaluation of the matter before the court. The court should grant such petition unless it finds the expert is unnecessary.

12. Subpoenas. Upon request of any party, a subpeona should be issued by the court (or its clerk), commanding the attendance and testimony of any person at any proceeding conducted pursuant to this Part, or commanding the production of documents for use in any such proceeding.

13. Public access to adjudication proceedings. The court should honor any request by the parents or child that specified members of the public be permitted to observe the hearing.

14. Burden of proof. The burden should rest on the petitioner to prove by clear and convincing evidence allegations sufficient to support the petition.

15. Evidence. Only legally relevant material and competent evidence, subject to cross-examination by all parties, may be

admissible to the hearing, pursuant to the principles governing evidence in civil matters in the courts of general jurisdiction in the state.

16. Findings. If the trier of fact, after a hearing, determines
that facts exist sufficient to terminate parental rights pursuant to the standards set out in Standard 8.3 C., the court
should convene a dispositional hearing in accordance with
Standard 8.5.

If the finder of fact determines that facts sufficient to
terminate parental rights have not been established, the court
should dismiss the petition.

C. Basis for involuntary termination.

Before entering an interlocutory order of termination of
parental rights, a court, after a hearing, must find one or more of
the following facts:

1. The child has been abandoned. For the purposes of this
Part, a child has been abandoned when:

a. his/her parents have not cared for or contacted
him/her, although the parents are physically able to do so,
for a period of [sixty] days, and the parents have failed to
secure a living arrangement for the child that assures the
child protection from harm that would authorize a judicial
declaration of endangerment pursuant to Standard 2.1;

b. he/she has been found to be endangered pursuant to
Part V and has been in placement, and the parents for a
period of more than [one] year have failed to maintain
contact with the child although physically able to do so,
notwithstanding the diligent efforts of the agency to encourage and strengthen the parental relationship; or

c. he/she has been in the custody of a third party without
court order pursuant to Standard 10.7, for a period of
[eighteen] months, and the parents for a period of more
than [eighteen] months have failed to maintain contact with
the child although physically able and not prevented from
doing so by the custodian.

2. The child has been removed from the parents previously
under the test established in Standard 6.4 C., has been
returned to his/her parents, has been found to be endangered
a second time, requiring removal, has been out of the home for
at least [six] months, and there is a substantial likelihood that
sufficient legal justification to keep the child from being
returned home, as specified in Standard 6.4 C., will continue
to exist in the foreseeable future.

3. The child has been found to be endangered in the manner

specified in Standard 2.1 A., more than [six] months earlier another child in the family had been found endangered under 2.1 A., the child has been out of the home for at least [six] months, and there is a substantial likelihood that sufficient legal justification to keep the child from being returned home, as specified in Standard 6.4 C., will continue to exist in the foreseeable future.

4. The child was found to be endangered pursuant to Standard 5.4, the child has been in placement for [two] or more years if under the age of three, or [three] or more years if over the age of three, the agency has fulfilled its obligations undertaken pursuant to Standard 6.5 B., and there is a substantial likelihood that sufficient legal justification to keep the child from being returned home, as specified in Standard 6.4 C., will continue to exist in the foreseeable future.

5. The child has been in the custody of a third party without court order, or by court order pursuant to Standard 10.7, for a period of [three] years, the third party wishes to adopt the child, and

a. the parents do not want or are unable to accept custody at the present time;

b. return of the child to the parents will cause the child to suffer serious and sustained emotional harm; or

c. the child is twelve years or older and wants to be adopted.

6. The child has been in voluntary placement by court order pursuant to Standard 10.7 for a period of [three] years and

a. the parents do not want or are unable to accept custody at the present time;

b. return of the child to the parents will cause the child to suffer serious and sustained emotional harm; or

c. the child is twelve years or older and wants to be adopted.

8.4 Situations in which termination should not be ordered.

Even if a child comes within the provisions of Standard 8.2 or 8.3, a court should not order termination if it finds by clear and convincing evidence that any of the following are applicable:

A. because of the closeness of the parent-child relationship, it would be detrimental to the child to terminate parental rights;

B. the child is placed with a relative who does not wish to adopt the child;

C. because of the nature of the child's problems, the child is placed in a residential treatment facility, and continuation of parental rights will not prevent finding the child a permanent family placement if the parents cannot resume custody when residential care is no longer needed;

D. the child cannot be placed permanently in a family environment and failure to terminate will not impair the child's opportunity for a permanent placement in a family setting;

E. a child over age ten objects to termination.

8.5 Dispositional proceedings.
A. Predisposition report.

Upon a finding that facts exist sufficient to terminate parental rights, the court should order a complete predisposition report prepared by the probation department for the dispositional hearing. A copy of the report should be provided to each of the parties to the proceeding. The report should include:

1. the present physical, mental, and emotional conditions of the child and his/her parents, including the results of all medical, psychiatric, or psychological examinations of the child or of any parent whose relationship to the child is subject to termination;

2. the nature of all past and existing relationships among the child, his/her siblings, and his/her parents;

3. the proposed plan for the child;

4. the child's own preferences; and

5. any other facts pertinent to determining whether parental rights should be terminated.

B. Dispositional hearing.

A dispositional hearing should be held within [forty-five] days of the finding pursuant to Standard 8.3 B. 16. All parties to the proceedings should be able to participate in this hearing, and all matters relevant to the court's determination should be presented in evidence.

8.6 Interlocutory order for termination of parental rights; appeals.

A. If the court after a hearing finds that one or more of the bases exist pursuant to Standard 8.3 C. and that none of the bases in Standard 8.4 C. is applicable, it should enter an interlocutory order terminating parental rights. An interlocutory order terminating parental rights may be made final or vacated in accordance with the provisions in Standard 8.7 B.

B. Appeals. An appeal may be taken as of right from a court

order entered pursuant to Standard 8.3 B. 16., 8.6, or 8.7. The standards governing appeals from proceedings under this Part should be the same as those set out in the *Appeals and Collateral Review* standards, except that the parties entitled to take an appeal under *Appeals and Collateral Review* Standard 2.2 should include the petitioner, pursuant to Standard 8.3 B. 2. and 4. above.

**8.7 Actions following termination.**

A. When parental rights are terminated, a court should order the child placed for adoption, placed with legal guardians, or left in long-term foster care. Where possible, adoption is preferable. However, a child should not be removed from a foster home if the foster parents are unwilling or unable to adopt the child, but are willing to provide, and are capable of providing, the child with a permanent home, and the removal of the child from the physical custody of the foster parents would be detrimental to his/her emotional well-being because the child has substantial psychological ties to the foster parents.

B. When an adoption or guardianship has been perfected, the court should make its interlocutory order final and terminate its jurisdiction over the child. If some other long-term placement for the child has been made, the court should continue the hearing to a specific future date not more than one year after the date of the order of continued jurisdiction. After the hearing, the court should extend the interlocutory order to a specified date to permit further efforts to provide a permanent placement, or vacate the interlocutory order and restore parental rights to the child's parents.

The standards for voluntary placements do not disregard the fact that the "voluntary" aspect applies to the parent and not to the child. Protection of the child's interest is paramount, yet parents must not be discouraged from using a procedure that may be best for all concerned parties at a time of crisis. An important safeguard for parents and children is the requirement that there be an unambiguous statement of the rights and obligations of the parents and the agency with which the child is placed and of the consequences that can result from failure to observe all requirements, such as the parents' commitment to maintain contact with the child during placement. Maximum participation of parents and children in selection of the placement and other decisions concerning custody and appropriate services is required of the agencies. Standard 10.4 G. was amended to describe the consequences of the child's remaining in placement for eighteen months without contact and three years in any case. Standard 10.5 was revised to add a preference for the placement chosen by the parents and the child.

**10.2 Need for statutory regulation.**

All states should adopt a statutory structure regulating voluntary placements.

**10.3 Preplacement inquiries.**

Prior to accepting a child for voluntary placement, the agency worker should:

A. Explore fully with the parents the need for placement and the alternatives to placement of the child.

B. Prepare a social study on the need for placement; the study should explore alternatives to placement and elaborate the reasons why placement is necessary. However, a child may be placed prior to completion of the social study if the child would be endangered if left at home or the parents cannot care for the child at home even if provided with services.

C. Review with an agency supervisor the decision to place the child.

D. Determine that an adequate placement is in fact available for the child.

**10.4 Placement agreements.**

When a child is accepted for placement, the agency should enter into a formal agreement with the parents specifying the rights and obligations of each party. The agreement should contain at least the following provisions:

A. a statement by the parents that the placement is completely voluntary on their part and not made under any threats or pressure from an agency;

B. a statement by the parents that they have discussed the need for placement, and alternatives to placement, with the agency worker and have concluded that they cannot care for their child at home;

C. notice that the parents may resume custody of their child within forty-eight hours of notifying the agency of their desire to do so;

D. a statement by the parents that they will maintain contact with the child while he/she is in placement;

E. a statement by the agency that it will provide the parents with services to enable them to resume custody of their child;

F. notification to the parents of the specific worker in charge of helping them resume custody and an agreement that the agency will inform the parents immediately if there is a change in workers assigned to them;

G. a statement that if the child remains in placement longer than six months, the case will automatically be reviewed by the juvenile court, and that termination of parental rights might occur if the child remains in placement for eighteen months if the parents have failed to maintain contact or three years even if the parents have maintained contact.

### 10.5 Parental involvement in placement.

The agency should involve the parents, and the child, in the placement process to the maximum extent possible, including consulting with the parents, and the child if he/she is of sufficient maturity, in the choice of an appropriate placement, and should request the parents to participate in bringing the child to the new home or facility. Preference should be given to the placement of choice of the parents and the child, in the absence of good cause to the contrary.

### 10.6 Written plans.

Within two weeks of accepting a child for placement, the agency and parents should develop a written plan describing the steps that will be taken by each to facilitate the quickest possible return of the child and to maximize parent-child contact during placement. The plan should contain at least the following elements:

A. provisions for maximum possible visitation;

B. a description of the specific services that will be provided by the agency to aid the parents;

C. a description of the specific changes in parental condition or home environment that are necessary in order for the parents to resume custody; and

D. provisions for helping the parents participate in the care of the child while he/she is in placement.

### 10.7 Juvenile court supervision.

No child should remain in placement longer than six months unless the child is made a ward of the juvenile court, and the court, at a hearing in which both the parents and child are represented by counsel, finds that continued placement is necessary.

**10.8 Termination of parental rights.**

**If a child is brought under court supervision, the standards for termination of parental rights contained in Part VIII should apply.**

### 4.5.3 Nature of limited coercion for noncriminal behavior.

The thrust of the *Noncriminal Misbehavior* volume is avoidance of coercive intervention for juvenile misconduct that does not constitute criminal action. The standards nonetheless recognize that certain activity either will not be tolerated by a community or will place juveniles in situations that may endanger their health or safety. They further concede that even if an ideal system of voluntary services is available, juveniles or their families might not apply for them. Therefore the delicate balance must be struck anew between the protection of legitimate community concerns (state interest) and the freedom of the individual from coercive intervention (individual liberty), even if the individual has not as yet harmed any person or property.

As discussed in the preceding section on grounds for intervention, the balance achieved by the standards is to permit restricted incursions, such as six hours of limited custody for juveniles found in dangerous circumstances who refuse to return home (Standard 2.1), the same six-hour limited custody for taking a runaway to a nonsecure shelter, expending conscientious efforts to persuade the child to agree to an additional twenty-one days (if returning home remains unacceptable) to arrange for an alternative residential placement (Standard 5.1), court hearings for approval of alternative residences (Standard 5.1), and seventy-two hour emergency medical or psychiatric services for juveniles in crisis (Standard 6.5).

In these instances, the grounds and nature of the intervention are intertwined, so the standards were set forth in the preceding section on agency intervention. Perhaps it should be observed that there is an arbitrary quality in these standards—i.e., why six hours and not ten or twenty-four?—because they are untested. There are no models for official nonintervention in noncriminal misbehavior, so the project could not be certain about community, juvenile, and family reaction to the absence of a judicial alternative. Services might be developed and used voluntarily; schools, civic organizations, and churches might pick up the slack; or families and children might heal themselves if left to their own devices. Some of the objectionable behavior might be reclassified by the state legislatures into delinquency or neglect causes of action. Or some failures of nonfeasance might have to be absorbed as the trade-off for freedom. A number of runaways who refuse to stay in shelters might be permanently damaged, while others return home from the streets ready to adjust to the normal demands of society, unscathed by the experience. People do walk around with pneumonia, stubbornly refusing assistance: some die and some survive. The price of liberty for children is harder for adults to tolerate. But the effort so apparent in the standards to seek a compromise between pure nonintervention and unjustifiable control has resulted in a mutation that may need time and experience before it assumes an acceptable final form for the species juvenile justice.

### 4.5.4 Guidelines for police handling of juveniles.

Frequently, the first mechanism for official intervention is the police, although it is not necessarily the initiator of the intervention. However, police officers often are the first official contact with the juvenile justice system for juveniles, outside of school disciplinary action. They also most commonly are the first screening and diversion source, since police officers often prefer to use their law enforcing authority to warn children of the dangers of misconduct rather than to involve them prematurely with the courts or other institutions. The police have been in the forefront of those in the system who believe there should be well articulated and precise guidelines for the extensive discretionary powers they are obliged to exercise in their daily activities. A quick curbstone decision as to whether to apprehend a ten-year-old shoplifter or let him or her go with a severe reprimand involves innate sensitivity and judgment, but it could be greatly aided by objective criteria. Both society and the juvenile can be gravely affected by that decision for years to come. Therefore, one of the most important *Police Handling of Juvenile Problems* standards requires specially trained personnel for dealing with juveniles (Standard 4.1). Other standards stress the formulation of policy guidelines to assist officers in handling criminal and noncriminal juvenile problems (Standard 5.1 B.). The standards for police personnel are set forth in Part IV.

## PART IV: IMPLICATIONS OF THE POLICE ROLE FOR POLICE ORGANIZATION AND PERSONNEL

**4.1 All police departments should establish a unit or officer specifically trained for work with juveniles. The nature of the allocation must necessarily vary from department to department.**
  **A. In departments where small size, the nature of community**

needs, or other considerations do not justify the assignment of even one officer to work with juveniles on a full-time basis, one officer should nevertheless be explicitly assigned the principal responsibility for the task, even while he or she might be expected to work in other areas.

B. Wherever resources permit even minimal specialization of function, the full-time appointment of a juvenile officer should receive highest priority.

C. Departments capable of staffing bureaus specializing in work with juveniles should consider the adequate staffing of them as a matter of highest priority.

D. A formalized network of connection for the communication of information and the transfer of cases between the juvenile bureau (or the juvenile officer) and other segments of the department should be established.

E. A formalized network of connection for the communication of information and the transfer of cases between the juvenile bureau (or the juvenile officer) and analogues in departments of adjoining jurisdiction should be established.

4.2 The juvenile officer or the supervising officer of a juvenile bureau should, in conjunction with the chief administrator of the department and other relevant juvenile justice agencies, formulate policies and training relative to police work with juveniles, implement established policies, and oversee their implementation throughout the department.

A. Juvenile officers should be selected from among officers who have mastered the craft of basic police work, and who have acquired, beyond that, the skill and knowledge their specialization calls for.

B. In departments having juvenile bureaus, the supervising officer should be of sufficiently high rank to convey the importance of both the position and the area of responsibility.

C. The juvenile officer or the supervising officer of a juvenile bureau should have the principal responsibility for the development and maintenance of relations within the department, with other agencies within the juvenile justice process, such as the court, the prosecutor, and intake staff, and with other community youth-serving agencies. He or she should have the principal responsibility for the development and maintenance of relations across jurisdictional boundaries with other departments.

D. The juvenile officer or members of juvenile bureaus should represent the police department in most matters connected with juveniles, vis-a-vis other institutions. In situations where such representation calls for the participation of other officers, juvenile officers should supervise or assist in such representations, depending on circumstances, and they should receive information about all representations that take place without their knowledge at the earliest possible opportunity.

E. Juvenile officers should take charge of all cases that go beyond an initial and informal handling that might have been administered by other officers. When the primary responsibility falls upon other segments of the department, as in cases involving serious crimes, juvenile officers should participate in investigations and prosecutions.

F. In cases that have gone beyond the initial and informal treatment accorded to them by other officers, but are judged upon investigation not to require referrals to other institutions, juvenile officers should be responsible for all counseling, guidance, and advice that might be incidentally required to reach a disposition of the case.

4.3 Since most juvenile cases begin by interventions of the uniformed patrol and a large share of these do not go beyond the initial intervention, standard police practices should be planned and instituted for patrol officers along lines of policies developed by the juvenile officers or the juvenile bureau.

A. As a rule, members of the uniformed patrol should assume full responsibility for the handling of all problems and disturbances subject to on-site abatement. In this capacity, they are to employ the least coercive measures of control and they should avail themselves of the aid of such nonpolice resources as are directly available in the context of the problem or disturbance.

B. While it is in the nature of patrol that all uniformed officers are expected to deal with any problem they encounter, at least provisionally, every patrol unit should contain at least one officer to whom the handling of problems involving juveniles will be assigned, to the fullest extent possible. This officer should remain under the administrative control of his or her patrol unit and should function as a formal link between the unit and the juvenile officer or the juvenile bureau.

C. Police should transfer cases in which further work is indicated to juvenile officers. When circumstances make it mandatory that a juvenile be arrested, detained, placed, or referred to an outside institution, the juvenile officer or the juvenile bureau should be notified without delay about the action taken and the reasons for taking it.

4.4. The principal task of police policy-making concerning juveniles should be to maintain flexible response readiness toward actually existing and emerging service and control needs in the community, and an assurance of maximum possible availability of alternative remedial resources to which problem cases can be referred for further care.

A. The juvenile officer or the supervising officer of the juvenile bureau should formulate policy in close coordination with the community relations officer or the community relations unit of the department.

B. Policy formulation should include recognition of the role of the uniformed patrol in police work involving juveniles, and orientation of its potential effectiveness to the proper aims of service and control.

C. The juvenile officer or the supervising officer of the juvenile bureau should formulate procedures and set standards for the transfer of cases from the uniformed patrol to the juvenile bureau; set limits for counseling, advice, and guidance provided by the juvenile unit; and provide guidance for the transfer of cases from the police to other institutions.

D. The basic principle of police policy concerning juveniles should be to rely on least coercive measures of control while maintaining full regard for considerations of legality, equity, and practical effectiveness.

4.5 Adequate staffing of programs for policing juveniles should be a matter of overriding significance.

A. Officers should be selected and appointed to work with juveniles as patrol officers and as juvenile officers on the basis of demonstrated aptitude and expressed interest.

B. To qualify for appointments as juvenile officers, officers should be fully competent members of the police and possess an educational background equivalent to graduation from college. The educational background standard should not be applied retroactively.

C. The initial assignment should be on a probationary basis during which the officers work under supervision and with restricted decision-making authority, and are given inservice training that should include internship placements in several institutions, the juvenile courts, schools, and social service agencies among them.

D. In the selection of patrol officers to work with juveniles, and of juvenile officers, first consideration should be given to otherwise eligible officers who share the racial, ethnic, and social background of the juveniles with whom they will work.

E. The practice of appointing responsible and interested young people to function in the role of paraprofessional aids in police work with juveniles should be encouraged.

In Part V, the *Police Handling of Juvenile Problems* standards recommend that police departments provide incentives to encourage personnel to deal effectively with juveniles by giving recognition to juvenile officers, creative recruitment and training, and inclusion of questions on juvenile problems in police promotional examinations.

5.1 Police agencies should establish positive incentives to encourage their personnel to support the thrust of these and other standards in the Juvenile Justice Standards series. These incentives should include:

A. appropriate status and recognition for the juvenile bureau and juvenile officers, given the importance of their task;

B. formulation of policy guidelines in the juvenile area that assist officers in handling juvenile problems, both criminal and noncriminal in nature;

C. provision of creative recruit, inservice, and promotional training that explores both juvenile policy guidelines and the philosophy behind them;

D. establishment of criteria for measuring effectiveness in handling juvenile problems that are consistent with departmental policy guidelines and with these standards; and

E. use in promotional examinations of material relating to the role of police in handling juvenile problems.

Part V also stresses the need for public accountability through periodic review of police policies for the handling of juvenile problems.

An interesting comment lightly disguised as a standard provides a frame of reference for the *Police Handling of Juvenile Problems* volume. Standard 1.3 states:

1.3 Most police work consists of inherently provisional procedures. In this work, the police function consists largely of mobilizing remedies for various problems, to be administered by other institutions. It is evident that what police can accomplish in this regard depends largely on what is available to them. Thus, many improvements in police handling of juvenile problems can only result from the availability of more appropriate and effective resources and services, both within and outside of the juvenile justice field, to which police can make referrals. This fact, too, introduces a degree of uncertainty into the formulation of proposed standards for police.

### 4.5.5. Youth services as a community resource.

The Commission usually avoided such admonitions as those appearing in the *Police Handling of Juvenile Problems* volume concerning the availability of resources because it was agreed in the early stages of the project that, within the bounds of reason, the standards were designed to define an ideal system toward which the various jurisdictions should aim. It also was decided that the prevailing lack of appropriate resources was more a reflection of inefficient and misguided allocation of funds than the inability to obtain sufficient public support to finance a system with proper services, facilities, and personnel. Therefore, the assumption is that the adoption of the proposed standards will carry with it the funding for necessary resources.

One product of that optimistic attitude is the *Youth Service Agencies* volume. Standards cannot supply funds, although they might inspire appropriations by Congress and state legislatures and contributions from private charitable organizations. Rather, the standards must describe the services and facilities that should be available for the effective functioning of the juvenile justice system.

### 5.3 Refusal by the juvenile to participate.

If a formally referred juvenile refuses to participate in a service program after the initial planning sessions, the youth service agency should have the authority to file a recommendation with the police and the court that the juvenile not be diverted if apprehended subsequently unless the juvenile enters into a written agreement for services of a specified duration (termed a participation agreement), which should also specify that failure to abide by the agreement will allow referral back to the court. The youth service agency should make use of the nondiversion recommendation only in exceptional circumstances. The juvenile should be informed of the existence and meaning of the agency action.

### 5.4 Limits on formal participation.

No formally referred juvenile who has attended an agency program for one year should be penalized by the filing of a recommendation against future diversion pursuant to Standard

5.3. Similarly, no participation agreement should require a juvenile to agree to participate in a youth service agency program for more than one year.

**5.5 Resource evaluation.**

The development of service priorities should be preceded in the planning stage by a complete and realistic evaluation of existing community resources and of the availability of such services to juveniles and families.

**5.6 Service development.**

When the resource evaluation indicates the absence of a needed service, such as a drug rehabilitation program, the youth service agency should establish and administer or provide support for the establishment of the service in the community.

**5.7 Service provision.**

The youth service agency should ensure the receipt of a mix of services rather than specializing in only one. The priorities will vary in each community; however, at a minimum the following should probably be available:

A. individual and marital counseling;
B. individual and family therapy;
C. residential facilities;
D. job training and placement;
E. medical services;
F. psychiatric services;
G. educational programs;
H. legal services;
I. recreational and athletic programs;
J. day care;
K. crisis intervention services that are available twenty-four hours a day;
L. bilingual services in communities with non-English-speaking residents.

The agency should, as an objective, honor personal preferences in selecting the services to be received by a particular individual or in developing new ones. Services should always be distributed in a manner that evidences respect for the participants and enhances the ability of participants to direct their own lives.

The close relationship between available voluntary services and police referrals of juveniles to the courts is further demonstrated in the

*Youth Service Agencies* volume, which refers frequently to the need for police liaison with the agencies and police diversion standards to encourage, as well as mandate, the use of community agencies in preference to formal court proceedings in all appropriate cases.

In the previous section on the grounds for intervention we described the standards for informal self-referrals, parent referrals, and police referrals, reserving the details of formal referrals to this section because of the greater degree of coerciveness involved and the commensurate increase in concern for the protection of the juvenile's rights. Thus, Standard 4.7 requires a statement by the intake official of the reasons why a juvenile was *not* diverted to the agency and Standard 4.10 authorizes a motion to appeal the decision not to divert, as well as matters related to the participation agreement that may be required after a formally referred juvenile has refused to participate in a service program. Standard 4.11 was amended by inserting a reference to Standard 5.1, which *requires* attendance at two program planning sessions. Standard 4.12 was revised to require that privileged communications to intake, counseling, and supervisory personnel, instead of to all program staff or participants, be kept confidential. The relevant standards follow:

### 4.10 Court review.

**Decisions by the court intake official 1. not to divert a juvenile, or 2. in the case of a previously diverted juvenile, to require the signing of a participation agreement (see Standards 5.3 and 5.4) as a condition of diversion, or 3. to resume proceedings against a juvenile who has allegedly violated the terms of a participation agreement, may be appealed by motion of the juvenile by his or her attorney to the juvenile court at any time prior to the fact-finding hearing. A judge who hears such a motion should not also preside at the fact-finding hearing(s) for that juvenile.**

### 4.11 Legal consequences of diversion to YSA.

**Formal referral to a youth service agency should represent an alternative to prosecution; such referral therefore should be accompanied by a formal termination of all legal proceedings against the juvenile which were the subject of the referral, except as provided in Standard 5.1. Mere suspension or deferral of prosecution pending participation in a youth service program is inconsistent with the concept of a youth service agency as a voluntary option. Referral in exchange for a guilty plea is inconsistent with the goal of stigma avoidance.**

4.12 Confidentiality.

To encourage full participation by juveniles and their families in youth service agency programs, any statements made during participation in a youth service agency program to intake, counseling, and supervisory personnel in the agency should be confidential and privileged. Appropriate legislation should prohibit their use in subsequent civil or criminal proceedings involving the juvenile or family or their divulgence to anyone without the written permission of the juvenile.

4.13 Right to refuse diversion.

Any juvenile should have the right at any time to request processing by the juvenile court in lieu of formal diversion to a youth service agency. Before a juvenile can be required to elect diversion to a YSA or to sign a participation agreement as a condition of diversion (see Standards 5.3 and 5.4), the juvenile and his or her parents or guardian should be advised that the juvenile has a right to first consult with an attorney, who, among other things, may appeal the requirement of a participation agreement to the court (see Standard 4.10).

## PART V: THE SERVICE SYSTEM

5.1 Voluntarism.

A fundamental premise in the administration of a youth service agency should be that participation by the juveniles should be voluntary. In the case of formal referrals, therefore, juveniles should only be required to attend two program planning sessions. Such attendance should be ensured by allowing further juvenile court proceedings in the event of nonattendance. Except as provided in Standard 5.3, the youth service agency should not have the authority to refer juveniles back to the court on the ground of nonparticipation after the initial planning sessions. Juveniles and families who are informally referred to the youth service agency should be free to drop out of the program without penalty at any time.

5.2 Initial planning sessions.

A key purpose of the initial planning sessions should be to inform the juvenile and his or her family of the voluntary nature of continued participation in the program. If the juvenile has been formally referred, such assurance may properly be coupled with a realistic appraisal of the effect nonparticipation could have in the event of subsequent apprehension.

**5.3 Refusal by the juvenile to participate.**

If a formally referred juvenile refuses to participate in a service program after the initial planning sessions, the youth service agency should have the authority to file a recommendation with the police and the court that the juvenile not be diverted if apprehended subsequently unless the juvenile enters into a written agreement for services of a specified duration (termed a participation agreement), which should also specify that failure to abide by the agreement will allow referral back to the court. The youth service agency should make use of the nondiversion recommendation only in exceptional circumstances. The juvenile should be informed of the existence and meaning of the agency action.

**5.4 Limits on formal participation.**

No formally referred juvenile who has attended an agency program for one year should be penalized by the filing of a recommendation against future diversion pursuant to Standard 5.3. Similarly, no participation agreement should require a juvenile to agree to participate in a youth service agency program for more than one year.

Among the concerns connected with diverting juveniles from formal court proceedings to community programs under the supervision of the youth service agencies are questions of loss of public control over records and information, accountability for and evaluation of the quality of the programs, and integrated planning with the more formal components of the juvenile justice system. These issues are addressed in the *Youth Service Agencies* standards contained in Part VI, Monitoring and Assessment System, and Part VII, Organization/Administration, which should be compared to the standards for administration of the system as a whole adopted by Drafting Committee IV, Administration.

### 4.5.6 Minors and capacity to act.

The *Rights of Minors* standards are not designed so much to limit intervention in the lives of children as to establish affirmative rights in juveniles that had been denied to them because of their status as minors. Therefore, these standards propose to liberate the minors who come within its coverage (by meeting prescribed conditions set forth above in section 4.4, Rights of Minors to Prevent Intervention) from the constraints against their freedom to act as individuals. They are granted capacity to decide for themselves to take certain initiatives: to maintain their own households; bring their own lawsuits against a parent to enforce support obligations; obtain necessary medical care without parental knowledge or consent; get a job; enter into a valid contract; and assert first amendment constitutional rights. The conditions precedent to qualifying for these privileges of citizenship are stipulated in the standards and generally are based on age and demonstrated maturity. However, some of the rights provided are unrelated to the apparent capacity of the juvenile, but apply to all children who find themselves in a particular situation (need for emergency health care) or satisfy statutory prerequisites (e.g., an illegitimate child of a financially able parent).

### 4.5.7 School regulations.

The *Schools and Education* standards are vitally important to juveniles, who are obliged to spend most of their childhood in school. The duty to attend school is not construed as a coercive intervention, however, because the standards not only support the compulsory education laws but feature as Standard 1.1 an affirmative right to an education. The procedures to encourage attendance involve little compulsion. Intervention standards are those concerned with the school regulatory power, disciplinary sanctions, interrogation of students, and searches and seizure. Related standards cover the parental role and student consent or waiver.

In general, as stated in Standard 2.1 B., the standards do not allocate control of decisions, in which students are expected to take an action or exercise discretion, between student and parent. Students should participate in decisions affecting their interests to the extent appropriate in view of the circumstances, interest involved, and the age and experience of the student.

Standard 2.2 prescribes the conditions for consent to otherwise prohibited actions of school officials, police, or other government officials, as follows:

1. **the consent or waiver is voluntary in fact;**
2. **the student is clearly advised**
   **a. that the consent or waiver may be withheld, and**
   **b. of any possible adverse consequences that might result from such consent or waiver;**

3. the student's parent, except when a reasonable effort to inform the parent is unsuccessful,

a. is informed of the fact that the student's consent or waiver will be sought,

b. has the opportunity to be present before the consent or waiver is given (unless a student over fourteen years of age objects to the parent's presence), and

c. expressly approves of the consent or waiver (unless a student over sixteen years of age has knowledge of the parent's lack of approval and gives or repeats his or her consent or waiver thereafter); and

4. either

a. there is no evidence of coercion, or

b. any evidence of coercion that exists is satisfactorily rebutted.

B. In addition to the requirements specified in Standard 2.2 A., a student who is entitled to counsel (retained or provided) under these standards may give an effective consent or waiver only if the student:

1. is advised of his or her right to counsel;

2. is given an opportunity to obtain counsel; and

3. either

a. makes the consent waiver through counsel, or

b. waives the right to counsel in accordance with Standard 2.2 A.

C. The burden of proving that a student's consent or waiver meets the requirements of Standard 2.2 A. should be carried by any party relying upon the consent or waiver to establish the validity of an action, the inapplicability of a right, or the admissibility of evidence.

D. In determining whether the consent or waiver was voluntary in fact, each of the following should be considered as evidence tending to indicate that the consent or waiver was involuntary:

1. the student's parent was not informed of the fact that the student's consent or waiver would be sought;

2. the parent was not present when the consent or waiver was given;

3. the parent did not approve of the consent or waiver;

4. the consent or waiver was given in the school building;

5. the consent or waiver was given in the office of the school principal or some other administrative official of the school;

6. the consent or waiver was given in the presence of the school principal or some other administrative official of the

school (unless there is unambiguous evidence that the school official acted in a manner that would have been understood by the student as attempting to help the student to make a voluntary choice);

7. the consent or waiver was given without the assistance of counsel;

8. the consent or waiver was requested by a school official, a police officer, or other government official;

9. the consent or waiver was not in writing;

10. the consent or waiver was given by a student under twelve years of age.

E. Standard 2.2 A. applies to any consent or waiver under these standards, including but not limited to:

1. consent to a search otherwise proscribed by Part VIII;

2. consent to interrogation otherwise proscribed by Part VII (except that the prohibition of Standard 7.2 cannot be avoided by consent or waiver);

3. waiver of a right to object to any excludable evidence;

4. waiver of any procedural right provided by Part V; and

5. consent to the administration of any drug, physical test (such as a urinalysis), psychological test, or any other procedure not required of all students by a general rule promulgated pursuant to the school board's authority in accordance with Part III.

F. If the student's opportunity to enjoy any right or privilege otherwise available is conditioned, in whole or in part, upon the student's consent or waiver, the consent or waiver should be conclusively presumed to be invalid.

The standards on school regulatory power prohibit certain forms of school authority, in Standards 3.4 to 3.8.

3.4 No student should be denied access to any school activity whether or not the activity is denominated "extracurricular," except as provided in these standards.

3.5 Neither the education per se function nor the host function of schools justifies the complete or partial exclusion of a student from any school program or activity solely on the basis of such student's status of being married or being a parent (wed or unwed).

3.6 Neither the education per se function nor the host function of schools justifies:

A. the exclusion of a student from any school activity based solely on the fact that such student is pregnant unless her participation in such activity presents a clear and imminent threat of harm to the student or foetus involved that cannot be eliminated by other means; or

B. the exclusion of a student from school based solely on a student's hair style, unless the relationship between the particular activity involved and the student's hair style is such that the student's participation creates a clear and imminent threat of harm to the student or other persons involved in the activity, or is clearly incompatible with performance of the particular activity involved.

**3.7** School authorities should not, without the prior informed consent of the affected students or their parents, obtained pursuant to the terms of Standard 2.2 hereof:

A. compel any student to respond to psychological or other tests, or otherwise supply information, that involves the disclosure of intimate details of a student's personal or family life or the personal or family life of other members of the student's family; or

B. compel any student to take any drug the purpose of which is to alter or control the behavior of the student.

**3.8** Schools may reasonably restrict access to school premises by persons who are other than students or school personnel.

Other restraints on sanctions are set forth in Standards 6.1 to 6.6.

**6.1** School disciplinary sanctions against student conduct or status should be imposed only if consistent with the limitations contained in these standards as to a school's authority to regulate student conduct and status, and only to the extent that is reasonably necessary to accomplish legitimate school objectives that cannot otherwise be reasonably effectuated.

**6.2** Corporal punishment should not be inflicted upon a student, but school authorities may use such force as is reasonable and necessary:

A. to quell a disturbance threatening physical injury to persons or property; or

B. to protect persons (including school authorities themselves) or property from physical injury; or

C. to remove a pupil causing or contributing to a disturbance in the classroom or disruption of the educational process who refuses to leave when so ordered by the school authority in charge; or

D. to obtain possession of weapons or other dangerous objects upon the person or within the control of a student.

E. Such acts do not constitute corporal punishment.

6.3 A. No student should be permanently excluded from school. No student should be excluded from school for a period in excess of one school year. No student should be suspended or otherwise excluded from school for more than one school month, unless the student's presence in school presents a clear and imminent threat of harm to students or other persons on school premises, property, or to the educational process, and that threat cannot be eliminated by other, less restrictive, means.

B. Prior to suspending or otherwise excluding a student from school for more than one school month, the student should be provided with a hearing de novo before the state commissioner of education or equivalent officer. In such a hearing the burden of proving that the requirements for exclusion under Standard 6.3 A. have been met should be on the local school authorities.

6.4 A. No student should be suspended from regular school attendance unless the student's continued presence in school presents a demonstrable threat of harm to students, or other persons on school premises, property, or to the educational process, and that threat cannot be eliminated by other, less restrictive means.

B. Suspensions should not exceed in duration the time that is necessary to accomplish the purposes of the suspension.

6.5 When a student is suspended from regular school attendance for any period of time, the school authorities should provide the student with equivalent education during the period of the suspension.

6.6 Academic sanctions should not be imposed on any student where the student's conduct involves a nonacademic disciplinary offense.

When students are subject to disciplinary sanctions, their procedural protections should be commensurate with the seriousness of the sanction that might be imposed.

5.3 A student who is threatened with a serious disciplinary sanction is entitled to receive the following procedural safeguards:

A. prior to the hearing described in subsection B.;

1. notice in writing that

a. is received long enough before the hearing to enable the student to prepare a defense,

b. factually describes the misconduct charged,

c. identifies the procedural safeguards to which the student is entitled under these standards, and

d. identifies the rule making such misconduct subject to sanction;

2. receipt of a summary of all testimonial evidence to be used against him or her;

3. right to examine all documents to be used against him or her;

B. a hearing that is private (unless the student expressly requests a public hearing), that is presided over by an impartial hearing officer or tribunal, and at which the student is entitled,

1. to be represented by counsel,

2. to present testimonial or other evidence,

3. to hear the evidence against him or her (or, if presented in the form of affidavits, to see the affidavits),

4. to cross-examine witnesses who testify against him or her (and to challenge adverse affidavits),

5. to make oral and written argument relating to any aspect of the student's position and the case against him or her, and

6. to obtain, at the completion of the proceeding, a record of the hearing proceedings;

C. a decision,

1. concerning the questions whether

a. the student in fact engaged in the conduct charged,

b. a valid rule was violated by that conduct, and

c. the sanction to be imposed is appropriate for that conduct, and

2. that is

a. made by an impartial decision maker or decision making tribunal,

b. based solely on the facts and arguments presented at the hearing, and

c. if against the student, supported by clear and convincing evidence that the student engaged in the misconduct charged and explained in a written opinion; and

D. a right to judicial review within a reasonable time by a court of general jurisdiction to challenge the hearing decision on the ground that the decision is not supported by substantial evidence, is arbitrary and unreasonable, or is contrary to any constitutional or other legal provision.

5.3.1 As used in these standards, the right to be represented by counsel includes:
  A. 1. the right to be advised by the presiding officer of
     a. the right to counsel and
     b. the channels through which counsel might be obtained;
    2. the right to be represented by counsel in preparing for and participating in the hearing specified in Standard 5.3 B.; and
    3. in the case of a student who is indigent and is threatened with expulsion or a transfer to a school used or designated as a school for problem children of any kind, the right to have counsel provided at state expense.
  B. In advising a student of the right to counsel pursuant to Standard 5.3.1 A., it should be the duty of the presiding officer:
    1. to use reasonable efforts to obtain and provide information concerning channels through which counsel might be obtained;
    2. to refuse to proceed with a hearing until satisfied that the student
     a. has voluntarily waived the right to counsel, or
     b. (1) in cases within 5.3.1 A. 3. is represented by counsel who has had adequate opportunity to prepare the student's case,
      (2) in cases not within 5.3.1 A. 3. has been given adequate notice of the right to obtain counsel but has failed to do so; and
    3. in any proceeding at which the student is not represented by counsel, to use reasonable efforts to protect the student from any disadvantage that would result from not being so represented.
  C. Nothing in Standard 5.3, 5.3.1 A. or B. should prevent a student from being represented, at the student's option, by a person who is not a graduate of a law school or admitted to the practice of law, but the option to be so represented should have no effect upon the student's right to counsel except insofar as the right to counsel was waived pursuant to the provisions of Standard 2.2.

5.4 In determining whether a student has violated a student conduct rule, evidence of student misconduct obtained in violation of these standards or the student's constitutional rights should not be considered.

5.5 A. To provide a basis for a sanction under these standards, a rule governing student conduct should be:
    1. in a published writing describing with specificity
      a. the conduct prohibited, and
      b. the sanctions that may be imposed by reason of a violation of the rule; or
    2. based on a general understanding, in the light of past practice, with respect to which understanding there is objective evidence that a reasonable student to whom the rule applied under the circumstances involved in the particular case would have been aware of both the rule and the likelihood of a resulting sanction of comparable nature and degree to that now threatened.
    B. In determining whether a written rule is sufficiently specific, considerations tending to indicate the validity of the rule include:
    1. a relatively high degree of precision of the words actually used in the written statement,
    2. the difficulty of using more precise words,
    3. the likelihood that the students who were subject to the rule would understand that the conduct alleged to violate the rule was covered by the rule and that the sanction now threatened might be imposed,
    4. the lack of opportunity given to school officials by the rule to apply the rule in a discriminatory fashion,
    5. the lack of probability that the rule has in fact been applied in a discriminatory fashion to the student now subjected to the rule or to any other student,
    6. the relatively low degree of seriousness of the sanction threatened by reason of the misconduct charged or relative lack of importance of permissible conduct discouraged by the rule,
    7. the proportionality of the sanction threatened and the misconduct charged,
    8. the fact that reasonable efforts were made to bring to the student's attention the nature and significance of the misconduct covered by the rule in view of the age of the students to whom the rule applies.
    C. In determining whether a student conduct rule that is not in writing may be imposed:
    1. the presumption should be that

a. unwritten rules are invalid, and

b. rules that do not specify a sanction are invalid for purposes of imposing a serious disciplinary sanction; and

2. in determining whether the presumption has been overcome, consideration should be given to

a. the persuasiveness of the reasons for not stating the rule in writing,

b. the improbability that a student has been prejudiced by reason of the fact that the rule is not in writing, and

c. subsections 3.-8. of Standard 5.5 B.

**5.6** A student who is threatened with a disciplinary sanction that is not a serious disciplinary sanction is entitled to procedural safeguards equivalent or comparable to those specified in Standard 5.3 except insofar as lesser safeguards are justified by:

A. the relative lack of severity of the sanctions threatened; and

B. the substantial burden imposed upon the school's interest by reason of making greater safeguards available.

**5.7** Unless special circumstances bring the case within Standard 5.8, the hearing and hearing procedures required by this chapter should be provided prior to the imposition of a disciplinary sanction.

**5.8** A. Notwithstanding any other provision in these standards, a student may be excluded temporarily from a classroom or a school prior to the operation or availability of procedures otherwise required if such an exclusion is clearly justified by an imminent danger of harm to:

1. any person (including the student),

2. the educational process of a substantial and continuing or repetitive nature, or

3. property that is extensive in amount.

B. The determination of the existence of an imminent danger of harm may be made in the first instance by a teacher, counselor, administrator, or other school official in a position both to make such determination and to be required to act to protect persons, the educational process, or property.

C. The exclusion authorized under Standard 5.8 should be for the shortest possible time consistent with the circumstances justifying exclusion.

D. 1. As soon as possible after the temporary exclusion, an

emergency hearing should be held to determine whether the exclusion may be continued.

2. The sole question to be determined at the emergency hearing should be whether there is substantial evidence to support the exclusion of the student, pending a full hearing in compliance with Standard 5.3, on the ground that readmission would pose a threat of imminent danger or harm as provided in Standard 5.8 A.

E. In addition to the emergency hearing required by Standard 5.8 D.1., the excluded student is entitled to a preliminary hearing within a reasonable time after requesting it, if:

1. such a hearing can be held substantially sooner than the full hearing required by Standard 5.3;

2. the procedures that could be made available at such a preliminary hearing would be substantially more extensive than those available at the emergency hearing.

F. At the preliminary hearing the student may challenge both the grounds of the exclusion and the determination that the student's presence in school (or the classroom) pending the outcome of the full hearing would present a threat of imminent danger of harm as provided in Standard 5.8.

G. Both the emergency and preliminary hearings should be conducted by an impartial presiding officer and result in a decision by an impartial decision maker and, to the extent possible, should conform to the requirements of Standard 5.3.

H. A determination adverse to the student in either an emergency or preliminary hearing should not prejudice the student in any way nor preclude the assertion of any of the rights required by Standard 5.3.

I. A student may request judicial review of the decision made at either the emergency hearing or preliminary hearing or both, but such judicial review should be available only at the discretion of the reviewing court.

5.9 Every school should provide a procedure through which a student can initiate and obtain an appropriate resolution of grievances.

Disciplinary sanctions are defined as follows:

9.3 A. As used in these standards, a "disciplinary sanction" means any action required of a student or any action taken by the school upon or with respect to a student that:

1. would be regarded by a reasonable person in the stu-

dent's circumstances as substantially painful, unpleasant, stigmatizing, restrictive, or detrimental, or a denial of a substantial benefit; and

2. would not occur but for the misconduct with which the student is charged.

B. Action is not prevented from being a disciplinary sanction because:

1. it is taken (or characterized as taken) in the best interest of the student, or

2. the student is given choices between two or more courses of action, any of which, if the sole option, would be a disciplinary sanction.

9.4 A "serious disciplinary sanction" includes

A. the following specified disciplinary sanctions:

1. expulsion;*

2. suspension for a period that either

a. in the aggregate is in excess of five days during any one academic year, or

b. is of indefinite length by reason of either

(1) the failure of the school to specify the duration of the suspension or

(2) the student's being directed to do or cease doing something when the student desires not to obey that direction;

3. a transfer to a different school;

4. corporal punishment;

5. denial of any opportunity ordinarily available to students to participate in activities or to engage in conduct if

a. the denial extends beyond three weeks and

b. the denial would be regarded by a reasonable person in the student's circumstances as a substantial detriment; or

6. reduction of grade or loss of academic credit in any course, including action that inevitably results in such reduction or loss; or

B. any disciplinary sanction reasonably likely to have consequences for the student comparable to the consequences of any of the sanctions specified in Standard 9.4 A.

Parts VII and VIII cover protections against interrogation and searches or seizures. Standards 7.1 and 8.1 provide that police

*But see Standard 6.3 A. and commentary thereto.

interrogation of a student concerning a crime and searches and seizures by police are not less protected because of student status.

Standards 7.1, 7.2, and 7.3 prescribe the conditions for permissible police interrogation of a student.

**7.1 If an interrogation of a student by a police officer concerning a crime of which the student is a suspect occurs off school premises and not in connection with any school activity, the validity of the interrogation should in no way be affected by the student status.**

**7.2 The interrogation of a student by a police officer for any purpose should not take place in school, or away from school when the student is engaged in a school related activity under the supervision of a school official, except:**

**A. when it is urgently necessary to conduct the interrogation without delay in order to avoid,**

**1. danger to any person,**

**2. flight from the jurisdiction of a person who is reasonably believed to have committed a serious crime, or**

**3. destruction of evidence; or**

**B. when there is no other reasonably available place or means of conducting the interrogation.**

**7.3 A. When, pursuant to Standard 7.2, a police officer interrogates a student who is on school premises or engaged in a school activity and who is suspected of a crime, the student should be advised of this suspicion in terms likely to be understood by a student of the age and experience involved; should be advised of the right to counsel (including state-appointed counsel if the student is indigent), the right to have a parent present, and the right to remain silent; and should be advised that any statement made may be used against the student.**

**B. If, pursuant to Standard 7.2, a police officer interrogates a student who had not theretofore been suspected of conduct covered by Standard 7.3 A. but during such interrogation information is obtained, either from that student or from any other source, that would lead a reasonable person to suspect the student of such conduct, the interrogation should immediately thereafter be governed by Standard 7.3 A.**

Standards 8.2 and 8.3 define a reasonable search and protected student areas.

8.2 A search by a police officer of a student, or a protected student area, is unreasonable unless it is made:
A. 1. under the authority and pursuant to the terms of a valid search warrant,
2. on the basis of exigent circumstances such as those that have been authoritatively recognized as justifying warrantless searches,
3. incident to a lawful arrest,
4. incident to a lawful "stop," or
5. with the consent of the student whose person or protected student area is searched; and
B. in a manner entailing no greater invasion of privacy than the conditions justifying the search make necessary.

8.3 As used in these standards, a protected student area includes (but is not limited to):
A. 1. a school desk assigned to a student if
a. the student sits at that desk on a daily, weekly, or other regular basis,
b. custom, practice, or express authorization the student does in fact store or is expressly permitted to store, in the desk, papers, equipment, supplies, or other items that belong to the student, and
c. the student does in fact lock or is permitted to lock the desk whether or not
(1) any school official or a small number of other students have the key or combination to the lock,
(2) school officials have informed the student or issued regulations calculated to inform the student either that only certain specified items may be kept in the desk or that the desk may be inspected or searched under specified conditions.
(3) the student has consented to or entered into an agreement acknowledging the restrictions described in Standard 8.3 A. 1. c. (1) and (2) above, or
(4) the student has paid the school for the use of the desk;
B. 1. a school locker assigned to a student if
a. the student has either exclusive use of the locker or jointly uses the locker with one or two other students and
b. the student does in fact lock or is permitted to lock the locker whether or not
(1) school officials or a small number of other students have the key or combination to the lock,

(2) school officials have informed the student or issued regulations calculated to inform the student either that only certain specified items may be kept in the locker or that the locker may be inspected or searched under specified conditions,

(3) the student has consented to or entered into an agreement acknowledging the restrictions described in Standard 8.3 B. 1. b. (1) and (2), or

(4) the student has paid the school for the use of the locker;

C. 1. a motor vehicle located on or near school premises if
a. it is owned by a student, or
b. has been driven to school by a student with the owner's permission.

Evidence obtained as a result of interrogations or searches conducted in violation of these standards should be inadmissible (without the student's express consent) in proceedings that might result in criminal or disciplinary sanctions against the student. Interrogations or searches conducted by school officials that might result in serious disciplinary sanctions are subject to all of the requirements of police interrogations or searches, including inadmissibility if in violation of the standards.

# PART V: COURT ROLES AND PROCEDURES

## 5.1 Dominant Themes.

Drafting Committee II, Court Roles and Procedures, had a difficult task. The members and reporters were charged with the responsibility of examining the operation of the various juvenile courts functioning in the states and evaluating the effectiveness of their structure, personnel, relationship to other parts of the system, judicial and nonjudicial procedures, and underlying policies. After studying both traditional and innovative practices, the Committee recommended standards for a reformed juvenile court.

There are many types of juvenile court systems. In most states, the juvenile court is a special session of a lower court of limited jurisdiction. Some states have independent juvenile courts operating statewide or in selected areas. Others combine forms, with independent courts in some areas and special sessions of trial courts of limited or general jurisdiction in other areas. The standards recommend the establishment of a family court, with original jurisdiction over all family matters, including divorce, adoption, and separation, as a division of the highest court of general trial jurisdiction. Matrimonial matters currently are handled in most states separately from juvenile court, occasionally with concurrent jurisdiction over such peripheral matrimonial issues as support and custody of children.

Critical issues also addressed by Drafting Committee II were the roles of the principals in the court process: judges, referees, probation workers, counsel for respondents and other private parties, counsel for the state, and the community service agencies to which referrals for services and treatment are made.

Closely related to the roles of the participants are the procedures prescribed for the juvenile court process, both judicial and nonjudicial. These include not only the fact-finding and dispositional hearings, but the probation intake process, motions and other preadjudication procedures, and transfer, appellate, and postdispositional procedures.

The dominant themes in the standards prepared by Drafting

147

Committee II are the right to counsel at every stage of the proceeding and the equally significant obligation of the court to advise the juvenile and other parties with substantial interests of that right; the requirements of rule making and specific criteria to govern proceedings and decisions; the need for written statements of all orders and the reasons on which they are based; the related emphasis on restraining arbitrary official action; thoughtful attention to the respective roles of juveniles and parents, with full participation of both in the court process; a traditional "lawyer-client" relationship for counsel and mature juveniles; allowance for possible conflict or adversity of interests between juveniles and parents, and provision for the appointment of guardians *ad litem* to protect immature juveniles and to take the place of hostile or absent parents; appellate review of juvenile court orders as a matter of right; improved status of the juvenile court, expanded to a family court, with original jurisdiction over all family matters, organized as a division of the highest court of general trial jurisdiction, with judges rotated among the divisions; and a significant role at every stage of the court process for the prosecuting attorney, as well as counsel for private parties. Many other important positions were adopted, but the fundamental principle is the preservation of a separate juvenile court to deal with the problems of youth and their families in a just and equitable manner. The standards encourage experimentation and innovation, as in predisposition hearings, voluntary participation of persons in its treatment programs, and waiver of jurisdiction over intractable cases of serious juvenile crimes to adult courts only after every effort has been made, every safeguard provided, and ample proof presented of the capacity of the criminal justice system to deal with the matter.

The following volumes were prepared under the supervision of Drafting Committee II:

*Adjudication*
*Appeals and Collateral Review*
*Counsel for Private Parties*
*Court Organization and Administration*
*The Juvenile Probation Function: Intake and Predisposition Investigative Services*
*Pretrial Court Proceedings*
*Prosecution*
*Transfer Between Courts*

All eight volumes released by Drafting Committee II were approved by the House of Delegates of the American Bar Association with the understanding that certain modifications adopted by the executive committee of the IJA-ABA Joint Commission would appear in the approved drafts. Although there were no changes in principle, the executive committee agreed to amendments in the standards and commentary after consideration of the comments received from ABA sections and other groups. Those revisions are enumerated in detail in the Appendix, in which the Addenda published in each of the final approved drafts appear in alphabetical order, and in the discussion of the standards that follows.

In this part we will review the standards proposed for court structure; the roles of counsel, juveniles, parents, guardians, and other participants; and the court process, from reporting a complaint through appeal and postdispositional review. The dispositional stage will be covered in the next part on treatment and corrections.

## 5.2 A Restructured Court and the Enlarged Role of Counsel.

The dangerous fiction that the juvenile court process is nonadversarial because all those involved are concerned only with the best interests of the child no longer stands unchallenged, although its vestiges remain. After *Kent, Gault,* the President's Task Force Report, and other critical reappraisals, even its staunchest defenders concede that there are points at which the court's dual responsibilities to help children and protect society inevitably must come into conflict. Through these fissures in the wall, the right to counsel for respondents at least at the trial or adjudicatory stage and the resultant enhanced role of the prosecuting attorney have entered and begun to expand. With adjustments adapted to the special nature of a juvenile court, the standards have attempted to define vital roles for counsel for all parties, drawing on criminal, civil, and equitable precedents as they appear relevant to the proceedings.

### 5.2.1 Court organization and administration.

The structure of the court itself is drastically changed by its comprehensive jurisdiction over family matters, its upgraded status, and its emphasis on formal guidelines prescribing rules of procedure, administration, and case decision making. *Court Organization and Administration* Standard 1.1 was amended by deleting "nonjudicial" before "probation" in subdivision D. It now provides as follows:

**1.1 Organizational structure: general principles.**
**The traditional juvenile court jurisdiction should be included in a family court division of the highest court of general trial jurisdiction.**
**A. The exclusive original jurisdiction of this division should encompass: juvenile law violations; cases of abuse and neglect;**

cases involving the need for emergency medical treatment; voluntary and involuntary termination of parental rights proceedings; adoption proceedings; appointment of legal guardians for juveniles; proceedings under interstate compacts on juveniles and on the placement of juveniles; intrafamily criminal offenses; proceedings in regard to divorce, separation, annulment, alimony, custody, and support of juveniles; proceedings to establish paternity and to enforce support; and proceedings under the Uniform Reciprocal Enforcement of Support Act. Mental illness and retardation commitment proceedings concerning juveniles and adults should be governed by the law of the jurisdiction applicable to such proceedings for nonadjudicated persons.

B. Calendaring methods should follow the general principle that the same judge should consider the different legal issues that relate to all members of the same family. Further, the judge who presides at an adjudicatory hearing should conduct the disposition hearing of the case.

C. General intake procedures to determine the need for formal judicial consideration of juvenile delinquency referrals should be adapted and applied to the different types of cases within the jurisdiction of the family court division.

D. The court should encourage probation and social service agencies working with court clientele to maximize single staff member responsibility for an entire family.

The volume also proposes case processing time standards. Standard 3.3 states:

Time standards for judicial hearing of juvenile cases should be promulgated and monitored. These should include:

A. detention and shelter hearings: not more than twenty-four hours following admission to any detention or shelter facility;

B. adjudicatory or transfer (waiver) hearings:

1. concerning a juvenile in a detention or shelter facility: not later than fifteen days following admission to such facility;

2. concerning a juvenile who is not in a detention or shelter facility: not later than thirty days following the filing of the petition;

C. disposition hearings: not later than fifteen days following the adjudicatory hearing. The court may grant additional time in exceptional cases that require more complex evaluation.

Formal rules for the operation of the court are required by Standard 3.1 on Rulemaking, which states: "The Family Court Division should operate under formally adopted: A. rules of procedure; B. rules of administration; and C. guidelines."

Standard 3.2 on Case Decisionmaking provides in part as follows: "A judge should render all judicial decisions on cases before the court. No judicial proceedings should be heard by nonjudicial personnel. Adjudicatory proceedings should be conducted in a formal manner...."

However, formal judicial action is not the only outcome recommended in the standards on court organization. Diversion to community agencies is encouraged for families in appropriate cases, as in Standard 1.1 C. and D. above.

The *Court Organization and Administration* volume describes a broad original jurisdiction over family matters for the family court division, but it should be observed that the other volumes generally concentrate on traditional juvenile problems, leaving standards for matrimonial matters to specialists in that field. The purpose of bringing all family issues within a single court is to avoid the duplication of consideration of related problems, which leads to inconsistent court orders and insensitivity to the totality of a family's situation. For that reason, the standards urge calendaring methods to enable the same judge to hear the different legal issues that relate to all members of the same family. The standards also recommend appointment of a court administrator for each family court division with four or more judges and specify the functions the family court administrator should administer or perform. However, Standards 2.1 C. and 2.3 were amended by adding brackets around "on a modified rotation system" in Standard 2.1 C. and "four" in Standard 2.3 to make rotation of judges and appointment of an administrator for courts with four or more judges discretionary with each jurisdiction.

The doctrine of inherent powers in the judiciary with regard to compelling the provision of resources is supported, but carefully proscribed as follows:

# PART IV: RESPONSIBILITY OF THE FAMILY COURT DIVISION TO EFFECTUATE ITS DUTIES AND ORDERS

## 4.1 General principles.

The family court division should have available those personnel, facilities, and services necessary for the effective discharge of its responsibilities. The doctrine of inherent powers should be employed only when the court can show all of the following:

A. all possible approaches to obtain the necessary resource have been tried and have failed;

B. the expense in question is a necessary as opposed to a desirable expense; and

C. failure to obtain this resource would render the court unable to fulfill its legal duties.

Finally, *Court Organization and Administration* sets standards for the assignment and appointment of judges.

**2.1 Judges.**
Judges of the family court division should be assigned from among the judges of the highest court of general trial jurisdiction. Their assignment to the family court division should be:

A. by appointment of the presiding judge of the highest court of general trial jurisdiction;

B. with special consideration given to the aptitude, demonstrated interest, and experience of each judge;

C. [on a modified rotation system,] with indefinite tenure discouraged;

D. if at all practical, on a full-time basis; and

E. accompanied by the supporting personnel, equipment, and facilities necessary for effective functioning.

**5.2.2 Counsel for private parties and the prosecution.**

The emphasis in the *Court Organization and Administration* standards on formal rules to govern judicial and nonjudicial proceedings reinforces the need for extensive involvement of counsel to ensure the protection of the rights of the parties. To some extent, the presence of counsel may be undesirable because studies have shown that fewer cases are dismissed in the preadjudicatory stage if counsel are active in the case (although those cases might have concerned more serious offenses). Nevertheless, the more rules and regulations are operative, the more essential attorneys are. The *Counsel for Private Parties* and *Prosecution* volumes define those rules.

Thus, *Counsel for Private Parties* Standard 1.1 states:

**1.1 Counsel in juvenile proceedings, generally.**
The participation of counsel on behalf of all parties subject to juvenile and family court proceedings is essential to the admin-

istration of justice and to the fair and accurate resolution of
issues at all stages of those proceedings.

And *Prosecution* Standard 1.1 states:

**1.1 The role of the juvenile prosecutor.**
   **A. An attorney for the state, hereinafter referred to as the
juvenile prosecutor, should participate in every proceeding of
every stage of every case subject to the jurisdiction of the family
court, in which the state has an interest.**
   **B. The primary duty of the juvenile prosecutor is to seek
justice: to fully and faithfully represent the interests of the state,
without losing sight of the philosophy and purpose of the family
court.**

The more complex guideline appears in subsection B. of *Prosecution*
Standard 1.1, since it interjects concern for the "philosophy and
purpose of the family court," thereby placing the prosecutor in the
classic double bind of simultaneously protecting the interests of the
state and the child. In the section entitled Statement of General
Principles, this potential conflict is resolved by assigning primary
responsibility to the prosecutor to represent the state's interest when
"the interests of the state and those of the youth are in irreconcilable
conflict.... However, if the interests of the youth can be advanced
without damage to the interests of the state, the juvenile prosecutor
should not feel that the inherently adversarial nature of the office
requires him or her to oppose the accommodation of the interests of the
youth."
   That would seem to reflect the prevailing view in jurisdictions that
give prosecutors an active role in juvenile court proceedings. It must be
much easier to state than to implement. The defense counsel's task is
an easier one to understand and execute. Standard 3.1 in *Counsel for
Private Parties* is unambiguous, stating in part, "Client's interests
paramount. However engaged, the lawyer's principal duty is the
representation of the client's legitimate interests." It adopts the
traditional position that the "determination of the client's interests in
the proceedings, and hence the plea to be entered, is ultimately the
responsibility of the client after full consultation with the attorney"—
traditional for adult court, not juvenile court.
   Consideration also is given to the stage of the proceeding. *Prosecution* Standard 6.2 stipulates that "At the adjudicatory hearing the
juvenile prosecutor should assume the traditional adversary position
of a prosecutor."

Therefore, two points are clear—counsel for both sides should participate at every stage of the proceeding and the interest of the client (whether juvenile, parent, or state) is paramount. In the prosecutor's case, this role is compounded by a duty to consider the child's interest as well if there is no unreconcilable conflict with the state's interests. However, adversity of interests can be a problem for juvenile's counsel and that is convoluted further by questions of the juvenile's capacity to make responsible lawyer-client decisions. *Counsel for Private Parties* Standard 3.1 (b) (ii) [c] [2] was amended by deleting "other than himself or herself" from the provision requiring counsel to request appointment of a guardian *ad litem,* thereby making it possible for counsel to be so designated. *Counsel for Private Parties* provides the following:

**3.1 The nature of the relationship.**
    **(a) Client's interests paramount.**
    **However engaged, the lawyer's principal duty is the representation of the client's legitimate interests. Considerations of personal and professional advantage or convenience should not influence counsel's advice or performance.**
    **(b) Determination of client's interests.**
        **(i) Generally.**
    **In general, determination of the client's interests in the proceedings, and hence the plea to be entered, is ultimately the responsibility of the client after full consultation with the attorney.**
        **(ii) Counsel for the juvenile.**
        **[a] Counsel for the respondent in a delinquency or in need of supervision proceeding should ordinarily be bound by the client's definition of his or her interests with respect to admission or denial of the facts or conditions alleged. It is appropriate and desirable for counsel to advise the client concerning the probable success and consequences of adopting any posture with respect to those proceedings.**
        **[b] Where counsel is appointed to represent a juvenile subject to child protective proceedings, and the juvenile is capable of considered judgment on his or her own behalf, determination of the client's interest in the proceeding should ultimately remain the client's responsibility, after full consultation with counsel.**
        **[c] In delinquency and in need of supervision proceedings where it is locally permissible to so adjudicate very**

young persons, and in child protective proceedings, the respondent may be incapable of considered judgment in his or her own behalf.

[1] Where a guardian ad litem has been appointed, primary responsibility for determination of the posture of the case rests with the guardian and the juvenile.

[2] Where a guardian ad litem has not been appointed, the attorney should ask that one be appointed.

[3] Where a guardian ad litem has not been appointed and, for some reason, it appears that independent advice to the juvenile will not otherwise be available, counsel should inquire thoroughly into all circumstances that a careful and competent person in the juvenile's position should consider in determining the juvenile's interests with respect to the proceeding. After consultation with the juvenile, the parents (where their interests do not appear to conflict with the juvenile's) and any other family members or interested persons, the attorney may remain neutral concerning the proceeding, limiting participation to presentation and examination of material evidence or, if necessary, the attorney may adopt the position requiring the least intrusive intervention justified by the juvenile's circumstances.

(iii) Counsel for the parent.

It is appropriate and desirable for an attorney to consider all circumstances, including the apparent interests of the juvenile, when counseling and advising a parent who is charged in a child protective proceeding or who is seeking representation during a delinquency or in need of supervision proceeding. The posture to be adopted with respect to the facts and conditions alleged in the proceeding, however, remains ultimately the responsibility of the client.

The role of parents and guardians *ad litem* will be discussed in the next section. Client decisions are covered in *Counsel for Private Parties* Standard 5.2.

## 5.2 Control and direction of the case.

(a) Certain decisions relating to the conduct of the case are in most cases ultimately for the client and others are ultimately for the lawyer. The client, after full consultation with counsel, is ordinarily responsible for determining:

(i) the plea to be entered at adjudication;

(ii) whether to cooperate in consent judgment or early disposition plans;

(iii) whether to be tried as a juvenile or an adult, where the client has that choice;

(iv) whether to waive jury trial;

(v) whether to testify on his or her own behalf.

(b) Decisions concerning what witnesses to call, whether and how to conduct cross-examination, what jurors to accept and strike, what trial motions should be made, and any other strategic and tactical decisions not inconsistent with determinations ultimately the responsibility of and made by the client, are the exclusive province of the lawyer after full consultation with the client.

(c) If a disagreement on significant matters of tactics or strategy arises between the lawyer and the client, the lawyer should make a record of the circumstances, his or her advice and reasons, and the conclusion reached. This record should be made in a manner which protects the confidentiality of the lawyer-client relationship.

To add to the complexity of the role of both counsel is another relationship peculiar to juvenile court—the key role of probation workers. Standard 1.4 of *Counsel to Private Parties* provides:

**1.4 Relations with probation and social work personnel.**

A lawyer engaged in juvenile court practice typically deals with social work and probation department personnel throughout the course of handling a case. In general, the lawyer should cooperate with these agencies and should instruct the client to do so, except to the extent such cooperation is or will likely become inconsistent with protection of the client's legitimate interests in the proceeding or of any other rights of the client under the law.

*Prosecution* Standards 3.7, 4.1, and 4.2 provide as follows:

**3.7 With intake officers, probation officers, and social workers.**

An atmosphere of mutual respect and trust should exist among the juvenile prosecutor and intake officers, probation officers, and social workers. He or she should be available to advise them concerning any matters relevant to their functions.

**4.1 Responsibilities of the juvenile prosecutor and intake officer at the intake stage.**

A. The juvenile prosecutor should be available to advise the intake officer whether the facts alleged by a complainant are legally sufficient to file a petition of delinquency.

B. If the intake officer determines that a petition should be filed, he or she should submit a written report requesting that a petition be filed to the juvenile prosecutor. The intake officer should also submit a written statement of the decision and the reasons therefor to the juvenile and his or her parents or legal guardian. All petitions should be countersigned and filed by the juvenile prosecutor. The juvenile prosecutor may refuse the request of the intake officer to file a petition. Any determination by the prosecutor that a petition should not be filed should be final and not appealable to the family court.

C. If the intake officer determines that a petition should not be filed, the officer should notify the complainant of the decision and of the reasons therefor and should advise the complainant that he or she may submit the complaint to the juvenile prosecutor for review. Upon receiving a request for review, the juvenile prosecutor should consider the facts presented by the complainant, consult with the intake officer who made the initial decision, and then make the final determination as to whether a petition should be filed.

D. In the absence of a complainant's request for a review of the intake officer's determination that a petition should not be filed, the intake officer should notify the juvenile prosecutor of a determination that a petition should not be filed. The juvenile prosecutor then has the right, after consultation with the intake officer, to file a petition.

**4.2 Withdrawal of petition upon a subsequent finding of lack of legal sufficiency.**

If, subsequent to the filing of a petition with the family court, the juvenile prosecutor determines that there is insufficient evidence admissible in a court of law under the rules of evidence to establish the legal sufficiency of the petition, he or she should move to withdraw the petition.

The role of probation intake and investigative workers will be discussed in the next section. However, it can be seen that the prosecutor and other counsel have a more fragile and sensitive relationship with other juvenile court personnel than is the case in other courts. Juvenile courts traditionally abhor formality and rules encumbering individualized decision making by court officials. Judges and probation workers in juvenile courts value their perceived obligation to respond impressionistically to juvenile problems. Many resent the intrusion of formal rules, added paper work, and legalistic pyrotechnics, which they regard as frequently obstructing their primary concern—the treatment and care of children identified as suffering from severe behavior problems and family pathology, regardless of the original grounds for court intervention. The standards radically curtail their discretionary powers and circumscribe their areas of concern by imposing criteria and requiring written decisions.

In most other respects, the standards are consistent with the Rules of Professional Conduct for attorneys and with the customary roles for prosecution and defense counsel in criminal matters and in some areas, as in discovery procedures, in civil matters for plaintiff and defense counsel. One significant area of difference is in plea bargaining and admissions, although several revisions have brought the juvenile standards closer to criminal law practices, e.g., *Prosecution* Standard 5.1 and *Adjudication* Standard 3.3 B. have been changed to include dispositions as matters subject to plea negotiations. Here the standards impose a heavier burden on all adult participants—judges, lawyers, parents, and guardians *ad litem*—to ascertain the ability of the juveniles to comprehend the implications of their admissions or other pleas and also to consider possible adversity in the interests of their parents. Another anomaly of juvenile court practice is the intense reliance on the results of social investigations at the preadjudication and dispositional stages. Finally, the availability of transfer of a delinquency case from the juvenile court to the adult criminal court also is a departure in juvenile law.

*Prosecution* Part V covers uncontested adjudication proceedings as follows:

### 5.1 Propriety of plea agreements.

**A. A plea agreement concerning the petition or petitions that may be filed against a juvenile may properly be entered into by the juvenile prosecutor.**

**B. Plea agreements should be entered into with both the interests of the state and those of the juvenile in mind, although the primary concern of the juvenile prosecutor should be the protection of the public interest, as determined in the exercise of traditional prosecutorial discretion.**

### 5.2 Plea discussions when a juvenile maintains factual innocence.

The juvenile prosecutor should neither initiate nor continue plea discussions if he or she is aware that the juvenile maintains factual innocence.

### 5.3 Independent evidence in the record.

A plea agreement should not be entered into by the juvenile prosecutor without the presentation on the record of the family court of independent evidence indicating that the juvenile has committed the acts alleged in the petition.

### 5.4 Fulfillment of plea agreements.

If juvenile prosecutors find that they are unable to fulfill a plea agreement they should promptly give notice to the juvenile and cooperate in securing leave of court for the withdrawal of the admission, and take such other steps as may be appropriate and effective to restore the juvenile to the position he or she was in before the plea was entered.

*Counsel for Private Parties* deals with admissions in Standard 6.3 and adjudication without trial in Standard 7.1.

### 6.3 Early disposition.

(a) When the client admits the acts or conditions alleged in the juvenile court proceeding and after investigation the lawyer is satisfied that the admission is factually supported and that the court would have jurisdiction to act, the lawyer should, with the client's consent, consider developing or cooperating in the development of a plan for informal or voluntary adjustment of the case.

(b) A lawyer should not participate in an admission of responsibility by the client for purposes of securing informal or early disposition when the client denies responsibility for the acts or conditions alleged.

### 7.1 Adjudication without trial.

(a) Counsel may conclude, after full investigation and preparation, that under the evidence and the law the charges involving the client will probably be sustained. Counsel should so advise the client and, if negotiated pleas are allowed under prevailing law, may seek the client's consent to engage in plea discussions with the prosecuting agency. Where the client denies guilt, the lawyer cannot properly participate in submitting a plea of involvement where the prevailing law requires that such a plea be supported by an admission of responsibility in fact.

(b) The lawyer should keep the client advised of all developments during plea discussions with the prosecuting agency and should communicate to the client all proposals made by the prosecuting agency. Where it appears that the client's participation in a psychiatric, medical, social or other diagnostic or treatment regime would be significant in obtaining a desired result, the lawyer should so advise the client and, when circumstances warrant, seek the client's consent to participation in such a program.

The standards governing plea bargaining and admissions will be considered in greater detail in the section on court procedures in connection with the *Pretrial Court Proceedings* volume.

*Prosecution* Standard 4.3 A. 3. was amended in regard to the juvenile's age and offense charged for motions to transfer to criminal court in order to conform to changes in the *Transfer Between Courts* standards. With respect to reliance on social investigations, *Prosecution* Standard 4.3 states:

**4.3 Investigation: proper subject for family court jurisdiction.**

**A. The juvenile prosecutor should determine, by investigating the juvenile's past record with the police and the court, whether he or she is a proper subject for family court jurisdiction.**

**1. Where the juvenile prosecutor's inquiry into the conduct alleged and the juvenile's circumstances warrant it, the complaint may be transferred to the intake agency for a preadjudication disposition.**

**2. If the juvenile prosecutor determines that the state's interest requires the formal adjudicative process of the family court, a petition should be filed as soon as possible with the family court.**

**3. A motion to transfer the case to criminal court may be filed with the petition if the juvenile is at least fifteen years of age but under the age of eighteen at the time of the conduct alleged in the petition, and if there is clear and convincing evidence that**

**a. the alleged conduct would constitute a class one or class two juvenile offense, and**

**b. the juvenile alleged to have committed a class two offense has a prior record of adjudicated delinquency involving the infliction or threat of significant bodily injury, and**

**c. previous dispositions of the juvenile have demon-**

strated the likely inefficacy of the dispositions available to the family court, and

d. the services and dispositional alternatives available in the criminal justice system are more appropriate for dealing with the juvenile's problems and are, in fact, available.

B. If a petition is filed, the information obtained in the course of this investigation should be made available to the juvenile or to the counsel for the juvenile.

*Counsel for Private Parties* Standard 4.3 conforms more closely to conventional defense practice, as follows:

### 4.3 Investigation and preparation.

(a) It is the duty of the lawyer to conduct a prompt investigation of the circumstances of the case and to explore all avenues leading to facts concerning responsibility for the acts or conditions alleged and social or legal dispositional alternatives. The investigation should always include efforts to secure information in the possession of prosecution, law enforcement, education, probation and social welfare authorities. The duty to investigate exists regardless of the client's admissions or statements of facts establishing responsibility for the alleged facts and conditions or of any stated desire by the client to admit responsibility for those acts and conditions.

(b) Where circumstances appear to warrant it, the lawyer should also investigate resources and services available in the community and, if appropriate, recommend them to the client and the client's family. The lawyer's responsibility in this regard is independent of the posture taken with respect to any proceeding in which the client is involved.

(c) It is unprofessional conduct for a lawyer to use illegal means to obtain evidence or information or to employ, instruct or encourage others to do so.

The dispositional phase will be examined in the chapter on treatment and corrections. But the standards on the role of counsel in dispositions are of interest here in considering the duty of prosecutors and counsel for private parties. *Prosecution* Standard 7.1 states:

### 7.1 Permissibility of taking an active role.

A. Juvenile prosecutors may take an active role in the dispositional hearing. If they choose to do so, they should make their

own, independent recommendation for disposition, after reviewing the reports prepared by their own staff, the probation
department, and others.

B. While the safety and welfare of the community is their
paramount concern, juvenile prosecutors should consider alternative modes of disposition which more closely satisfy the
interests and needs of the juvenile without jeopardizing that
concern.

Of even greater interest is Standard 7.2, especially in view of the
customary non-involvement of the state's counsel in dispositional
decisions.

**7.2 Duty to monitor the effectiveness of various modes of
disposition.**
A. Juvenile prosecutors should undertake their own periodic
evaluation of the success of particular dispositional programs
that are used in their jurisdiction, from the standpoint of the
interests of both the state and the juvenile.

B. If juvenile prosecutors discover that a juvenile or class of
juveniles is not receiving the care and treatment contemplated
by the family court in making its dispositions, they should
inform the family court of this fact.

*Counsel for Private Parties* Standard 9.2 states:

**9.2 Investigation and preparation.**
(a) Counsel should be familiar with the dispositional alternatives available to the court, with its procedures and practices at
the disposition stage, and with community services that might
be useful in the formation of a dispositional plan appropriate to
the client's circumstances.

(b) The lawyer should promptly investigate all sources of
evidence including any reports or other information that will be
brought to the court's attention, and interview all witnesses
material to the disposition decision.

(i) If access to social investigation, psychological, psychiatric or other reports or information is not provided voluntarily
or promptly, counsel should be prepared to seek their disclosure and time to study them through formal measures.

(ii) Whether or not social and other reports are readily
available, the lawyer has a duty independently to investigate
the client's circumstances, including such factors as previous

**history, family relations, economic condition and any other information relevant to disposition.**

**(c) The lawyer should seek to secure the assistance of psychiatric, psychological, medical or other expert personnel needed for purposes of evaluation, consultation or testimony with respect to formation of a dispositional plan.**

The standards for transfer of an alleged delinquent from juvenile to criminal court will be part of the discussion on court procedures in a later section. As for the prosecutor's part in the decision, *Prosecution* Standard 4.3 A. 3. sets forth the criteria to be applied by the prosecutor in deciding whether to file a motion to transfer the case to criminal court for juveniles who are fifteen to seventeen years of age at the time of the alleged commission of a class one or class two juvenile offense. The text of *Prosecution* Standard 4.3 appears at pages 160–61.

There can be no dispute that greater formality and regulation in juvenile court proceedings must result in an enlarged role for counsel. It also restricts the free exercise of discretion by court officials by stipulating the criteria that must be met by decisions at every stage of the court process. By training, lawyers are the professionals to whom parties and workers must turn to determine whether the rules and regulations have been satisfied. Nevertheless, formality and rulemaking need not unduly restrain court officials in the performance of their duties if they are prepared to furnish reasonable accounts of the basis for their actions. Innovation, experimentation, even risktaking, can flourish in an atmosphere of openness and reason. It is only capricious, discriminatory, or irrational conduct that order and formality are designed to eliminate by exposing the decision making process to scrutiny and review.

## 5.3 The Role of Probation.

One of the most crucial elements of the juvenile justice system and one of its greatest disappointments is the role of the probation services. Probation officials, usually trained social workers, may be involved at four stages of the court process—(1) at intake to screen complaints by deciding whether to adjust the matter at intake, refer it to an agency for service, or refer it to the court for judicial action; (2) during the interim status or predisposition stage when participating in the release or detention decision; (3) at postadjudication when investigating a juvenile and family to report to the court in order to assist it in reaching its dispositional decision; and (4) during the postdisposition term when supervising juveniles placed on probation by the court. The role of probation would appear to be central to the operation of the juvenile justice system. Unfortunately, its performance has been so erratic, unreliable, and ineffective that the standards adopted to govern its work have greatly reduced its authority.

The concept of probation intake, investigation, and supervision remains essential to a functioning juvenile justice system. But the range of discretion and the available nonjudicial remedies are curtailed by the standards.

After a complaint is reported, the matter is referred to intake. Standard 2.1 of *The Juvenile Probation Function: Intake and Predisposition Investigative Services* requires that intake services be available to all juvenile courts.

The dispositional alternatives available at intake after the complaint is received and intake interviews have taken place are set forth in Standards 2.2 to 2.5 as unconditional dismissal, judicial disposition, nonjudicial disposition of a complaint, and a consent decree. Dismissal of a complaint at intake terminates all proceedings against the juvenile. Judicial disposition is the initiation of formal judicial proceedings through the filing of a petition. The choice between dismissal and referral to the court for a hearing is a pure screening decision. Less pure and far more controversial is the probation intake choice of a nonjudicial disposition of the complaint. It is at this point that the Commission gave expression to its disappointment in the performance of probation services and its uncertainty as to their beneficial effects on juveniles and families by restricting nonjudicial dispositions to referral to community programs, presumably under the aegis of the local youth service agency, and by insisting upon the juvenile's nonwaivable right to counsel at the intake stage. Short-term crisis intervention by probation intake was approved, but probation service on a continuing basis was expressly excluded as a nonjudicial disposition.

Aside from the alternatives of unconditional dismissal, court referral, and nonjudicial disposition, a fourth intake disposition is the execution of a consent decree. A consent decree is described in Standard 2.5 as follows:

**2.5 Consent decree.**

**A. A consent decree is a court order authorizing supervision of a juvenile for a specified period of time during which the juvenile may be required to fulfill certain conditions or some other disposition of the complaint without the filing of a petition and a formal adjudicatory proceeding.**

**A consent decree should be permissible under the following conditions:**

**1. The juvenile and his or her parents or legal guardian should voluntarily and intelligently consent to the decree.**

2. The intake officer and the judge should advise the juvenile and his or her parents or legal guardian that they have the right to refuse to consent to the decree and to request a formal adjudication.

3. The juvenile should have an unwaivable right to the assistance of counsel in connection with an application for a consent decree. The intake officer should advise the juvenile of this right.

4. The terms of the decree should be clearly stated in the decree and a copy should be given to all parties to the decree.

5. The decree should not remain in force for a period in excess of six (6) months. Upon application of any of the parties to the decree, made before expiration of the decree, the decree, after notice and hearing, may be extended for not more than an additional three (3) months by the court.

6. The juvenile and his or her parents or legal guardian should be able to terminate the agreement at any time and to request the filing of a petition and formal adjudication.

7. Once a consent decree has been entered, the subsequent filing of a petition based upon the events out of which the original complaint arose should be permitted for a period of [three (3)] months from the date the decree was entered. If no petition is filed within that period its subsequent filing should be prohibited. The juvenile's compliance with all proper and reasonable terms of the decree should be an affirmative defense to a petition filed within the [three-month] period.

Other safeguards at the intake stage, in addition to the right to counsel, are the requirement that the agencies responsible for intake services should issue written guidelines and rules to establish criteria for intake dispositional decisions and the juvenile's privilege against self-incrimination at intake. Any statement or information divulged to an intake officer is inadmissible in evidence until after the adjudication unless made after consultation with and in the presence of counsel.

The intake officer should make an initial determination of the legal sufficiency of a complaint and if uncertain, should ask the prosecutor for a determination of its legal sufficiency. If the complaint is deemed legally sufficient, the intake officer should determine what disposition is in the best interests of the juvenile and the community according to the following criteria set forth in Standard 2.8 B.:

1. The seriousness of the offense that the alleged delinquent conduct constitutes should be considered in making an intake dispositional decision. A petition should ordinarily be filed

against a juvenile who has allegedly engaged in delinquent conduct constituting a serious offense, which should be determined on the basis of the nature and extent of harm to others produced by the conduct.

2. The nature and number of the juvenile's prior contacts with the juvenile court should be considered in making an intake dispositional decision.

3. The circumstances surrounding the alleged delinquent conduct, including whether the juvenile was alone or in the company of other juveniles who also participated in the alleged delinquent conduct, should be considered in making an intake dispositional decision. If a petition is filed against one of the juveniles, a petition should ordinarily be filed against the other juveniles for substantially similar conduct.

4. The age and maturity of the juvenile may be relevant to an intake dispositional decision.

5. The juvenile's school attendance and behavior, the juvenile's family situation and relationships, and the juvenile's home environment may be relevant to an intake dispositional decision.

6. The attitude of the juvenile to the alleged delinquent conduct and to law enforcement and juvenile court authorities may be relevant to an intake dispositional decision, but a nonjudicial disposition of the complaint or the unconditional dismissal of the complaint should not be precluded for the sole reason that the juvenile denies the allegations of the complaint.

7. A nonjudicial disposition of the complaint or the unconditional dismissal of the complaint should not be precluded for the sole reason that the complainant opposes dismissal.

8. The availability of services to meet the juvenile's needs both within and outside the juvenile justice system should be considered in making an intake dispositional decision.

9. The factors that are not relevant to an intake dispositional decision include but are not necessarily limited to the juvenile's race, ethnic background, religion, sex, and economic status.

Prior to making the intake decision, the officer is authorized to conduct a preliminary investigation consisting of interviews with the complainant, victim, witness or co-participant; checking public records; interviews with the juveniles and their parents or guardians. Additional inquiries require the consent of the juveniles and their parents or guardians. The guidelines for the intake interviews and dispositional conferences are proposed in Standard 2.14.

2.14 Intake interviews and dispositional conferences.

A. If the intake officer deems it advisable, the officer may request and arrange an interview with the juvenile and his or her parents or legal guardian.

B. Participation in an intake interview by the juvenile and his or her parents or legal guardian should be voluntary. They should have the right to refuse to participate in an interview, and the officer should have no authority to compel their attendance.

C. At the time the request to attend the interview is made, the intake officer should inform the juvenile and his or her parents or legal guardian either in writing or orally that attendance is voluntary and that the juvenile has the right to be represented by counsel.

D. At the commencement of the interview, the intake officer should:

1. explain to the juvenile and his or her parents or legal guardian that a complaint has been made and explain the allegations of the complaint;

2. explain the function of the intake process, the dispositional powers of the intake officer, and intake procedures;

3. explain that participation in the intake interview is voluntary and that they may refuse to participate; and

4. notify them of the right of the juvenile to remain silent and the right to counsel as heretofore defined in Standard 2.13.

E. Subsequent to the intake interview, the intake officer may schedule one or more dispositional conferences with the juvenile and his or her parents or legal guardian in order to effect a nonjudicial disposition.

F. Participation in a dispositional conference by a juvenile and his or her parents or legal guardian should be voluntary. They should have the right to refuse to participate, and the intake officer should have no authority to compel their attendance.

G. The intake officer may conduct dispositional conferences in accordance with the procedures for intake interviews set forth in subsections D. and E.

The intake decision should be made within thirty days after the complaint is filed if the juvenile is not in detention or shelter care. If the officer decides a petition should be filed, the officer should send a written report to the prosecutor with a statement of the reasons for the decision, also submitted to the juvenile and parents. A decision by the prosecutor to file or not to file should be final. If the officer decides not to file, the notice of the decision and reasons should also go to the complainant, advising that the complainant may submit the complaint to the prosecutor for a final determination as to whether a petition should be filed.

Juvenile probation services also have a role at the predisposition stage to conduct investigations and prepare predisposition reports, pursuant to written guidelines and rules for such investigations and reports, and in accordance with Standard 3.3.

**3.3 Scope of investigation; formulation of postdisposition plan; format, contents, length, and disclosure of report.**

A. The scope of a predisposition investigation that the investigating officer conducts should be carefully tailored to the needs of the individual case and should vary depending upon the type of case and the issues involved. The officer should only collect evidence relevant to the court's dispositional decision.

B. When it is appropriate for the investigating officer to conduct a comprehensive investigation, the officer may secure information from existing records of the juvenile court, law enforcement agencies, schools, and other agencies with which the juvenile has come in contact and from interviews and conferences with the juvenile, the juvenile's family, school personnel, and individuals having knowledge of the juvenile.

C. An officer conducting a predisposition investigation may refer a juvenile for a physical or mental examination to a physician, psychiatrist, or psychologist only if a court order authorizing an examination is obtained. Such a court order should be issued only after a hearing on the need for such an examination.

D. The officer conducting a predisposition investigation should explore community resources as well as other resources that might be available to assist the juvenile. The officer should then formulate a postdisposition plan for the care and, where appropriate, for the treatment of the juvenile.

E. A written predisposition report summarizing the significant findings of the investigation should be prepared. The format, contents, and length of the report should be flexible. A comprehensive report should ordinarily include the following:

　　1. a summary of the facts with respect to the conduct of the juvenile that led to the adjudication;

　　2. a summary of the juvenile's prior contacts with the juvenile court and law enforcement agencies, including the disposition following each contact and the reasons therefor;

　　3. a summary of the juvenile's home environment, family relationships and background;

4. a summary of the juvenile's school and employment status and background;

5. a summary of the juvenile's interests and activities;

6. a summary of any significant physical problems of the juvenile and description of any behavior problems of the juvenile that the officer learns of or observes in the course of the investigation, provided the officer is careful not to represent these observations as qualified professional evaluations;

7. a summary of the results and recommendations of any significant physical and mental examinations; and

8. an evaluation of the foregoing information, a recommendation as to disposition, and a suggested postdisposition plan of care and treatment.

F. The predisposition report should contain only information that is relevant to the court's dispositional decision, and all information should be presented in a concise, factual, and unbiased manner. The report should indicate how much time and effort was expended upon the investigation and the sources of information in the report.

G. The predisposition report should not be open to public inspection, but the juvenile's counsel and the attorney representing the state in connection with dispositional proceedings should be given access to the report.

The report should be submitted to the court after adjudication and prior to disposition.

The probation intake, investigation, and supervision roles should be treated as separate functions. Intake and investigation should be administered by a statewide agency, with some local administrative functions. Officers should be qualified by formal education or training, prior work experience and job performance of a certain quality, and appropriate personal characteristics and skills. Minority group members and women should be included in recruitment efforts. The agencies should establish reasonable workloads and staff ratios. Training and educational incentives and use of paraprofessionals and volunteers should be encouraged.

## 5.4 Court Procedures.

The court process adopted in the standards and followed in many juvenile courts today begins with the reporting of a complaint (by police, parents, alleged victims, child care, child protective, or other social agency); issuance of a summons or a citation with notice of charges; probation intake screening resulting in adjustment at intake through intake services or dismissal of the charges, referral to a youth service agency, or execution of a consent decree, or referral to the court for judicial proceedings; filing the petition; preadjudication proceedings such as transfer, probable cause, detention, or discovery hearings; the dispositional hearing; appeals or collateral attacks; corrections; and possible postdispositional proceedings, such as modification of a disposition.

Diversion through referral to a treatment program or other services through a youth service agency can take place at any stage of the proceedings. Counsel or a guardian *ad litem* also can be appointed at any stage as needed, although the standards call for a nonwaivable right to counsel at intake and adjudication. The police process of apprehension, arrest, release, diversion, or referral to the court is treated separately in section 4.3.3.

### 5.4.1 Preadjudication standards.

*Pretrial Court Proceedings* standards are analogous to pretrial procedures for adults, drawing on both criminal and civil law, but also adding certain features related specifically to juvenile court needs, for example, the appointment of guardians *ad litem*. The standards cover the report, petition, and summons; notification of rights and initial appearance; discovery; probable cause hearings; respondent's right to counsel; waiver of the juvenile's rights; the role of parents and guardians *ad litem;* and juvenile court calendaring. The volume covers delinquency proceedings only.

After the report of the complaint has been filed with and screened by probation intake and the decision is made to file a petition with the court, Standard 1.4 directs that the petition be prepared and filed by the prosecuting attorney. This standard is consistent with the volumes on prosecution and probation intake. Standard 1.3 specifies the details to be set forth in the petition:

### 1.3 Contents of the petition.
**A. The petition should set forth with particularity all factual and other allegations relied upon in asserting that the juvenile is within the juvenile court's jurisdiction, including:**
    **1. the name, address, and date of birth of the juvenile;**
    **2. the name and address of the juvenile's parents or guardian and, if the juvenile is in the custody of some other person, such custodian;**
    **3. the date, time, manner, and place of the acts alleged as the basis of the court's jurisdiction;**
    **4. a citation to the section and subdivision of the juvenile court act relied upon for jurisdiction; and**

5. a citation to the federal, state, or local law or ordinance, if any, allegedly violated by the juvenile.

B. The petition should state the kinds of dispositions to which the respondent could be subjected if the allegations of the petition were proven, such as transfer for criminal prosecution, probation, or removal from the home.

*Pretrial Court Proceedings* Standard 1.2 C. also requires that a statement advising the parties of their legal rights be included in or appended to the summons or the petition. The thrust of both standards is to ensure adequate notice of the charges and possible consequences to the affected persons.

Standards 2.1 and 2.2 are even more precise with respect to notification of rights. Standard 2.1 B. was amended to require that the juvenile's rights be explained in open court. Standard 2.2 was amended to add jury trial to the specific rights the judge should recite.

## 2.1 Notification of rights.

At every stage in the proceedings at which these standards require the giving of notice of rights, the following requirements should be satisfied:

A. notification of the juvenile's rights should always be given to both the juvenile and the parent and/or guardian or custodian who is present at the proceedings;

B. the notice should be in writing but should be explained to the recipient by the judge personally in open court at the regularly scheduled hearing in all circumstances where notice is given in the recipient's presence;

C. notification should be given in simple language calculated to ensure the recipient's understanding;

D. in bilingual and multilingual communities, notification should be given in English and in the dominant language of the recipient; and

E. the official record of the proceedings should record the fact that such notice was given and the contents of the notice.

## 2.2 Initial appearance.

A. The initial appearance of a delinquency respondent before a judge of the juvenile court should be not later than [five] days after the petition has been filed.

B. At the first appearance in court the juvenile should be notified by the judge of the contents of the petition, and of his or her rights, including:

1. the right to counsel as provided in Standard 5.2;

2. the right to have parents present at all stages of the proceedings;
3. the right to a probable cause hearing;
4. the right to trial by jury;
5. the right to confrontation and cross-examination of witnesses; and
6. the privilege against self-incrimination.

C. At the initial appearance, counsel should be appointed if necessary, and a date should be set for the fact-finding hearing.

Finally, the concern that the parties be fully informed is further supported by Standard 2.3 on multilingual communication, as follows:

2.3 Multilingual communications.

In bilingual and multilingual communities, the court and counsel should take appropriate steps to ensure that language barriers do not deprive the respondent, parents, and other appropriate persons of the ability to understand and effectively participate in all stages of the proceedings. Such steps should include the provision of interpreters at all stages of the proceedings, at public expense.

To facilitate full access to all possible procedural safeguards, *Pretrial Court Proceedings* standards adopt broad discovery practices from civil courts, as provided in Standard 3.1:

3.1 Scope of discovery.

In order to provide adequate information for informed intake screening, diversion, and pleas in delinquency cases, and to expedite trials, minimize surprise, afford opportunity for effective cross-examination, and meet the requirements of due process, discovery prior to trial and other judicial hearings should be as full and free as possible consistent with protection of persons and effectuation of the goals of the juvenile justice system.

The *Pretrial Court Proceedings* standards further stress disclosure by defining the petitioner's obligations to disclose to respondent as follows:

3.3 Petitioner's obligations.

A. Except as otherwise provided as to matters not subject to disclosure (Standard 3.8) and protective orders (Standard 3.17), the petitioner should disclose to respondent's counsel the following material and information within his or her possession or control:

1. the names and addresses of persons whom the petitioner intends to call as witnesses at the hearing or trial, together with their relevant written or recorded statements;

2. any written or recorded statements and the substance of any oral statements made by the respondent, or made by a corespondent if the trial is to be a joint one;

3. any reports or statements of experts, made in connection with the particular case, including scientific tests, experiments or comparisons, and results of physical or mental examinations, behavioral observations, and investigations of the respondent's school, social, or family background;

4. any reports or records, whether or not made in connection with the particular case, of the respondent's involvement with law enforcement, judicial, welfare, school or other public agencies, which might assist counsel in representing the respondent before the court at any stage of the proceedings;

5. any books, papers, records, documents, photographs, or tangible objects which the petitioner intends to use in the hearing or trial or which were obtained from or belong to the respondent;

6. any record of prior criminal convictions of persons whom the petitioner intends to call as witnesses at the hearing or trial; and

7. those portions of grand jury minutes containing testimony of the respondent and relevant testimony of persons whom the petitioner intends to call as witnesses at the hearing or trial.

B. Subject to Standards 3.8 and 3.17, the respondent should have the right to obtain discovery by way of deposition.

C. The petitioner should inform respondent's counsel:

1. whether there is any relevant recorded grand jury testimony which has not been transcribed; and

2. whether there has been any electronic surveillance (including wiretapping) of conversations to which the respondent was a party or of the respondent's premises.

D. Subject to Standard 3.17, the petitioner should disclose to respondent's counsel any material or information within his or her possession or control which tends to negate the allegations of the petition or would tend to mitigate the seriousness thereof.

E. The petitioner's obligations under this standard extend to material and information in the possession or control of members of the petitioner's staff and of any others who have participated in the screening, investigation, or evaluation of the case and who either regularly report, or who have reported with reference to the particular case, to the petitioner's office.

There are other provisions for additional disclosure upon request, disclosure within the court's discretion, and denial of a request for disclosure:

**3.7 Discretionary disclosures.**
   A. Upon a showing of materiality to the preparation of the respondent's case and if the request is reasonable, the court, in its discretion, may require disclosure to respondent's counsel of relevant material and information not covered by Standards 3.3, 3.5, and 3.6.
   B. The court may deny disclosure authorized by this standard if it finds that there is a substantial risk to any person of physical harm, intimidation, bribery, economic reprisals, or unnecessary annoyance or embarrassment resulting from such disclosure which outweighs any usefulness of the disclosure to respondent's counsel.

Matters not subject to disclosure specified in Standard 3.8 are work products and informant's identity.

Standard 3.14 makes the rules governing depositions in criminal proceedings applicable to delinquency proceedings, but recommends enacting special rules on depositions for delinquency cases.

Sanctions for failure to comply with discovery rules or orders are authorized in Standard 3.20.

Although the broad pretrial discovery rights provided in the standards exceed those available in adult criminal proceedings and far surpass those provided in most juvenile courts, depositions are reluctantly granted.

An equally hard fought battle in juvenile courts is the right to a probable cause hearing. Many courts are granting that right for juveniles who are detained, detained beyond a specified period, or charged with more serious offenses, as well as in cases where transfer to criminal court is contemplated. Standard 4.1 provides as follows:

**4.1 The right to a probable cause hearing.**
   A. In all delinquency proceedings the respondent should have the right to a judicial determination of probable cause, unless the adjudicatory hearing is held within [five] days after the filing of the petition if the juvenile is detained, and within [fifteen] days if the juvenile is not detained. Unless it appears from the

evidence that there is probable cause to believe that an offense has been committed and that the respondent committed it, the petition should be dismissed.

B. Unless there has been a prior judicial determination of probable cause, detention and transfer hearings should commence with consideration of that issue.

The role of counsel is discussed in a preceding section. The standards with respect to the time at which the right to counsel attaches, notice of that right, the effect of apparent conflict between juveniles and their parents, and the position that no means test is imposed in appointing counsel for a juvenile if private counsel has not been retained, appear in Standards 5.1 to 5.3. Parents with means are expected to pay for their own counsel. Standard 5.1 C. was amended to clarify and limit the juvenile's counsel's authority to waive the inadmissibility of statements made to intake officers or social service workers prior to adjudication.

## PART V: RESPONDENT'S RIGHT TO COUNSEL

5.1 Scope of the juvenile's right to counsel.

A. In delinquency cases, the juvenile should have the effective assistance of counsel at all stages of the proceeding.

B. The right to counsel should attach as soon as the juvenile is taken into custody by an agent of the state, when a petition is filed against the juvenile, or when the juvenile appears personally at an intake conference, whichever occurs first. The police and other detention authorities should have the duty to ascertain whether a juvenile in custody has counsel and, if not, to facilitate the retention or provision of counsel without delay.

C. Unless waived by counsel, the statements of a juvenile or other information or evidence derived directly or indirectly from such statements made to the intake officer or social service worker during the process of the case, including statements made during intake, a predisposition study, or consent decree, should not be admissible in evidence prior to a determination of the petition's allegations in a delinquency case, or prior to conviction in a criminal proceeding.

5.2 Notification of the juvenile's right to counsel.

As soon as a juvenile's right to counsel attaches under Standard 5.1 B. the authorities should advise the juvenile that representation by counsel is mandatory, that there is a right to employ private counsel, and that if private counsel is not retained counsel will be provided without cost.

**5.3 Juvenile's eligibility for court-appointed counsel; parent-juvenile conflicts.**

A. In any delinquency proceeding, if counsel has not been retained for the juvenile, and if it does not appear that counsel will be retained, the court should appoint counsel. No reimbursement should be sought from the parent or the juvenile for the cost of court-appointed counsel for the juvenile, regardless of the parent's or juvenile's financial resources.

B. At the earliest feasible stage of a delinquency proceeding the intake department should determine whether a conflict of interest exists between the juvenile and the parent, and should notify the court and the parties of any finding that a conflict exists.

C. If a parent has retained counsel for a juvenile and it appears to the court that the parent's interest in the case conflicts with the juvenile's interest, the court should caution both the parent and counsel as to counsel's duty of loyalty to the juvenile's interests. If the parent's dominant language is not English, the court's caution should be communicated in a language understood by the parent.

Finally, the standards in Part VI of *Pretrial Court Proceedings* cover the complex and delicate area of the role of parents and guardians *ad litem* in delinquency proceedings. Using the terminology of a "mature" or "immature" respondent, the test of the ability of juveniles to make client decisions in delinquency cases, especially the power to waive rights on their own behalf, is defined as the capacity to adequately comprehend and participate in the proceedings. If counsel believes a juvenile is immature, the court should be requested to appoint a guardian *ad litem* with power to make waiver decisions on behalf of the juvenile. It should be noted that the right to counsel is nonwaivable. Standard 6.2 describes the conditions for waiver of rights by a mature respondent:

**6.2 Waiver of the rights of mature respondents.**

A. A respondent considered by counsel to be mature should be permitted to act through counsel in the proceedings. However, the juvenile may not personally waive any right:

1. except in the presence of and after consultation with counsel; and

2. unless a parent has first been afforded a reasonable opportunity to consult with the juvenile and the juvenile's counsel regarding the decision. If the parent requires an interpreter for this purpose, the court should provide one.

B. The decision to waive a mature juvenile's privilege against self-incrimination; the right to be tried as a juvenile or as an adult where the respondent has that choice; the right to trial, with or without a jury; and the right to appeal or to seek other postadjudication relief should be made by the juvenile. Counsel may decide, after consulting with the juvenile, whether to waive other rights of the juvenile.

Waiver of rights of immature respondents is carefully protected by Standard 6.3.

## 6.3 Waiver of the rights of immature respondents.

A. A respondent considered by counsel to be immature should not be permitted to act through counsel, nor should a plea on behalf of an immature respondent admitting the allegations of the petition be accepted. The court may adjudicate an immature respondent delinquent only if the petition is proven at trial.

B. The decision to waive the following rights of an immature respondent should be made by the guardian *ad litem,* after consultation with the respondent and counsel: the privilege against self-incrimination; the right to be tried as a juvenile or as an adult, where the respondent has that choice; the right to a jury trial; and the right to appeal or seek other postadjudication relief. Subject to subsection A. of this standard, other rights of an immature respondent should be waivable by counsel after consultation with the juvenile's guardian *ad litem.*

Express waivers should be executed in writing and recorded. Assurance that the following conditions existed when administering the waiver should be the responsibility of the judge or other official:

## 6.4 Recording.

A. Express waivers should be executed in writing and recorded. When administering a waiver of the juvenile's right, the judge or other official should:

1. ascertain whether the waiver is being made by the juvenile or by the guardian *ad litem* on the juvenile's behalf;

2. if the juvenile is waiving a right on his or her own behalf, require counsel to affirm belief in the juvenile's

**capacity to do so, and affirm that counsel has otherwise complied with the requirements of this part; and**

**3. ascertain that the juvenile or guardian** *ad litem,* **as the case may be, is voluntarily and intelligently waiving the right in the presence of and after advice of counsel.**

The waiver should be executed in the dominant language of the waiving party or be accompanied by a translator's affidavit. The affidavit should be recorded.

*Pretrial Court Proceedings* Standard 6.5 prescribes the role of parents in delinquency proceedings. "Parents" are defined to include natural or adoptive parents whose parental rights have not been terminated, guardians, custodians, and separated or divorced parents. The parent's participation can be limited by the court if it finds their interests are adverse to the respondent's or that their presence will adversely affect the respondent's interests. Standards 6.8 A. and 6.9 A. were amended to make the appointment of counsel for indigent parents discretionary with the court, rather than mandatory. The parent's role at the proceedings is defined as follows:

**1. the parent of a delinquency respondent should have the right to notice, to be present, and to make representations to the court either** *pro se* **or through counsel at all stages of the proceedings;**

**2. parents should be encouraged by counsel, the judge, and other officials to take an active interest in the juvenile's case. Their proper functions include consultation with the juvenile and the juvenile's counsel at all stages of the proceedings concerning decisions made by the juvenile or by counsel on the juvenile's behalf, presence at all hearings, and participation in the planning of dispositional alternatives. Subject to the consent of the mature juvenile, parents should have access to all records in the case. If the juvenile does not consent, the court should nevertheless grant the parent access to records if they are not otherwise privileged, and if the court determines,** *in camera,* **that disclosure is necessary to protect the parent's interests.**

Guardians *ad litem* are appointed if the juvenile is immature, no parent or other responsible adult is present, conflict of interest appears to exist between parents and juvenile, or the juvenile's interest otherwise requires it. The guardian *ad litem's* function is to act as a concerned parent with the procedural rights accorded to parents. Certain persons may not be appointed as guardians *ad litem*—the juvenile's parents if they appear to have adverse interests, an agent or other representative of an institution having custody or guardianship of the juvenile, and an employee of the court or intake agency.

Standard 7.1 sets priorities in scheduling juvenile court cases.

**B. Insofar as is practicable, hearing priorities should favor the following categories:**

**1. young, immature, and emotionally troubled juveniles;**

**2. juveniles who are detained or otherwise removed from their usual home environment; and**

**3. juveniles whose pretrial liberty appears to present unusual risks to themselves or the community.**

As a general rule, all juvenile court cases should be processed without unnecessary delay. In calendaring cases, every effort should be made to have the same judge preside at the adjudication and postadjudication proceedings, but to avoid having the same judge at the adjudication hearing who has had prejudicial prior contacts with the case.

*Pretrial Court Proceedings* Standard 7.4 recommends an omnibus hearing prior to adjudication to:

**1. ascertain whether the parties have completed the discovery authorized in Part III and, if not, make appropriate orders to expedite completion;**

**2. make rulings on any motions or other requests then pending, and ascertain whether any additional motions or requests will be made at the hearing;**

**3. ascertain whether there are any procedural or constitutional issues which should be considered before trial; and**

**4. ensure compliance with the standards regarding provision of counsel.**

It also urges pretrial conferences with counsel present to consider matters to promote fair and expeditious proceedings if the trial is likely to be protracted or complicated, or at the request of counsel.

### 5.4.2 Transfer between courts.

Among the most controversial issues in the juvenile justice field is the authority to transfer jurisdiction over certain juveniles to the criminal courts. A number of states have responded to community concern over violent juvenile crimes by lowering the age at which an alleged delinquent can be waived to adult court on the theory that the possibility of incarceration in prisons may reduce the incidence of crime. The standards project has found no evidence to support that expectation. It has adopted the position that waiver of jurisdiction should be a last resort after all other efforts have failed and handling as an adult appears the only approach with any possibility of success in a particular case. Strict limitations as to age, prior record, and seriousness of the offense are prescribed. Fundamentally, the Commission regards transfer of a juvenile to criminal court as an admission of failure of the juvenile justice system to confront its sternest challenge. Therefore, the standards for *Transfer Between Courts* permit waiver of juvenile court jurisdiction only under the following conditions:

1. Age limits. The juvenile should be fifteen to seventeen years old at the time the offense is alleged to have occurred.

2. Limitations period. No waiver decision should be based on an offense alleged to have occurred more than three years prior to the filing of the petition, unless such offense would not be subject to a statute of limitations if committed by an adult. If the adult statutory limit for such offense is less than three years, the lesser period also applies to juvenile court proceedings.

3. The offense. The conduct alleged should constitute a class one or class two juvenile offense.

4. Notice. The clerk of the juvenile court should advise the prosecutor in writing of the possibility of waiver within two court days of filing any petition for a class one or two juvenile offense. The prosecutor should give the juvenile written notice of that possibility within three court days. The prosecutor should file a motion within seven court days and deliver a signed, acknowledged copy of the waiver motion within twenty-four hours after filing it.

5. Hearing requirements. The court should initiate the hearing within ten days of the filing of the waiver motion. The juvenile should be informed of a right to counsel at least five days before commencement of the hearing.

6. Necessary findings. The prosecutor has the burden of proving that probable cause exists to believe that the juvenile has committed the class one or class two juvenile offense alleged and that the juvenile is not a proper person for handling by the juvenile court by clear and convincing evidence of: the seriousness of the alleged offense; a prior record of adjudicated delinquency involving infliction or threat of significant bodily injury if accused of a class two offense; the inefficacy of the available dispositions as demonstrated by previous dispositions; and the appropriateness of the dispositional alternatives that are in fact available in the criminal justice system for dealing with the juvenile's problems.

No admission during the waiver hearing should be admissible to establish guilt or impeach testimony in any subsequent criminal proceeding. The juvenile may disqualify the presiding officer from any subsequent criminal trial or juvenile court adjudicatory hearing relating to any action alleged in the petition.

The waiver decision may be appealed by the juvenile or the prosecutor within seven days after it is rendered.

It might be noted that the standards originally limited waiver to juveniles sixteen or over accused of committing class one offenses. In addition, brackets were added to all time periods in the final approved version of these standards.

### 5.4.3 Adjudication standards.

The adjudication phase of juvenile delinquency proceedings would seem to be the most settled area following *In re Gault*, 387 U.S. 1 (1967), and subsequent judicial decisions. Unfortunately, *Gault* resolved some procedural issues and challenged the complacency of many traditional juvenile court practitioners, but created almost as much confusion as it eliminated. Which procedural safeguards are sufficient to provide an alleged delinquent with due process? Justice Fortas declined to rule on "whether ordinary due process requirements must be observed with respect to hearings to determine the disposition of the delinquent child." 387 U.S. at 27. Yet he insisted on facing the reality of the juvenile court process, labeling the titles "receiving home" or "industrial school" as euphemisms for the institutions in which juveniles are incarcerated. Reciting the protection that would have been afforded to an adult similarly charged under the guarantees of the Constitution, he said, "So wide a gulf between the State's treatment of the adult and of the child requires a bridge sturdier than mere verbiage, and reasons more persuasive than cliché can provide." 387 U.S. at 29-30. But the Court narrowed its decision to specified rights at the adjudicatory stage of a delinquency proceeding in which the juvenile may be deprived of liberty, those rights being notice of charges, right to counsel, confrontation and cross-examination of witnesses, and the privilege against self-incrimination. The Court did not rule on a right to appellate review, to be provided with a transcript, or to have the judge state the grounds for his or her conclusions.

The Court appeared to be citing with disapproval such concepts as the nonadversary nature of the proceedings, the *parens patriae* doctrine, and the assertion that a child has a right "not to liberty but to custody." The Court said:

> Accordingly, the highest motives and most enlightened impulses led to a peculiar system for juveniles, unknown to our law in any

comparable context. The constitutional and theoretical basis for this peculiar system is—to say the least—debatable. And in practice, as we remarked in the *Kent* case, *supra,* the results have not been entirely satisfactory. Juvenile court history has again demonstrated that unbridled discretion, however benevolently motivated, is frequently a poor substitute for principle and procedure. In 1937, Dean Pound wrote: "The powers of the Star Chamber were a trifle in comparison with those of our juvenile courts...." The absence of substantive standards has not necessarily meant that children receive careful, compassionate, individualized treatment. The absence of procedural rules based upon constitutional principle has not always produced fair, efficient, and effective procedures. Departures from established principles of due process have frequently resulted not in enlightened procedure, but in arbitrariness. 387 U.S. at 17-19.

But only some elements of the adversary system were introduced and the image of the kindly juvenile judge has not been abandoned, as demonstrated in *McKeiver v. Pennsylvania,* 403 U.S. 441 (1971).

The *Adjudication* standards have gone a bit further. Such requirements as a written petition, counsel for the respondent and the government, and the presence of the respondent have been covered in other sections. The presence of both parents also is urged and appointment of a guardian *ad litem* authorized if the parents are absent or excluded. A verbatim transcript is required, with the record preserved and kept confidential, but preservation is made paramount to confidentiality and expungement if the record may be needed for use in subsequent legal proceedings. Plea alternatives are discussed, with refusal to plead entered as a denial. The effects of admissions and denials are covered more fully under uncontested and contested proceedings. Standard 2.2 A. was revised to provide that amendment of a petition should be governed by the same rules as would be applied to the amendment of the charge in a criminal case.

*Adjudication* Standards 3.1 through 3.8 cover uncontested adjudication proceedings and are reproduced in their entirety below. Standard 3.3 B. was changed to add dispositions to plea bargaining.

## PART III: UNCONTESTED ADJUDICATION PROCEEDINGS

**3.1 Capacity to plead.**

**A. The juvenile court should not accept a plea admitting an allegation of the petition without determining that the respondent has the mental capacity to understand his or her legal rights in the adjudication proceeding and the significance of such a plea.**

B. In determining whether the respondent has the mental capacity to enter a plea admitting an allegation of the petition, the juvenile court should inquire into, among other factors:

1. the respondent's chronological age;

2. the respondent's present grade level in school or the highest grade level achieved while in school;

3. whether the respondent can read and write; and

4. whether the respondent has ever been diagnosed or treated for mental illness or mental retardation.

**3.2 Admonitions before accepting a plea admitting an allegation of the petition.**

The judge of the juvenile court should not accept a plea admitting an allegation of the petition without first addressing the respondent personally, in language calculated to communicate effectively with the respondent, and:

A. determining that the respondent understands the nature of the allegations;

B. informing the respondent of the right to a hearing at which the government must confront respondent with witnesses and prove the allegations beyond a reasonable doubt and at which respondent's attorney will be permitted to cross-examine the witnesses called by the government and to call witnesses on the respondent's behalf;

C. informing the respondent of the right to remain silent with respect to the allegations of the petition as well as of the right to testify if desired;

D. informing the respondent of the right to appeal from the decision reached in the trial;

E. informing the respondent of the right to a trial by jury;

F. informing the respondent that one gives up those rights by a plea admitting an allegation of the petition; and

G. informing the respondent that if the court accepts the plea, the court can place respondent on conditional freedom for (__) years or commit respondent to (the appropriate correctional agency) for (__) years.

**3.3 Responsibilities of the juvenile court judge with respect to plea agreements.**

A. Subject to the qualification contained in subsection B. of this standard, the juvenile court judge should not participate in plea discussions.

B. If a plea agreement has been reached that contemplates entry of a plea admitting an allegation of the petition in the expectation that other allegations will be dismissed or not filed, or that dispositional concessions will be made, the juvenile court judge should require disclosure of the agreement and the reasons therefor in advance of the time for tender of the plea. Disclosure of the plea agreement should be on the record in the presence of the respondent. The court should then indicate whether it will concur in the proposed agreement. If the court concurs, but later decides not to grant the concessions contemplated by the plea agreement, it should so advise the respondent and then call upon the respondent either to affirm or withdraw the plea.

C. When a plea admitting an allegation of the petition is tendered as a result of a plea agreement, the juvenile court judge should give the agreement due consideration, but notwithstanding its existence, should reach an independent decision whether to grant the concessions contemplated in the agreement.

3.4 Determining voluntariness of a plea admitting the allegations of the petition.

A. The juvenile court should not accept a plea admitting an allegation of the petition without determining that the plea is voluntary.

B. By inquiry of the attorneys for the respondent and for the government, the juvenile court should determine whether the tendered plea is the result of a plea agreement and, if so, what agreement has been reached.

C. If the attorney for the government has agreed to seek concessions that must be approved by the court, the court should advise the respondent personally that those recommendations are not binding on the court and follow the procedures provided in Standard 3.3 B.

D. The court should then address the respondent personally and determine whether any other promises or inducements or any force or threats were used to obtain the plea.

3.5 Determining accuracy of a plea admitting the allegations of the petition.

The juvenile court should not accept a plea admitting an allegation of the petition without making an inquiry and satisfying itself that the allegation admitted is true. The inquiry should be conducted:

A. by requiring the attorney for the government to describe the proof that the government would expect to produce if the case were tried; or

B. by personally questioning the respondent as to respondent's conduct in the case.

**3.6 Inquiry concerning effectiveness of representation.**
A. The juvenile court should not accept a plea admitting an allegation of the petition unless it determines that the respondent was given the effective assistance of an attorney.
B. The juvenile court should make that determination upon tender of a plea admitting an allegation of the petition and should do so by inquiring:
    1. of the respondent and respondent's attorney concerning the number and length (but not the content) of conferences the attorney has had with respondent;
    2. of the attorney for the respondent concerning the factual investigation, if any, that the attorney conducted in the case;
    3. of the attorney for the respondent concerning the legal preparation, if any, that the attorney made on behalf of respondent;
    4. of the respondent and respondent's attorney concerning what advice the attorney gave respondent concerning whether to admit or deny the allegations of the petition;
    5. of the respondent and respondent's attorney concerning whether there has been any conflict between them as to whether respondent should admit an allegation of the petition, and if there was, subject to the attorney-client privilege, the nature of that conflict.

**3.7 Parental participation in uncontested cases.**
A. Except when a parent is the complainant, the judge of the juvenile court should not accept a plea admitting an allegation of the petition without inquiring of the respondent's parent or parents who are present in court whether they concur in the course of action the respondent has chosen.
B. The judge of the juvenile court should consider the responses of the respondent's parents to the court's inquiry in exercising discretion on whether to reject the tendered plea.

**3.8 Plea withdrawal.**
A. The juvenile court should allow the respondent to withdraw a plea admitting an allegation of the petition whenever the respondent proves that withdrawal is necessary to correct a manifest injustice.
    1. A motion for withdrawal is not barred because made subsequent to adjudication or disposition.

2. Withdrawal is necessary to correct a manifest injustice when the respondent proves:

a. denial of the effective assistance of counsel guaranteed by constitution, statute, or rule;

b. that the plea was not entered or ratified by the respondent;

c. that the plea was involuntary, or was entered without knowledge of the allegations or that the disposition actually imposed could be imposed;

d. that respondent did not receive the concessions contemplated by the plea agreement and the attorney for the government failed to seek or not to oppose those concessions as promised in the plea agreement; or

e. that respondent did not receive the concessions contemplated by the plea agreement concurred in by the court, and did not affirm the plea after being advised that the court no longer concurred and after being called upon to either affirm or withdraw the plea.

3. The respondent should be permitted to move for withdrawal of the plea without alleging innocence of the allegations to which the plea has been entered.

B. Before the disposition of the case, the court should allow the respondent to withdraw the plea for any fair and just reason without proof of manifest injustice as defined in subsection 2. of this standard.

Contested proceedings are covered in *Adjudication* Standards 4.1 through 4.5. Standard 4.1 was amended to add brackets around "six" for the number of persons on a jury.

### 4.1 Trial by jury.

A. Each jurisdiction should provide by law that the respondent may demand trial by jury in adjudication proceedings when the respondent has denied the allegations of the petition.

B. Each jurisdiction should provide by law that the jury may consist of as few as [six] persons and that the verdict of the jury must be unanimous.

### 4.2 Rules of evidence.

The rules of evidence employed in the trial of criminal cases should be used in delinquency adjudication proceedings when the respondent has denied the allegations of the petition.

**4.3 Burden of proof.**
Each jurisdiction should provide by law that the government is required to adduce proof beyond a reasonable doubt that the respondent engaged in the conduct alleged when the respondent has denied the allegations of the petition.

**4.4 Social information.**
A. Except in preadjudication hearings in which social history information concerning the respondent is relevant and admissible, such as a detention hearing or a hearing to consider transfer to criminal court for prosecution as an adult, the judge of the juvenile court should not view a social history report or receive social history information concerning a respondent who has not been adjudicated delinquent.

B. Each jurisdiction should provide by law that when a jury is the trier of fact it should not view a social history report or receive social history information concerning the respondent.

**4.5 Role of parents in contested proceedings.**
A respondent's parents or other persons required by law to be served with a copy of the petition should be permitted to make representations to the court either pro se or through counsel in a jury-waived contested adjudication proceeding.

Standard 5.3 describes the legal consequences of adjudication.

**5.3 Legal consequences of adjudication.**
A. Each jurisdiction should provide by law that a juvenile court adjudication is not a conviction of crime and should not be viewed to indicate criminality for any purpose.

B. Each jurisdiction should provide by law that a juvenile court adjudication is not a proper subject for inquiry in applications for public or private employment and in applications for public or private educational or licensing programs.

C. Each jurisdiction should provide by law that a plea admitting the allegations of the petition, an adjudication by the juvenile court, or evidence adduced in a juvenile court adjudication proceeding is not admissible in any other judicial or administrative proceeding except subsequent juvenile proceedings concerning the same respondent to the extent otherwise admissible.

Among the most disputed standards is the right to a public trial provided in Standard 6.1. The standards on public access to adjudication proceedings should be examined in their entirety.

### 6.1 Right to a public trial.

Each jurisdiction should provide by law that a respondent in a juvenile court adjudication proceeding has a right to a public trial.

### 6.2 Implementing the right to a public trial.

A. Each jurisdiction should provide by law that the respondent, after consulting with counsel, may waive the right to a public trial.

B. Each jurisdiction should provide by law that the judge of the juvenile court has discretion to permit members of the public who have a legitimate interest in the proceedings or in the work of the court, including representatives of the news media, to view adjudication proceedings when the respondent has waived the right to a public trial.

C. The judge of the juvenile court should honor any request by the respondent, respondent's attorney, or family that specified members of the public be permitted to observe the respondent's adjudication proceeding when the respondent has waived the right to a public trial.

D. The judge of the juvenile court should use judicial power to prevent distractions from and disruptions of adjudication proceedings and should use that power to order removed from the courtroom any member of the public causing a distraction or disruption.

### 6.3 Prohibiting disclosure of respondent's identity.

A. Each jurisdiction should provide by law that members of the public permitted by the judge of the juvenile court to observe adjudication proceedings may not disclose to others the identity of the respondent when the respondent has waived the right to a public trial.

B. Each jurisdiction should provide by law that the judge of the juvenile court should announce to members of the public present to view an adjudication proceeding when the respondent has waived the right to a public trial that they may not disclose to others the identity of the respondent.

### 5.4.4 Appeals and collateral review.

The standards provide for one appeal as a matter of right to all parties materially affected by a juvenile court order to review the facts found, law applied, and disposition ordered. Additional review may be had by leave of the court.

The goals of appellate review enumerated in Standard 1.1 are to correct errors, ensure substantial uniformity of treatment to persons in like situations, and provide for growth in keeping with the goals of the juvenile justice system.

Appeals from juvenile court should be heard by the court designated to hear initial appeals from the highest court of general trial jurisdiction. A person who becomes eighteen during the pendency of an appeal, except from a waiver order, may not be criminally prosecuted as an adult for the same transaction.

Standard 2.1 lists some of the orders deemed reviewable as final orders of the juvenile court. An appeal of any final order may be taken by the juvenile or the juvenile's parents, custodian, or guardian. Standard 2.1 C. was amended to give juveniles the option to request that an order finding the juvenile delinquent not become final. Under Standard 2.2 C. the state may take an appeal of any final order in *other than delinquency* cases and of the following orders in delinquency cases:

**a. an order adjudicating a state statute unconstitutional;**
**b. any order which by depriving the prosecution of evidence, by upholding the defense of double jeopardy, by holding that a cause of action is not stated under a statute, or by granting a motion to suppress, terminates a delinquency petition;**
**C. an order which denies a petition to waive juvenile court jurisdiction in favor of adult criminal prosecution.**

Standard 2.3 provides that review may be sought by leave of the appellate court from interlocutory orders of the juvenile court, including a finding that jurisdiction exists over the subject matter or juvenile.

The standards recommend adopting measures for expedited appeal, including the possibility of the parties agreeing to transmit to the appellate court a written stipulated statement of the facts and procedural developments without procuring a transcript of the minutes.

The appeals standards do not provide for automatic stay of a juvenile court order by the initiating of an appeal but authorize the party to request the juvenile court to stay the effect of its order and to release the juvenile pending appeal. Standard 5.3 on status during appeal states:

**5.3 Upon the filing of an appeal of judgment and disposition, the release of the appellant, with or without conditions, should issue in every case unless the court orders otherwise. An order of interim detention should be permitted only where the disposition imposed, or most likely to be imposed, by the court includes some form of secure incarceration; and the court finds one or more of the following on the record:**

**A. that the juvenile would flee the jurisdiction or not appear before any court for further proceedings during the pendency of the appeal;**

**B. that there is substantial probability that the juvenile would engage in serious violence prior to the resolution of the appeal.**

**Juveniles should be given credit at disposition for any time spent in a secure facility pending appeal.**

Standard 5.6 empowers the appellate court to grant the relief requested when the juvenile court has denied an application for a release or a stay.

Collateral review pertains to modification or reconsideration of juvenile court orders by the juvenile court itself, as distinguished from review by an appellate court. Part VI of *Appeals and Collateral Review* delineates the standards for collateral and supplementary proceedings as follows:

**6.1 Orders of the juvenile court may be modified by that court at any time when it has jurisdiction over the matter after notice and opportunity for hearing to all parties, upon the petition of a party or by the juvenile court sua sponte.**

**6.2 Modification of the court's dispositional orders should be governed by the *Dispositions* volume, Standard 5.1 A., and the *Corrections Administration* volume, Standard 5.1 A.**

**6.3 Every order committing any juvenile into the custody of the state and every order adjudicating a juvenile to be neglected, regardless of custody, should be reviewed by the**

juvenile court without the request of any party not less than once in every [six] months.

**6.4** The juvenile, his or her parents, custodian, or guardian may petition the juvenile court to inquire into the adequacy of the treatment being afforded the juvenile.

It may be observed that the standards covered in this part on court roles and procedures do not cover every stage of the court process. The crucial phases of detention, dispositions, and corrections have been reserved for the next part for both pragmatic and logical reasons. The practical reason is that the volumes on interim status, dispositions, and corrections were drafted by Drafting Committee III, the subject of Part VI of this volume. But an even greater compulsion for treating these standards separately derives from the common issues concerning the function of treatment and corrections and the positions adopted by the Commission.

# PART VI: TREATMENT AND CORRECTIONS

## 6.1 The Goals of Juvenile Justice.

In Part IV we considered the grounds for intervening in the lives of children. Issues related to voluntary and involuntary participation in programs and the jurisdiction of the juvenile courts and agencies were discussed. Standards proposed for the boundaries of permissible intrusion by the public and private sector were examined in the context of principles concerning the respective rights and obligations of juveniles, families, and the community.

Implicit in the standards for intervention and nonintervention were certain conclusions as to justifiable goals for a system of juvenile justice. For example, by eliminating court jurisdiction over juveniles whose misconduct would not constitute a crime if committed by adults, the standards declared that the courts could not compel such nonconforming youth to accept treatment or correction. However, the *Noncriminal Misbehavior* standards did not preclude other forms of intervention—some voluntary, some short-term, but *not* court-related treatment or corrections programs. In the *Abuse and Neglect* volume, the prerequisite of proving specific harm to the child barred coerced removal of a child if the presence or imminent danger of such harm could not be proved.

On the other hand, truancy could not be the basis of court jurisdiction, but could be a violation of regulations under *Schools and Education* standards for student disciplinary proceedings. Not all sanctions are court imposed. Nor is all treatment provided against the juvenile's wishes. The *Rights of Minors* standards prescribe the conditions for juveniles to obtain medical treatment, birth control devices, and other services without the knowledge or consent of their parents. *Youth Service Agencies* standards urge access to the full range of appropriate services for the children and families who seek help without a court order, but set restrictions on the commitments that can be made prerequisites for admission to the programs. Finally, the *Police Handling of Juvenile Problems* standards encourage diversion to

193

service programs in preference to court referral, but prescribe the adoption of criteria for the police officer's decision to arrest, release, or refer a juvenile alleged to have committed an offense.

The standards do reflect the Commission's rejection of a position held by many juvenile specialists. There is no assumption in the standards that coercive treatment is a benefit. A greater heresy is the refusal to accept a correlation between delinquency and a need for therapeutic care as a proven fact, as a basis for the court's jurisdiction, or as a primary determinant of the disposition imposed after adjudication. Although a need for treatment or services is a factor in selecting a placement or other disposition, other factors set the maximum sanction permitted for a particular offense and need does not mandate participation in any treatment program in the absence of a medical or psychiatric emergency. Moreover, certain types of treatment are barred for juveniles in correctional facilities or in detention regardless of need. The status of the juvenile—preadjudication, predisposition, or postdisposition—also affects the nature and degree of intervention allowable, including testing, social investigation, and supervision.

Drafting Committee III addressed itself to one of the ultimate questions in the project—what can and should be done with the children and families involved in the juvenile justice system? What are the legitimate goals of juvenile court or other agency jurisdiction? The members considered the meaning of treatment, rehabilitation, punishment, deterrence, sanctions, services, incapacitation, proportionality, care, and supervision. They distinguished among confinement, commitment, and placement; initiated guidelines for the architecture of secure and nonsecure facilities; debated the optimum size of detention and correction facilities; fixed time limits for custody and for hearings; agreed on procedural safeguards for court dispositional hearings and for disciplinary and grievance mechanisms in correctional institutions. Perhaps most significantly, they drafted the criteria for juvenile court dispositions following delinquency adjudications.

The volumes prepared under the supervision of Drafting Committee III, Treatment and Corrections, are:

*Architecture of Facilities*
*Corrections Administration*
*Dispositional Procedures*
*Dispositions*
*Interim Status: The Release, Control, and Detention of Accused Juvenile Offenders Between Arrest and Disposition*

In addition, the *Juvenile Delinquency and Sanctions* standards were drafted originally with Drafting Committee I, but later Commission action required extensive coordination with the *Dispositions* standards, including the incorporation of sections and the adaptation of terminology. Therefore, the Commission appointed a single editorial committee for the final revisions of the two volumes, chaired by the chairperson of Drafting Committee III, to ensure uniformity in the sanctions and disposition standards.

All of these volumes were approved by the House of Delegates of the American Bar Association with the revisions indicated below.

## 6.2 Contact Prior to Disposition: Interim Status.

The *Interim Status* standards cover the period during which an alleged delinquent makes initial contact with the juvenile justice system until final execution of the disposition decision. Standard 1.1 describes this period and the objectives of the volume succinctly.

### 1.1 Scope and overview.
The standards in this volume set out in detail the decision making process that functions between arrest of a juvenile on criminal charges and final disposition of the case. By limiting the discretion of officials involved in that process, and by imposing affirmative duties on them to release juveniles or bear the burden of justification for not having done so, the standards seek to reduce the volume, duration, and severity of detention, and of other curtailment of liberty during the interim period.

More detailed standards are described as basic principles. Standard 3.1 was amended by inserting "generally." Standard 3.3 was revised by the addition of new subdivision E.

### 3.1 Policy favoring release.
Restraints on the freedom of accused juveniles pending trial and disposition are generally contrary to public policy. The preferred course in each case should be unconditional release.

### 3.2 Permissible control or detention.
The imposition of interim control or detention on an accused juvenile may be considered for the purposes of:
A. protecting the jurisdiction and process of the court:
B. reducing the likelihood that the juvenile may inflict serious bodily harm on others during the interim period; or
C. protecting the accused juvenile from imminent bodily harm upon his or her request.
However, these purposes should be exercised only under the

circumstances and to the extent authorized by the procedures, requirements, and limitations detailed in Parts IV through X of these standards.

**3.3 Prohibited control or detention.**
Interim control or detention should not be imposed on an accused juvenile:
A. to punish, treat, or rehabilitate the juvenile;
B. to allow parents to avoid their legal responsibilities;
C. to satisfy demands by a victim, the police, or the community;
D. to permit more convenient administrative access to the juvenile;
E. to facilitate further interrogation or investigation; or
F. due to a lack of a more appropriate facility or status alternative.

**3.4 Least intrusive alternative.**
When an accused juvenile cannot be unconditionally released, conditional or supervised release that results in the least necessary interference with the liberty of the juvenile should be favored over more intrusive alternatives.

**3.5 Values.**
Whenever the interim curtailment of an accused juvenile's freedom is permitted under these standards, the exercise of authority should reflect the following values:
A. respect for the privacy, dignity, and individuality of the accused juvenile and his or her family;
B. protection of the psychological and physical health of the juvenile;
C. tolerance of the diverse values and preferences among different groups and individuals;
D. ensurance of equality of treatment by race, class, ethnicity, and sex;
E. avoidance of regimentation and depersonalization of the juvenile;
F. avoidance of stigmatization of the juvenile; and
G. ensurance that the juvenile receives adequate legal assistance.

**3.6 Availability of adequate resources.**
The attainment of a fair and effective system of juvenile justice requires that every jurisdiction should, by legislation,

court decision, appropriations, and methods of administration, provide services and facilities adequate to carry out the principles underlying these standards. Accordingly, the absence of funds cannot be a justification for resources or procedures that fall below the standards or unnecessarily infringe on individual liberty. Accused juveniles should be released or placed under less restrictive control whenever a form of detention or control otherwise appropriate is unavailable to the decision maker.

Fundamentally, the *Interim Status* standards are premised on the presumption of innocence of an accused juvenile prior to adjudication, a preference for release over detention whenever feasible and for the least restrictive alternative, and an insistence on accountability through written reasons and review for interim measures other than unconditional release. Tight controls are imposed on the use of social history information for the interim status release decision only, barring its use until after adjudication. Treatment or testing during interim status is restricted under Standard 4.5:

**4.5 Limitations on treatment or testing.**
   **A. Involuntary.**
      **1. Prior to adjudication, an accused juvenile should not be involuntarily subjected to treatment or testing of any kind by the state or any private organization associated with the interim process except:**
         **a. to test for the presence of a contagious or communicable disease that would present an unreasonable risk of infection to others in the same facility;**
         **b. to provide emergency medical aid; or**
         **c. to administer tests required by the court for determining competency to stand trial.**
      **2. After adjudication, an accused juvenile may be subjected to involuntary, nonemergency testing only to the extent found necessary by a court, after a hearing, to aid in the determination of an appropriate final disposition.**
   **B. Voluntary.**
      **1. While in detention, an accused juvenile should be entitled to a prompt medical examination and to provision of appropriate nonemergency medical care, with the informed consent of the juvenile and a parent in accordance with subsection 2. below. Requirements of consent should be governed by the** *Rights of Minors* **volume.**
      **2. Informed, written consent should be obtained before a juvenile may be required to participate in any program,**

designed to alter or modify behavior, that may have potentially harmful effects.

a. If the juvenile is under the age of sixteen, his or her consent and the consent of his or her parents both should be obtained.

b. If the juvenile is sixteen or older, only the juvenile's consent should be obtained.

c. Any such consent may be withdrawn at any time.

Money bail is prohibited as an alternative to detention or unconditional release.

The standards for police action during interim status are consistent with the general principles cited above: favoring release, requiring written reasons for not releasing a juvenile within *two to four hours* of arrest, and prohibiting holding of an arrested juvenile in any police detention facility prior to release or transportation to a juvenile facility. Standard 4.3 was amended by adding, as an alternative to a written statement, stating on the record the evidence relied on for an interim measure other than release. The duties of an arresting officer are described in Standard 5.3. Subdivision F., which originally restricted arrest time prior to release or transportation to a facility to two hours, was changed to two to four hours and bracketed.

## 5.3 Duties.

The arresting officer should have the following duties in regard to the interim status of an accused juvenile:

A. Inform juvenile of rights. The officer should explain in clearly understandable language the warnings required by the constitution regarding the right to silence, the making of statements, and the right to the presence of an attorney. The officer should also inform every arrested juvenile who is not promptly released from custody of the right to have his or her parent contacted by the department. In any situation in which the accused does not understand English, or in which the accused is bilingual and English is not his or her principal language, the officer should provide the necessary information in the accused's native language, or provide an interpreter who will assure that the juvenile is informed of his or her rights.

B. Notification of parent. The arresting officer should make all reasonable efforts to contact a parent of the accused juvenile during the period between arrest and the presentation of the juvenile to any detention facility. The officer should inform the parent of the juvenile's right to the presence of counsel, appointed if necessary, and of the juvenile's right to remain silent.

C. Presence of attorney. The right to have an attorney present should be subject to knowing, intelligent waiver by the juvenile following consultation with counsel. If the police question any arrested juvenile concerning an alleged offense in the absence of an attorney for the juvenile, no information obtained thereby or as a result of the questioning should be admissible in any proceeding.

D. Recording of initial status decision. If the arresting officer does not release the juvenile within two hours, the reasons for the decision should be recorded in the arrest report and disclosed to the juvenile, counsel, and parent.

E. Notification of facility. Whenever an accused juvenile is taken into custody and not promptly released, the arresting officer should promptly inform the juvenile facility intake official of all relevant factors concerning the juvenile and the arrest, so that the official can explore interim status alternatives.

F. Transportation to facility. The police should, within [two to four hours] of the arrest, either release the juvenile or, upon notice to and concurrence by the intake official, take the juvenile without delay to the juvenile facility designated by the intake official. If the intake official does not concur, that official should order the police to release the juvenile.

The interim status decision for the arrested juvenile should not be made by the police, but their recommendations and observations should be solicited by the intake official. Guidelines for the status decision by the police are specified in Standard 5.6. This standard was revised by bracketing "less than one year," eliminating the "clear and convincing" standard of proof, expanding the exception to mandatory release to include juveniles charged with a class one juvenile offense involving violence, instead of only first or second degree murder, and deleting the "one-bite rule"—i.e., the rule allowing a juvenile to be detained because he or she already is under the jurisdiction of the court. Protective custody is covered in Standard 5.7.

5.6 Guidelines for status decision.

A. Mandatory release. Whenever the juvenile has been arrested for a crime which in the case of an adult would be punishable by a sentence of [less than one year], the arresting officer should, if charges are to be pressed, release the juvenile with a citation or to a parent, unless the juvenile is in need of emergency medical treatment (Standard 4.5 A. 1. b.), requests protective custody (Standard 5.7), or is known to be in fugitive status.

B. Discretionary release. In all other situations, the arresting officer should release the juvenile unless evidence as defined below demonstrates that continued custody is necessary. The seriousness of the alleged offense should not, except in cases of a class one juvenile offense involving violence, be sufficient grounds for continued custody. Such evidence should only consist of one or more of the following factors as to which reliable information is available to the arresting officer:

1. that the arrest was made while the juvenile was in a fugitive status;

2. that the juvenile has a recent record of willful failure to appear at juvenile proceedings.

### 5.7 Protective Custody.

A. Notwithstanding the issuance of a citation, the arresting officer may take an accused juvenile to an appropriate facility designated by the intake official if the juvenile would be in immediate danger of serious bodily harm if released, and the juvenile requests such custody.

B. A decision to continue or relinquish protective custody shall be made by the intake official in accordance with Standard 6.7.

The responsibility for the interim status decision rests with the intake official once an arrested juvenile has been brought to a juvenile facility. The same mandatory release requirements apply as for the arresting officer. If the intake official does not release the juvenile, Standard 6.5 D. 2. and 3. applies as follows:

2. If the juvenile is not released, the intake official should prepare a petition for a release hearing before a judge or referee, which should be filed with the court no later than the next court session, or within twenty-four hours after the juvenile's arrival at the intake facility, whichever is sooner. The petition should specify the charges on which the accused juvenile is to be prosecuted, the reasons why the accused was placed in detention, the reasons why release has not been accomplished, the alternatives to detention that have been explored, and the recommendations of the intake official concerning interim status.

3. If the court is not in session within the twenty-four-hour period, the intake official should contact the judge, by telephone or otherwise, and give notice of the contents of the petition.

The court must review the detention at a status review hearing within seven days after the initial hearing.

Standard 6.6 prescribes the guidelines for the status decision by the intake official. As discussed with respect to Standard 5.6 above, the factors for continued custody were changed to substitute a class one juvenile offense for first or second degree murder and to eliminate the one-bite rule. Protective detention is described in Standard 6.7.

### 6.6 Guidelines for status decision.

A. Mandatory release. The intake official should release the accused juvenile unless the juvenile:

1. is charged with a crime of violence which in the case of an adult would be punishable by a sentence of one year or more, and which if proven is likely to result in commitment to a security institution, *and* one or more of the following additional factors is present:

a. the crime charged is a class one juvenile offense;

b. the juvenile is an escapee from an institution or other placement facility to which he or she was sentenced under a previous adjudication of criminal conduct; or

c. the juvenile has a demonstrable recent record of willful failure to appear at juvenile proceedings, on the basis of which the official finds that no measure short of detention can be imposed to reasonably ensure appearance; or

2. has been verified to be a fugitive from another jurisdiction, an official of which has formally requested that the juvenile be placed in detention.

B. Mandatory detention. A juvenile who is excluded from mandatory release under subsection A. should not, *pro tanto*, be automatically detained. No category of alleged conduct or background in and of itself should justify a failure to exercise discretion to release.

C. Discretionary situations.

1. Release vs. detention. In every situation in which the release of an arrested juvenile is not mandatory, the intake official should first consider and determine whether the juvenile qualifies for an available diversion program, or whether any form of control short of detention is available to reasonably reduce the risk of flight or misconduct. If no such measure will suffice, the official should explicitly state in writing the reasons for rejecting each of these forms of release.

2. Unconditional vs. conditional or supervised release. In order to minimize the imposition of release conditions on persons who would appear in court without them, and present no substantial risk in the interim, each jurisdiction should develop guidelines for the use of various forms of release based upon the resources and programs available, and analysis of the effectiveness of each form of release.

3. Secure vs. nonsecure detention. Whenever an intake official determines that detention is the appropriate interim status, secure detention may be selected only if clear and convincing evidence indicates the probability of serious physical injury to others, or serious probability of flight to avoid appearance in court. Absent such evidence, the accused should be placed in an appropriate form of nonsecure detention, with a foster home to be preferred over other alternatives.

### 6.7 Protective detention.

A. Placement in a nonsecure detention facility solely for the protection of an accused juvenile should be permitted only upon the voluntary written request of the juvenile in circumstances that present an immediate threat of serious bodily harm to the juvenile if released.

B. In reaching this decision, or in reviewing a protective custody decision made by the arresting officer, the intake official should first consider all less restrictive alternatives and all reasonably ascertainable factors relevant to the likelihood and immediacy of serious bodily harm resulting from interim release or control.

Similar standards are established to guide the juvenile court in detention hearings, continuing detention review (every seven days), speedy trial, and speedy appellate review of the detention decision. Guidelines for the court's status decisions are in Standard 7.7. These guidelines were amended to allow continued detention if the court is in possession of facts which justify that alternative.

### 7.7 Guidelines for status decisions.

A. Release alternatives. The court may release the juvenile on his or her own recognizance, on conditions, under supervision, including release on a temporary, non-overnight basis to the attorney if so requested for the purpose of preparing the case, or into a diversion program.

**B. Mandatory release.** Release by the court should be mandatory when the state fails to establish probable cause to believe that the juvenile committed the offense charged, in any situation in which the arresting officer or intake official was required to release the juvenile, but failed to do so, unless the court is in possession of additional information which justifies detention under these standards.

**C. Discretionary situations.** In all other cases, the court should review all factors that officials earlier in the process were required by these standards to have considered. The court should review with particularity the adequacy of the reasons for detention recorded by the police and the intake official.

**D. Written reasons.** A written statement of the findings of facts and reasons why no measure short of detention would suffice should be made part of the order and filed immediately after the hearing by any judge who declines to release an accused juvenile from detention. An order continuing the juvenile in detention should be construed as authorizing nonsecure detention only, unless it contains an express direction to the contrary, supported by reasons. If the court orders release under a form of control to which the juvenile objects, the court should upon request by the attorney for the juvenile, record the facts and reasons why unconditional release was denied.

Visitation to detention facilities is covered in several standards. Standard 7.8 requires every juvenile court judge to visit each secure facility under the court's jurisdiction at least once every sixty days, but "sixty days" was bracketed in the revised version. Standard 9.3 imposes the same requirement on prosecuting attorneys. Under Standard 8.3, the attorneys for accused juveniles held in detention are required to visit the juvenile at least every seven days to ascertain the juvenile's well-being and to review the conditions of the facility, as well as to explore the possibility of relaxing the conditions of detention or securing the juvenile's release.

Innovative standards for juvenile detention facilities designed to effectuate the general principles underlying the standards are provided in Part X. Standard 10.5 was amended to change the maximum population of a detention facility from twelve juveniles to twelve to twenty. Standard 10.8 was amended by adding new subdivisions K. and L.

**10.1 Applicability to waiver of juvenile court jurisdiction.**

When jurisdiction of the juvenile court is waived, and the juvenile is detained pursuant to adult pretrial procedures, the juvenile should be detained in a juvenile facility and in accordance with the standards in this part.

## 10.2 Use of adult jails prohibited.

The interim detention of accused juveniles in any facility or part thereof also used to detain adults is prohibited.

## 10.3 Policy favoring nonsecure alternatives.

A sufficiently wide range of nonsecure detention and nondetention alternatives should be available to decision makers so that the least restrictive interim status appropriate to an accused juvenile may be selected. The range of facilities available should be reviewed by all concerned agencies annually to ensure that juveniles are not being held in more restrictive facilities because less restrictive facilities are unavailable. A policy should be adopted in each state favoring the abandonment or reduction in size of secure facilities as less restrictive alternatives become available.

## 10.4 Mixing accused juvenile offenders with other juveniles.

A. In nonsecure facilities. The simultaneous housing in a nonsecure detention facility of juveniles charged with criminal offenses and juveniles held for other reasons should not be prohibited.

B. In secure facilities. Juveniles not charged with crime should not be held in any secure detention facility for accused juvenile offenders.

## 10.5 Population limits.

A. Individual facilities. The population of an interim detention facility during any twenty-four-hour period should not exceed [twelve to twenty] juveniles. This maximum may be exceeded only in unusual, emergency circumstances, with a written report presented immediately to each juvenile court judge and to the statewide agency described in Part XI.

B. Statewide. A primary goal of each assessment effort should be to establish, within one year, a quota of beds available in all facilities within the state for the holding of accused juveniles in secure detention. The quota should be reduced annually thereafter, as alternative forms of control are developed. The quota should be binding on the statewide agency as a mandatory ceiling on the number of accused juveniles who may be held in detention at any one time; provided that it may be exceeded temporarily for a period not to exceed sixty days in any calendar year if the agency certifies to the governor of the state and to the legislature, and makes available to the public, in a written report, that unusual emergency circumstances exist that require a specific new quota to be set for a limited period. The certification should state the cause of the temporary increase in the quota and the steps to be taken to reduce the population to the original quota.

### 10.6 Education.

All accused juveniles held in interim detention should be afforded access to the educational institution they normally attend, or to equivalent tutorial or other programs adequate to their needs, including an educational program for "exceptional children."

### 10.7 Rights of juveniles in detention.

Each juvenile held in interim detention should have the following rights, among others:

A. Privacy. A right to individual privacy should be honored in each institution. Because different children will desire different settings, and will often change their minds, substantial allowance should be made for individual choice, and for private as well as community areas, with due regard for the safety of others.

B. Attorneys. A private area within each facility should be available for conferences between the juvenile and his or her attorney at any time between 9 a.m. and 9 p.m. daily.

C. Visitors. Private areas within each facility should be available as contact visiting areas. The period for visiting, although subject to reasonable regulation by the facility staff, should cover at least eight hours every day of the week, and should conform to school regulations when the juvenile is attending school outside the facility. All regulations concerning visitors and visiting hours should be subject to review by the juvenile court.

D. Telephone. Each juvenile in detention should have ready access to a telephone between 9 a.m. and 9 p.m. daily. Calls may be limited in duration, but not in content nor as to parties who may be contacted, except as otherwise specifically directed by the court. Local calls should be permitted at the expense of the institution, but should under no circumstances be monitored. Long distance calls in reasonable number may be made to a parent or attorney at the expense of the institution, and to others, collect.

E. Restrictions on force. Reasonable force should only be used to restrain a juvenile who demonstrates by observed behavior that he or she is a danger to himself or herself or to others, or who attempts to escape. All circumstances concerning any use of force or unusual restrictions, including the circumstances that gave rise to such use, should be reported immediately to the juvenile facility administrator and the juvenile's attorney and parent.

F. Mail. Mail from or to an accused juvenile should not be opened by authorities. If reasonable grounds exist to believe that mail may contain contraband, it should be examined only in the presence of the juvenile.

10.8 Detention inventory.

The statewide interim agency should during its first year and annually thereafter, conduct an inventory of secure detention facilities to ascertain the extent of, reasons for, and alternatives to the secure detention of accused juveniles. The inventory should include:

A. the places of secure detention;
B. the daily population and turnover;
C. annual admissions;
D. range of duration of secure detention;
E. annual juvenile days of secure detention;
F. costs of secure detention;
G. trial status of those in secure detention;
H. reasons for termination of secure detention;
 I. disposition of secure detention cases;
 J. correlation of secure detention to post-adjudication disposition;
K. qualification and training of staff;
L. staffing patterns and deployment of staff resources.

The results of the inventory should be published annually. The agency should conduct a similar inventory of nonsecure detention facilities, beginning in the agency's second year. The inventory should draw attention to the differences in the use of detention by locality, and by characteristics of the detention population.

Finally, administrative standards for interim status are proposed, including centralized administration in a statewide executive agency with responsibility for consideration and review of all release and control of, and detention programs for, accused juveniles. However, "executive" was bracketed in the revised standard to give the states the option to choose judicial administration. Local intake officials would be representatives of the statewide agency. Semi-annual unannounced inspections of all facilities to ensure compliance with the standards, followed by reports filed within thirty days of the inspection, are prescribed in Standard 11.2 D. Standard 11.3 imposes a moratorium on construction or expansion of detention facilities until an inventory of existing facilities is completed and assessed.

Standard 11.4 states a policy encouraging experimentation, elevation of the statewide agency's standards, expanded use of alternatives to detention, and examination of innovative techniques from other jurisdictions.

The *Interim Status* standards leave no doubt as to the position being advanced—the absolute minimum of interference with the liberty of the juvenile during the period prior to implementation of the disposition consonant with the fair conduct of the trial, the safety of the community, and the protection of the juvenile under well-defined and reviewable criteria for the status decision. Incidental objectives are the phasing out of large institutions and the gradual substitution of community facilities for the juveniles for whom release is not an appropriate alternative. There had been conflict between the *Architecture of Facilities* volume and the *Interim Status* volume: the former prescribed twelve to twenty (in brackets, to reflect the flexibility of the number recommended) as the maximum population for detention facilities; the latter limited the size to twelve. These numbers were conformed in the revised drafts, adopting twelve to twenty, in brackets, as the standard.

## 6.3 Dispositions: Choices and Procedures.

Three volumes of standards should be considered together because they are functionally interconnected: *Juvenile Delinquency and Sanctions, Dispositions,* and *Dispositional Procedures.* The first volume prescribes the offenses for which juveniles may be sanctioned and the standards for maximum dispositions for each category of offense. The second volume establishes the guidelines for choosing the appropriate disposition within the maxima, describes the characteristics of the types of dispositions, and creates new standards for modification of a dispositional order. The third volume sets the standards for the dispositional hearing, the information to be gathered and used in arriving at the disposition, and the procedures to be followed in conducting the hearing and other aspects of the dispositional process.

The point is made in the *Dispositional Procedures* introduction that current dispositional hearings "often are merely ceremonial events and simply provide the judicial imprimatur for a decision arrived at earlier and elsewhere." The introduction to *Dispositions* refers to the dearth of materials and principles on the imposition of dispositions on juveniles, in contrast to the prominent concern manifested over adult sentencing and corrections criteria, and suggests that juvenile dispositional standards have "progressed little beyond the traditional formulation of the 'best interests of the child.'"

It might be said that the general sense of the project is that the greatest weakness in the juvenile system lies in the final stages of dispositions and corrections. That concern has produced bold and innovative results in the proposed standards, departing dramatically from the prevailing practices in the system.

However, one problem inherent in promulgating standards for juvenile offenses is the process of incorporating the penal law or criminal statutes applicable to adults under each state's laws. Although certain modifications of the penal law had been included, such as the elimination of victimless crimes (or "private offenses") except for narcotics violations, in *Juvenile Delinquency and Sanctions* Standard 2.4, and the proscription of sexual offenses according to the ages of the parties in Standard 4.1, both standards were deleted from the revised draft, so that the states' penal codes would prevail. Incorporation on a state-by-state basis does prevent uniformity and more comprehensive reform of the delinquency laws. Therefore, the revision process will rely in part on future changes in the substantive criminal law and adoption of a "Model Penal Code."

As discussed earlier in Part IV, Intervention in the Lives of Children, the *Juvenile Delinquency and Sanctions* standards establish a matrix consisting of the types of sanctions a juvenile court may impose in delinquency cases (which, in inverse order of severity, are nominal, conditional, and custodial in a nonsecure and in a secure facility), the classes of offenses (from class five up to class one juvenile offenses, based on the maximum sentence authorized upon conviction for such offenses under the adult criminal statute or ordinance), and the comparable limitations on type and duration of sanctions, or maximum dispositions that may be ordered by the juvenile court for each class of juvenile offense. The matrix is reproduced as Chart 1 on page 209. Maximum sanctions for confinement were increased from

## CHART 1

## MAXIMUM DURATION OF SANCTIONS (IN MONTHS)

*TYPE OF SANCTION\**

| | Conditional Freedom | | Placement in a Nonsecure Facility | | Confinement in a Secure Facility |
|---|---|---|---|---|---|
| One | 36 | OR | 36 | OR | 36 |
| Two | 24 | OR | 18 | OR | 18 |
| Three | 18 | OR | 6 | OR | 6 |
| Four | 12 | OR | 3 | OR | ·····3····· |
| Five | 6 | OR | ·····2····· | OR | XXXXXXXXXXX |

*CLASS OF JUVENILE OFFENSE*

Key:

∷ = Sanction authorized only if prior record.

XXX
XXX = Sanction not authorized.

\*Because nominal sanctions require no durational limits, that category is excluded from the chart.

two to three years for a class one offense and from twelve to eighteen months for a class two offense.

The types of sanctions are set forth in Standard 4.1 of *Juvenile Delinquency and Sanctions.*

## 4.1 Types of sanctions.

The sanctions that a juvenile court may impose upon a juvenile adjudged to have committed a juvenile offense should be of three types, from most to least severe, as follows.

A. Custodial, where the juvenile is ordered

1. to be confined in a secure facility as defined in these standards; or

2. to be placed in a nonsecure facility including a foster home or residence as defined in these standards.

B. Conditional, where the juvenile is ordered

1. periodically to report to probation or other authorities; or

2. to perform or refrain from performing certain acts; or

3. to make restitution to persons harmed by his or her offense or to pay a fine; or

4. to undergo any similar sanction not involving a change in the juvenile's residence or legal custody.

C. Nominal, where the juvenile is reprimanded, warned, or otherwise reproved and unconditionally released.

D. For purposes of this standard

1. the following institutions or designated portions thereof are secure facilities:

....[to be designated by the enacting jurisdiction]

2. the following types of facilities or designated portions thereof are nonsecure facilities:

....[to be designated by the enacting jurisdiction]

The classes of juvenile offenses are described in Standard 4.2.

## 4.2 Classes of juvenile offenses.

A. Offenses within the criminal jurisdiction of the juvenile court should be classified as class one through class five juvenile offenses.

B. Where, under a criminal statute or ordinance made applicable to juveniles pursuant to Standard 2.2, the maximum sentence authorized upon conviction for such offense is

1. death or imprisonment for life or for a term in excess of [twenty] years, it is a class one juvenile offense;

2. imprisonment for a term in excess of [five] but not more than [twenty] years, it is a class two juvenile offense;

3. imprisonment for a term in excess of [one] year but not more than [five] years, it is a class three juvenile offense;

4. imprisonment for a term in excess of [six] months but not more than [one] year, it is a class four juvenile offense;

5. imprisonment for a term of [six] months or less, it is a class five juvenile offense;

6. not prescribed, it is a class five juvenile offense.

The limitations on type and duration of sanctions are specified in Standard 5.2 A.

**5.2 Limitations on type and duration of sanctions.**

A. The juvenile court should not impose a sanction more severe than,

1. where the juvenile is found to have committed a class one juvenile offense,

   a. confinement in a secure facility or placement in a nonsecure facility or residence for a period of [thirty-six] months or

   b. conditional freedom for a period of [thirty-six] months;

2. where the juvenile is found to have committed a class two juvenile offense,

   a. confinement in a secure facility or placement in a nonsecure facility or residence for a period of [eighteen] months, or

   b. conditional freedom for a period of [twenty-four] months;

3. where the juvenile is found to have committed a class three juvenile offense,

   a. confinement in a secure facility or placement in a nonsecure facility or residence for a period of [six] months, or

   b. conditional freedom for a period of [eighteen] months;

4. where the juvenile is found to have committed a class four juvenile offense,

   a. confinement in a secure facility for a period of [three] months if the juvenile has a prior record, or

   b. placement in a nonsecure facility or residence for a period of [three] months, or

   c. conditional freedom for a period of [twelve] months;

5. where the juvenile is found to have committed a class five juvenile offense,

   a. placement in a nonsecure facility or residence for a period of [two] months if the juvenile has a prior record, or

   b. conditional freedom for a period of [six] months.

Standard 5.2 B.defines a "prior record" for our purposes here as an adjudication for a class one, two, or three juvenile offense within two years preceding the commission of the subject offense or adjudication for three class four or five offenses of which at least one was committed within the year preceding the subject offense.

Multiple juvenile offenses are covered in Standard 5.3.

### 5.3 Multiple juvenile offenses.

A. **When a juvenile is found to have committed two or more juvenile offenses during the same transaction or episode, the juvenile court should not impose a sanction more severe than the maximum sanction authorized by Standard 5.2 for the most serious such offense.**

B. **When, in the same proceeding, a juvenile is found to have committed two or more offenses during separate transactions or episodes, the juvenile court should not impose a sanction**

1. **more severe in nature than the sanction authorized by Standard 5.2 for the most serious such offense; or**

2. **longer in duration than a period equal to one and a half times the period authorized by Standard 5.2 for the most serious such offense.**

C. **When, at the time a juvenile is charged with an offense, the charging authority or its agents have evidence sufficient to warrant charging such juvenile with another juvenile offense, committed within the court's jurisdiction, the failure jointly to charge such offense should thereafter bar the initiation of juvenile court delinquency proceedings based on such offense.**

It should be noted that the Commission evidenced concern that the multiple offense provisions are not fully responsive to the problems of heinous crimes or intractable criminal behavior by juveniles, apparently leaving such problems to the waiver standards in the *Transfer Between Courts* volume. There is no provision for enhancement of sanctions.

Standard 5.4 terminates orders imposing sanctions no later than the juvenile's twenty-first birthday.

Special substantive provisions adapting the adult criminal law to make it more appropriate for juveniles relate to *mens rea* (mental capacity or intent), consent, parental authority, and responsibility (mental disease or defect—an equivalent of an insanity defense), in *Juvenile Delinquency and Sanctions* Standards 3.1 to 3.5, which appear in Part IV, section 4.2 above.

The standards provide that the burden of proof is on the prosecution to disprove affirmative defenses beyond a reasonable doubt (Standard

1.2). The *Juvenile Delinquency and Sanctions* Standard 1.1 initially describes as the purpose of the delinquency code:

**A. to forbid conduct that unjustifiably and without excuse inflicts or risks substantial harm to individual or public interests;**
**B. to safeguard conduct that is without fault or culpability from condemnation as delinquent;**
**C. to give fair warning of what conduct is prohibited and of the consequences of violation;**
**D. to recognize the unique physical, psychological, and social features of young persons in the definition and application of delinquency standards.**

The *Juvenile Delinquency and Sanctions* standards set clear limits on the official consequences that can flow from a delinquency adjudication. The *Dispositions* volume, which should be read as a companion to the delinquency sanctions standards, delineates the permissible purposes and goals of the juvenile correctional system, its services, programs, and facilities. *Dispositions* Standard 1.1 provides:

**The purpose of the juvenile correctional system is to reduce juvenile crime by maintaining the integrity of the substantive law proscribing certain behavior and by developing individual responsibility for lawful behavior. This purpose should be pursued through means that are fair and just, that recognize the unique characteristics and needs of juveniles, and that give juveniles access to opportunities for personal and social growth.**

Standard 1.2 defines a coercive disposition as one that limits the adjudicated juvenile's freedom of action in any way that is distinguishable from that of a nonadjudicated juvenile when noncompliance with the disposition may result in further enforcement action. The imposition of a coercive disposition carries the obligation to act with fairness and avoid arbitrariness, pursuant to a statute that prescribes the particular disposition with reasonable specificity.

The standard on coercive dispositions affirms the principle of proportionality—the requirement that the maximum severity and duration of the sanction should be determined by the legislature according to the seriousness of the offense. It also adopts determinate

sentences—a radical departure from the current dispositional system—in the following language:

**The nature and duration of all coercive dispositions should be
determined by the court at the time of sentencing, within the
limitations established by the legislature.**

Thus, the *Dispositions* standards reject indeterminate sentencing, a
cornerstone of the juvenile court scheme of individualized dispositions.
Indeterminate dispositions give discretion to the correctional authority to determine the rehabilitation of the juvenile as the criterion for
release or discharge from the correctional or treatment programs. The
*Dispositions* volume states:

> The lack of convincing data to support any single rationale for a
> correctional system (punishment, deterrence, or rehabilitation, for
> example) led to the adoption of two basic propositions: the imposition
> of coercive dispositions should be consistent with concepts of justice
> and fairness as well as with the aims of law enforcement and
> individual growth; and the correctional system for juveniles can be
> considered only as one modest component of a broader system of
> preventing crime by juveniles. Introduction at 1.

The necessary corollary of the principle of determinate sentencing is
that such dispositions may not be modified at the discretion of the
correctional authority. In other words, adjudicated juveniles may not
be discharged by the correctional agency because of administrative
convenience, predictions of future noncriminal behavior, or a system of
rewards for conformity to institutional norms. The standards for
modification and enforcement of dispositional orders do permit reduction of up to 5 percent of the term for good behavior, but otherwise
require a postdispositional judicial hearing on the application of the
agency, the juvenile, or the juvenile's parents alleging new information to show that *at the time of the application* the disposition is harsh
or inequitable. Standard 5.1 provides as follows:

**5.1 Reduction because disposition inequitable.**
  **A juvenile, his or her parents, the correctional agency with
responsibility for the juvenile, or the sentencing court on its own
motion may petition the sentencing court (or an appellate court)
at any time during the course of the disposition to reduce the
nature or the duration of the disposition on the basis that it
exceeds the statutory maximum; was imposed in an illegal
manner; is unduly severe with reference to the seriousness of the
offense, the culpability of the juvenile, or the dispositions given
by the same or other courts to juveniles convicted of similar**

**offenses; or if it appears at the time of the application that by doing so it can prevent an unduly harsh or inequitable result.**

An additional ground for reduction of the disposition is the failure of the correctional agency (or the state) to provide necessary services. Standard 5.2 requires the sentencing court to reduce the disposition or discharge the juvenile when access to required services is not being provided.

The standards impose a special obligation on the state, as in Standard 4.1, "to provide a full range of services aimed at facilitating normal growth and development of juveniles under correctional jurisdiction...." Thus, Standard 1.2 G. states:

**G. Availability of resources.**
**No coercive disposition should be imposed unless the resources necessary to carry out the disposition are shown to exist. If services required as part of a disposition are not available, an alternative disposition no more severe should be employed.**

Standard 4.1 also provides for a right to services.

**4.1 Right to services.**
**All publicly funded services to which nonadjudicated juveniles have access should be made available to adjudicated delinquents. In addition, juveniles adjudicated delinquent should have access to all services necessary for their normal growth and development.**
**A. Obligations of correctional agencies.**
**Correctional agencies have an affirmative obligation to ensure that juveniles under their supervision obtain all services to which they are entitled.**
**B. Purchase of services.**
**Services may be provided directly by correctional agencies or obtained, by purchase or otherwise, from other public or private agencies. Whichever method is employed, agencies providing services should set standards governing the provision of services and establish monitoring procedures to ensure compliance with such standards.**
**C. Prohibition against increased dispositions.**
**Neither the severity nor the duration of a disposition should be increased in order to ensure access to services.**
**D. Obligation of correctional agency and sentencing court.**
**If access to all required services is not being provided to a juvenile under the supervision of a correctional agency, the**

5

agency has the obligation to so inform the sentencing court. In addition, the juvenile, his or her parents, or any other interested party may inform the court of the failure to provide services. The court also may act on its own initiative. If the court determines that access to all required services in fact is not being provided, it should employ the following:

1. Reduction of disposition or discharge.

Unless the court can ensure that the required services are provided forthwith, it should reduce the nature of the juvenile's disposition to a less severe disposition that will ensure the juvenile access to the required services, or discharge the juvenile.

2. Affirmative orders.

In addition, the sentencing court, or any other court with the requisite jurisdiction, may order the correctional agency or other public agencies to make the required services available in the future.

4.2 Right to refuse services; exceptions.

Juveniles who have been adjudicated delinquent have the right to refuse all services, subject to the following exceptions:

A. Participation legally required of all juveniles.

Juveniles who have been adjudicated delinquent may be required to participate in all types of programs in which participation is legally required of juveniles who have not been adjudicated delinquent.

B. Prevention of clear harm to physical health.

Juveniles may be required to participate in certain programs in order to prevent clear harm to their physical health.

C. Remedial dispositions.

Juveniles subject to a conditional disposition may be required to participate in any program specified in the sentencing order, pursuant to Standard 3.2 D.

4.3 Requirement of informed consent to participate in certain programs.

Informed, written consent should be obtained before a juvenile may be required to participate in any program designed to alter or modify his or her behavior if that program may have harmful effects.

A. Juveniles below the age of sixteen.

If the juvenile is under the age of sixteen, his or her consent and the consent of his or her parent or guardian should be obtained.

B. Juveniles above the age of sixteen.

If the juvenile is sixteen or older, only the juvenile's consent need be obtained.

C. Withdrawal of consent.

Any such consent may be withdrawn at any time.

The following dispositional criteria were adopted:

### 2.1 Least restrictive alternative.

In choosing among statutorily permissible dispositions, the court should employ the least restrictive category and duration of disposition that is appropriate to the seriousness of the offense, as modified by the degree of culpability indicated by the circumstances of the particular case, and by the age and prior record of the juvenile. The imposition of a particular disposition should be accompanied by a statement of the facts relied on in support of the disposition and the reasons for selecting the disposition and rejecting less restrictive alternatives.

### 2.2 Needs and desires of the juvenile.

Once the category and duration of the disposition have been determined, the choice of a particular program within the category should be governed by the needs and desires of the juvenile.

Part III of *Dispositions* prescribes detailed standards for available remedies or categories of sanctions from the least restrictive alternative of a nominal disposition through the greatest restraint on the juvenile's freedom, a custodial disposition. Those standards follow.

## PART III: DISPOSITIONS

### 3.1 Nominal: reprimand and release.

The court may reprimand the juvenile for the unlawful conduct, warn against future offenses, and release him or her unconditionally.

### 3.2 Conditional.

The court may sentence the juvenile to comply with one or more conditions, which are specified below, none of which involves removal from the juvenile's home. Such conditions should not interfere with the juvenile's schooling, regular employment, or other activities necessary for normal growth and development.

A. Suspended sentence.

The court may suspend imposition or execution of a more

severe, statutorily permissible sentence with the provision that
the juvenile meet certain conditions agreed to by him or her and
specified in the sentencing order. Such conditions should not
exceed, in severity or duration, the maximum sanction permissible for the offense.

B. Financial.

  1. Restitution.

    a. Restitution should be directly related to the juvenile's
offense, the actual harm caused, and the juvenile's ability to
pay.

    b. The means to carry out a restitution order should be
available.

    c. Either full or partial restitution may be ordered.

    d. Repayment may be required in a lump sum or in
installments.

    e. Consultation with victims may be encouraged but not
required. Payments may be made directly to victims, or
indirectly, through the court.

    f. The juvenile's duty of repayment should be limited in
duration; in no event should the time necessary for repay-
ment exceed the maximum term permissible for the offense.

  2. Fine.

    a. Imposition of a fine is most appropriate in cases where
the juvenile has derived monetary gain from the offense.

    b. The amount of the fine should be directly related to the
seriousness of the juvenile's offense and the juvenile's
ability to pay.

    c. Payment of a fine may be required in a lump sum or
installments.

    d. Imposition of a restitution order is preferable to im-
position of a fine.

    e. The juvenile's duty of payment should be limited in
duration; in no event should the time necessary for payment exceed the maximum term permissible for the offense.

  3. Community service.

    a. In sentencing a juvenile to perform community ser-
vice, the judge should specify the nature of the work and
the number of hours required.

    b. The amount of work required should be related to the
seriousness of the juvenile's offense.

    c. The juvenile's duty to perform community service
should be limited in duration; in no event should the duty to
work exceed the maximum term permissible for the offense.

C. Supervisory.
   1. Community supervision.
   The court may sentence the juvenile to a program of community supervision, requiring him or her to report at specified intervals to a probation officer or other designated individual and to comply with any other reasonable conditions that are designed to facilitate supervision and are specified in the sentencing order.
   2. Day custody.
   The court may sentence the juvenile to a program of day custody, requiring him or her to be present at a specified place for all or part of every day or of certain days. The court also may require the juvenile to comply with any other reasonable conditions that are designed to facilitate supervision and are specified in the sentencing order.
D. Remedial.
   1. Remedial programs.
   The court may sentence the juvenile to a community program of academic or vocational education or counseling, requiring him or her to attend sessions designed to afford access to opportunities for normal growth and development. The duration of such programs should not exceed the maximum term permissible for the offense.
   2. Prohibition of coercive imposition of certain programs.
   This standard does not permit the coercive imposition of any program that may have harmful effects. Any such program should comply with the requirements of Standard 4.3 concerning informed consent.

3.3 Custodial.
   A. Custodial disposition defined.
   A custodial disposition is one in which a juvenile is removed coercively from his or her home.
   B. Presumption against custodial dispositions.
   There should be a presumption against coercively removing a juvenile from his or her home, and this category of sanction should be reserved for the most serious or repetitive offenses. It should not be used as a substitute for a judicial finding of neglect, which should conform to the standards in the *Abuse and Neglect* volume.
   C. Exclusiveness of custodial dispositions.
   A custodial disposition is an exclusive sanction and should not be used simultaneously with other sanctions. However, this

does not prevent the imposition of a custodial disposition for a specified period of time to be followed by a conditional disposition for a specified period of time, provided that the total duration of the disposition does not exceed the maximum term of a custodial disposition permissible for the offense.

D. Continuous and intermittent confinement.

Custodial confinement may be imposed on a continuous or an intermittent basis, not to exceed the maximum term permissible for the offense. Intermittent confinement includes:

1. night custody;
2. weekend custody.

E. Levels of custody.

Levels of custody include nonsecure residences and secure facilities.

1. Nonsecure residences.

No court should sentence a juvenile to reside in a nonsecure residence unless the juvenile is at least ten years old and unless the court finds that any less severe disposition would be grossly inadequate to the needs of the juvenile and that such needs can be met by placing the juvenile in a particular nonsecure residence.

2. Secure facilities.

a. A juvenile may be sentenced to a period of confinement in a secure facility; such a disposition, however, should be a last resort, reserved only for the most serious or repetitive offenses.

b. No court should sentence a juvenile to confinement in a secure facility unless the juvenile is at least twelve years old and unless the court finds that such confinement is necessary to prevent the juvenile from causing injury to the personal or substantial property interests of another.

c. Secure facilities should be coeducational, located near population centers as close as possible to the juvenile's home, and limited in population.

The *Dispositions* standards also provide for situations in which juveniles fail to comply with dispositional orders or commit a new offense.

5.4 Enforcement when juvenile fails to comply.

The correctional agency with responsibility for a juvenile may petition the sentencing court if it appears that the juvenile has willfully failed to comply with any part of the dispositional order. In the case of a remedial sanction, compliance is defined in terms of attendance at the specified program, and not in terms of performance.

If, after a hearing, it is determined that the juvenile in fact has not complied with the order and that there is no excuse for the noncompliance, the court may do one of the following:

A. Warning and order to comply.

The court may warn the juvenile of the consequences of failure to comply and order him or her to make up any missed time, in the case of supervisory, remedial, or custodial sanctions or community work; or missed payment, in the case of restitution or fines.

B. Modification of conditions and/or imposition of additional conditions.

If it appears that a warning will be insufficient to induce compliance, the court may modify existing conditions or impose additional conditions calculated to induce compliance, provided that the conditions do not exceed the maximum sanction permissible for the offense. The duration of the disposition should remain the same, with the addition of any missed time or payments ordered to be made up.

C. Imposition of more severe disposition.

If it appears that there are no permissible conditions reasonably calculated to induce compliance, the court may sentence the juvenile to the next most severe category of sanctions for the remaining duration of the disposition. The duration of the disposition should remain the same, except that the court may add some or all of the missed time to the remainder of the disposition.

D. Commission of a new offense.

Where conduct is alleged that constitutes a willful failure to comply with the dispositional order and also constitutes a separate offense, prosecution for the new offense is preferable to modification of the original order. The preference for separate prosecution in no way precludes the imposition of concurrent dispositions.

The third volume directly related to the dispositional stage following a delinquency adjudication is *Dispositional Procedures*. The current dispositional process is described there as follows: the dispositional judge's discretion is maximal; decisions are determined at a low level of visibility; expertise, real or presumed, dominates the decisional process; an identity of interest between the juvenile and the

222    STANDARDS FOR JUVENILE JUSTICE

state is presumed to exist; and the roles of the participants are blurred and confused, especially those of the judge, probation officer, and juvenile's attorney.

By contrast, the particular objectives of the standards for dispositional procedures are stated as being to: maximize accuracy in dispositional fact finding; maximize the opportunity for meaningful participation of all parties, including the victim, under certain conditions; minimize the significance attached to hearsay; use explicit fact finding and recorded reasons for selection of particular dispositions; encourage broad sharing of relevant information; limit dispositional facts to those directly relevant to dispositional objectives; balance formality with informality so that the hearing provides a fair opportunity to influence an impartial decision maker's judgment within the allowable limits of discretion; and fashion a disposition responsive to the individual condition or situation of the juvenile within the fixed legislative limits for the offense.

The standards carry out the enumerated objectives. Dispositional authority is vested in the juvenile court judge. Information relevant and material to disposition may be obtained only after adjudication, and any such information should not be considered a public record but should be broadly shared among the parties and others responsible for the care or custody of the juvenile. It should not be assumed that more information is better or that its accumulation is necessarily an aid to decision making.

The standards in this volume evidence a sharp concern for the possibility of compelling juveniles to testify against themselves at the dispositional stage under the guise of gathering relevant dispositional information. Therefore, in Standard 2.2 B. the following limitations are placed on obtaining information from the juvenile.

**B. Information in the form of oral or written statements relevant to disposition may be obtained from the juvenile, subject to the following limitations:**

**1. The statement should be voluntary as determined by the totality of circumstances surrounding the questioning and the juvenile should have full knowledge of the possible adverse dispositional consequences that may ensue.**

**2. In determining voluntariness, special consideration should be given to the susceptibility of the juvenile to any coercion, exhortations, or inducements which may have been used.**

**3. The juvenile should be afforded the right to consult with**

and be advised by counsel prior to any questioning by a representative of the state when such questioning is designed to elicit dispositional information.

4. It should clearly appear of record that the juvenile was advised that the information solicited may be used in a dispositional proceeding and that it may result in adverse dispositional consequences.

Standard 2.3 prescribes conditions for different types of information that may be deemed relevant to the dispositional decision, as well as the sources and methods by which the information may be sought. Please note that the *Dispositional Procedures* standards were amended by substituting "juvenile prosecutor" for "attorney for the state."

## 2.3 Information base.

A. The information essential to a disposition should consist of the juvenile's age; the nature and circumstances of the offense or offenses upon which the underlying adjudication is based, such information not being limited to that which was or may be introduced at the adjudication; and any prior record of adjudicated delinquency and disposition thereof.

B. Information concerning the social situation or the personal characteristics of the juvenile, including the results of psychological testing, psychiatric evaluations, and intelligence testing, may be considered as relevant to a disposition.

C. The social history may include information concerning the family and home situation; school records, in accordance with the *Juvenile Records and Information Systems* volume; any prior contacts with social agencies; and other similar items. The social history report should be in writing and should indicate clearly the sources of the information, the number of contacts made with such sources, and the total time expended on investigation and preparation.

D. When the state seeks to obtain and utilize information concerning the personal characteristics of the juvenile, such information should first be sought without resort to any form of confinement or institutionalization.

1. In the unusual case, where some form of confinement or institutionalization is represented by the state as being a necessary condition for obtaining this information, and the juvenile or his or her attorney objects, the court should

**conduct a hearing on the issue and determine whether the proposed confinement is necessary.**

**2. At such hearing the juvenile prosecutor should set forth the reasons for considering the information relevant to the dispositional decision. The juvenile prosecutor should also indicate what nonconfining alternatives were explored and demonstrate their inefficacy or unavailability. An order for examination and confinement under this standard should be limited to a maximum of thirty days, and should specify the nature and objectives of the examinations to be undertaken, as well as the place where such examinations are to be conducted.**

All information on which a disposition is based should be disclosed to the juvenile's attorney. If there is a compelling reason for nondisclosure to the juvenile, the court may so advise the attorney. Information should be made available to all parties sufficiently in advance of the hearing to permit investigation, verification, and rebuttal.

Consistent with other standards volumes, selection of a more severe dispositional alternative should be supported by a preponderance of the evidence.

Standard 3.1 requires the juvenile, the juvenile's attorney and parent or guardian or their attorney, and an attorney for the state to be present at all stages of the dispositional proceeding and permits others with a bona fide interest to be present at the court's discretion. The parents or guardian may be summoned to appear and if they fail to attend, the hearing may proceed but the court should determine whether to appoint a guardian *ad litem.*

The standards recommend experimentation with predisposition conferences to determine whether dispositional facts may be at issue and will require production of evidence, whether anyone who has prepared a report will be called to testify, to consider dispositional alternatives, and to arrive at an agreed upon disposition if possible. Such disposition agreements should be presented to the judge in writing for final approval.

If a predisposition conference does not produce an agreed upon disposition, a formal dispositional hearing should be conducted, with a full record preserved. The attorneys may present evidence in writing or by witnesses concerning the appropriate disposition, the juvenile and the juvenile's parent may address the court, and documents, witnesses, and preparers of reports may be challenged.

Standard 7.1 states the findings and formal requisites for imposition and correction of a disposition.

**7.1 Findings and formal requisites.**

A. The judge should determine the appropriate disposition as expeditiously as possible after the dispositional hearing, and when the disposition is imposed;

1. make specific findings on all controverted issues of fact, and on the weight attached to all significant dispositional facts in arriving at the disposition decision;

2. state for the record, in the presence of the juvenile, the reasons for selecting the particular disposition and the objective or objectives desired to be achieved thereby;

3. when the disposition involves any deprivation of liberty or any form of coercion, indicate for the record those alternative dispositions, including particular places and programs, that were explored and the reason for their rejection;

4. state with particularity the precise terms of the disposition that is imposed, including credit for any time previously spent in custody; and

5. advise the juvenile and the juvenile's attorney of the right to appeal and of the procedure to be followed if the appellant is unable to pay the cost of an appeal.

B. The court may correct an illegal disposition at any time and may correct a disposition imposed in an illegal manner within [120 days] of the imposition of the disposition.

**6.4 Administration of Corrections Programs.**

The department or agency responsible for administering the programs and facilities for juveniles under correctional supervision has less authority under the proposed standards than in the current system. Noncriminal misbehavior is removed from the jurisdiction of the court, so that only adjudicated delinquents are subject to corrections. The principle of determinate sentences is adopted, which eliminates the discretion of the correctional agency to determine the nature or duration of dispositions, restricting its role to selection of the program in which to place the juvenile within the category ordered by the court. Finally, juveniles are not subject to parole or to aftercare supervision after completion of the term of custody ordered by the court, unless community supervision had been part of the court's dispositional order.

Despite the reduced powers of corrections, the *Corrections Administration* volume is one of the longest in the series. The standards present in intricate detail the rights and duties of the juveniles and the corrections department during the period in which the court's disposition is implemented, listing the three central purposes of juvenile corrections: protection of the public, provision of a safe, human, caring environment, and access to required services for juveniles.

The term "safe, human, caring environment," chosen by the Commission in preference to the reporter's phrase, "basic level of care," is defined in Standard 4.9 as one designed to achieve normal growth and development by ensuring that programs provide opportunities for juveniles to:

1. enhance individuality and self-respect;
2. enjoy privacy;
3. develop intellectual and vocational abilities;
4. retain family and other personal ties;
5. express cultural identity;
6. relate and socialize with peers of both sexes;
7. practice religious beliefs;
8. explore political, social, and philosophical ideas;
9. enjoy a nutritious and varied diet;
10. receive dental and medical care, including birth control advice and services;
11. have a choice of recreational activities;
12. be safe from physical and psychological attack and abuse.

The five general principles to guide juvenile corrections administration are listed in Standard 1.2 as follows:

1.2 Five general principles.
The administration of juvenile corrections should be guided by five general principles:
A. Control and care.
The administration of programs for adjudicated juveniles should provide for the degree of control required for public protection, as determined by the court, and a safe, human, caring environment that will provide for normal growth and development.
B. Least possible restriction of liberty.
The liberty of a juvenile should be restricted only to the degree necessary to carry out the purpose of the court's order.
C. Fairness and legal rights.
Programs for adjudicated juveniles should be characterized by fairness in all procedures, and by a careful adherence to legal rights.
D. Accountability.

The administration of juvenile corrections should be accountable on three levels: to the courts for the carrying out of the dispositional order; to the public, through the appropriate legislative or other public body, for the implementation of the statutory mandate and expenditure of public funds; and to the juvenile for the provision of a safe, human, caring environment and access to required services.

E. Minimization of the scope of juvenile corrections.

The administration of juvenile corrections should aim to provide services and programs that will allow the court to reduce the number of juveniles placed in restrictive settings.

The standards for administration of juvenile corrections provide for a single statewide agency in the executive branch of government, separate from the administration of adult corrections or mental health facilities. For some purposes, programs may be subject to local control, but the statewide agency would be responsible for enforcing standards and providing assistance. If juveniles require mental health services, the department is responsible for providing them within the department's facilities directly or by outside contract. Transfer to a mental health agency would be pursuant to the laws governing admission or commitment of nonadjudicated juveniles to facilities for the mentally ill or mentally retarded. Standard 2.3 D. gives the court power to compel acceptance of a mentally ill or retarded delinquent by the agency best equipped to meet the juvenile's needs.

Standard 2.5 authorizes the department to provide directly or by purchase from the private sector programs required to carry out the disposition. Purchase from the private sector is permitted when it avoids duplication and provides a wider range and flexibility to meet the juvenile's needs more adequately. The department should monitor both public and private programs to ensure compliance with the standards.

The standards for correctional personnel allow for both career and short-term opportunities. Youth counsellors, who are in direct contact with juveniles, should demonstrate enthusiasm, sensitivity, and energy in working with the adjudicated juveniles in program settings. Recruitment policies should stress affirmative action to match racial and ethnic groups of juveniles and staff; equivalent appointment of men and women; and career appointments for ex-offenders, providing opportunities to augment experiential background. Extensive pre-service, probationary, and in-service training programs are prescribed.

The standards require the department to develop a code of conduct for all personnel, which should be part of the employment contract.

Standard 3.4 C. provides minimum requirements for the code of conduct.

1. **conformance with personnel requirements for public employees;**
2. **an emphasis on the essential role played by staff in ensuring the integrity of all aspects of the department's policy;**
3. **stress on the staff's responsibility to provide a safe, human, caring environment for the juvenile and to respect all rights of juveniles set forth in these standards;**
4. **a prohibition of any form of physical or verbal abuse of juveniles by staff members or by other juveniles with the tacit approval of the staff;**
5. **an affirmative obligation on the part of staff to report violations by personnel of the code of conduct.**

Private agencies also must observe the code of conduct as a condition to continuing contractual relations with the department. There should be judicial remedies for juveniles and their parents or guardians for violations of the code of conduct, with costs chargeable against the plaintiff in frivolous suits.

Volunteers should be involved to enrich and supplement programs and for advocacy, program planning, and monitoring activities.

An adjudicated delinquent under correctional supervision should suffer no loss in civil rights except those suspended or modified by the disposition imposed and any special conditions ordered by the court. Basic concepts of due process apply. Standard 4.5 provides in part that:

**Alterations in the status or placement of a juvenile that result in more security, additional obligations, or less personal freedom should be subject to regularized proceedings designed to allow for challenge through the presentation of evidence to an impartial tribunal. The relative formality of such proceedings should be based on the importance of the juvenile's interest at stake, the permissible sanction, and the nature of the setting in which the decision is to be made. The more restrictive the setting, or the greater the permissible restriction or sanction, the greater the degree of formality required.**

Standard 4.5 is augmented by the standards on disciplinary proceedings. Standard 4.8 prohibits all forms of corporal punishment.

Standard 4.8 B. prescribes limitations on the use of physical force by personnel, as follows:

**Personnel should be prohibited from the direct use or tacit approval of juveniles' use of physical force against other juveniles except:**
1. **as necessary in self defense or to prevent imminent injury to the juvenile, another person, or substantial property injury;**
2. **to prevent escape; or**
3. **when a juvenile's refusal to obey an order seriously disrupts the functioning of the facility. No more force should be used than is necessary to achieve the legitimate purpose for which it is used.**

The standards for the provision of services are set out in Standard 4.10. Subdivision F. was amended to require a procedure to monitor administration of drugs by an independent physician.

**A. The department's obligation to provide access to required services.**
Over and above the provision of a safe, human, caring environment the department should ensure that adjudicated juveniles have access to those services that are required for their individual needs.

**B. Services that all juveniles have an obligation to receive.**
The department should ensure that adjudicated juveniles obtain those services that nonadjudicated juveniles have an obligation to receive. Such services should be of no less quality than those provided to juveniles not under correctional supervision.

**C. Services necessary to prevent clear harm to physical health.**
The department should ensure that adjudicated juveniles obtain any services necessary to prevent clear harm to their physical health.

**D. Services mandated by the court as a condition to nonresidential disposition.**
The department should ensure that adjudicated juveniles obtain services determined by the court as a condition of a nonresidential disposition. As required by the *Dispositions* volume, such services should not be mandated by the court if they may have harmful effects.

E. Requirement of the juvenile's informed consent to all other services.

The department should ensure that the informed written consent of the juvenile is obtained by the program director for any services other than those described in subsections A., B., C., and D., above. Any such consent may be withdrawn at any time.

F. Limitations on the use of drugs.

Stimulant, tranquilizing, and psychotropic drugs should only be used when:

1. in addition to the consent of the juvenile, the consent of the parents or guardian of any juvenile under the age of sixteen is obtained;

2. such drugs are prescribed and administered by a licensed physician;

3. the program has a procedure, approved by the department, for recording all administrations of such drugs to juveniles, and for monitoring the short- and long-term effects of such drugs by a licensed physician who is independent of the department (the record maintained by the program should include the type and quantity of the drug administered, together with the date and time of day; the physician's reason for the prescription; the physician's observations of the effects of the drug, together with the written observations of other personnel and those of the juvenile);

4. personnel who directly administer drugs to juveniles have received specialized training.

Under no circumstances should stimulant, tranquilizing, or psychotropic drugs be used for purposes of program management or control, or for purposes of experimentation and research. In emergency situations and when the consent of the juvenile cannot be obtained, drugs may be administered subject to the seventy-two-hour emergency treatment provisions contained in the *Noncriminal Misbehavior* volume. Standard 4.10 G. 1. was revised to add court approval when parental consent is unavailable if the juvenile has consented to environmental modification techniques.

Criteria for program placement should include the location of the juvenile's home, the juvenile's age and sex, and the juvenile's need for services. A preference is stated for the use of *existing* relevant information for the placement decision, discouraging testing, and requiring the juvenile's informed consent to psychological tests and other means of obtaining information if nonadjudicated juveniles would not be obligated to take such tests.

Voluntary aftercare is permitted with the informed consent of the juvenile for a period not to exceed six months when such services are funded by the department.

Standard 4.14 covers work performed by adjudicated juveniles.

## 4.14 Work performed by adjudicated juveniles.

**A. Limitations on coerced work.**

**Juveniles under correctional supervision should have a right not to participate in coerced work assignments unless:**

**1. the work is performed in the community as a part of a conditional disposition; or**

**2. the work is reasonably related to the juvenile's housekeeping or personal hygienic needs; or**

**3. the work is part of an approved vocationally oriented program for the juvenile.**

**B. Compensation.**

**1. When the juvenile is required to work as part of a program under subsection A. 3., and to the extent that such work benefits the facility or program, the juvenile should be compensated for such work. The state should not make any set-off claim for care, custody, or services against such compensation. Such compensation should be guided by the appropriate minimum wage statutes with consideration given to the age and capability of the juvenile.**

**2. Juveniles who volunteer for work assignments not connected with personal housekeeping or hygienic needs should also be fairly compensated for such work and not be subject to set-off claims against such compensation.**

**3. Juveniles injured while performing work as described in this standard should be entitled to workmen's compensation benefits.**

**C. Juvenile's access to earnings.**

**A special account, in the nature of a trust fund, should be established for the juvenile's earnings, and reasonable rules established for periodic withdrawal, expenditure, and release of the entire fund when correctional supervision is terminated.**

Standards 5.1 and 5.2 relate to modification of dispositions and willful noncompliance with the court's order, as provided in the *Dispositions* and *Dispositional Procedures* volumes.

## 5.1 Procedure for reduction of a disposition.

A. A petition for reduction of a disposition may be filed with the dispositional court any time after the imposition of the order of disposition. The proper parties and the requisite grounds for such petition are set out in Part V of the *Dispositions* volume.

B. The court may reduce the disposition on the basis of the petition and any supportive documents that have been filed initially or subsequently at the request of the court.

C. If the court does not order the reduction of the disposition within [fifteen] days of the filing of the petition, then the petitioner should be entitled to a full dispositional hearing to be held within [thirty] days of the filing of the petition. Such hearings should be conducted in accordance with the relevant provisions of Part VI of the *Dispositional Procedures* volume.

D. Courts should develop rules which impose reasonable limits on the frequency with which such petitions may be filed by the juvenile or the juvenile's parents or guardian. Special provision should be made for additional filings when any subsequent petition raises a matter that was not previously brought to the attention of the court.

## 5.2 Procedure for willful noncompliance with order of disposition.

A. The department may petition the dispositional court charging the juvenile with a willful violation of the order of disposition.

B. Unless the petition is dismissed, the court should conduct a hearing on the petition in which the petitioner should have the burden of proving willful noncompliance by clear and convincing evidence. The juvenile and counsel for the juvenile should be given prior notice of the charges; should be present at all stages of such proceedings; and should have an opportunity to be heard, to be confronted with adverse witnesses, to cross-examine, and to offer evidence.

C. If the petition is sustained, the judge should make specific, written findings that are sufficient to provide effective appellate review.

D. Upon a finding of willful noncompliance, the court should determine the appropriate means to achieve compliance. If the court preliminarily determines that a disposition of the next most severe category may be imposed, the hearing should be conducted in accordance with Part VI of the *Dispositional Procedures* volume. If the court determines that only a warning or the modification of any previously imposed conditions may be imposed, the juvenile and his or her counsel should be present, have an opportunity to address the court, and be granted disclosure of any information in the court's possession bearing on disposition. No additional formality need be observed except as justice may require in appropriate cases.

Parts VI and VII are the crux of the *Corrections Administration* volume, providing standards for the full range of nonresidential and residential programs, respectively. The dispositions permitted pursuant to the *Juvenile Delinquency and Sanctions* and *Dispositions* standards are: (1) nonimal—reprimand and release; (2) conditional—suspended sentence, restitution, fine, and community supervision (probation); and (3) residential—nonsecure (foster home, group home) and secure placements. Community supervision, or probation, is classified as conditional freedom, which, for purposes of correctional responsibility, requires some form of correctional supervision in the community for adjudicated delinquents not removed from the home.

Standard 6.2 defines community supervision as follows:

Community supervision refers to the supervision of an adjudicated juvenile by a designated field worker under varying levels of intensity and in compliance with any other conditions included in the court's dispositional order. Community supervision involves the field worker in the combination of surveillance and service provision or brokerage tasks.

Field offices should be located in the area served, with community supervision generally administered by local offices of the statewide department. The standards authorize the court to specify conditions to carry out a community supervision order, observing the principles that the conditions be least restrictive of the juvenile's liberty or privacy or that of others consistent with the circumstances and offense involved; ensure a safe, human, caring environment; and provide for the juvenile's education, employment, or other activities necessary for normal growth and development. The conditions also may include curfew stipulations or prohibitions from specified places, determination of high, medium, or low levels of supervision, and payment of fines or restitution orders.

Standard 6.2 D. grants discretion to the department to modify the conditions in the supervision order after providing the court and the juvenile with written notice of the modification.

Standard 6.3 A. describes a program of day custody requiring a juvenile to be present at a specified place for all or part of every day or certain days. The same conditions as provided under community supervision may be attached to the day custody order.

Community service orders refer to work assignments, which should be for the general welfare of the community and, where possible, related to the nature of the juvenile's offense. The dispositional order should specify whether earnings should be withheld from the juvenile. The juvenile should be covered by workmen's compensation benefits.

Residential programs cover placement in secure and nonsecure facilities, the distinction deriving principally from staff control over residents' rights to leave the premises. Standard 7.1 defines facilities as follows:

**7.1 Secure and nonsecure facilities: definition and certification.**

**A secure facility is one that is used exclusively for juveniles who have been adjudicated delinquent and is characterized by exclusive staff control over the rights of its residents to enter or leave the premises on a twenty-four-hour basis.**

**A nonsecure facility refers to such residential programs as foster homes, group homes, and half-way houses, characterized by a small number of residents who have the freedom to enter or leave the premises under staff supervision.**

**The department should certify each residential program as secure or nonsecure and such certification, unless overturned in a court proceeding brought for that purpose, should determine any distinction in rights and responsibilities made in these standards.**

The much disputed but fundamental standard is 7.2, which limits the capacity of residential facilities to twelve to twenty adjudicated juveniles. Although the practicality, feasibility, and effectiveness of that standard was debated heatedly within the drafting committee and the Commission, the goal of reducing the size of facilities during interim status and corrections held firm throughout the life of the project, and the standards adopted in many of the volumes, such as *Interim Status, Dispositions,* and *Architecture of Facilities,* are contingent on a phasing out of large facilities. Standards for control, security, and disciplinary procedures in institutions are premised on the assumption that facilities will be small and relatively manageable, as homelike as possible, and will aim for the normalization of the residents. Thus, Standard 7.5 requires a presumption in favor of coeducational programs, or, if they are not available, opportunities for frequent social contact between juveniles of both sexes. The standards also seek location of the facilities as close to the juvenile's home community as possible to minimize disruption of the juvenile's cultural and geographical roots and ensure that links between the juvenile and his or her family and community are facilitated. Standard 7.4 prescribes strict limitations on the use of out-of-state programs, restricting such placements to programs conforming to the standards but not available within the state, and requiring written reasons showing why the programs are not provided within the state and why in-state programs are insufficient to meet the juvenile's needs.

A noteworthy model juvenile corrections Bill of Rights for residential facilities is provided in Standard 7.6, including liberal visitation, telephone access, uncensored mail, community involvement, religious freedom, non-institutional clothing, maximum privacy, varied diet, etc. Searches of the juvenile or the juvenile's property or room may not be routinely undertaken; the administrator of the facility may authorize a search only if reasonable grounds exist to suspect violations of the penal law or the regulations and a record is kept of the search. All regulations should be in writing and explained to the juvenile as soon as possible upon the juvenile's arrival at the facility. Access to legal counsel should be readily available to preserve or perfect any legal claims the juvenile may have.

The standards permit transfer between programs initiated in writing by the juvenile or the program director after notice to the juvenile's parents or guardian. Objections should be expeditiously reviewed. Proximity to the juvenile's home and possible reduction of services should be considered in the transfer decision.

Two changes in the *Corrections Administration* standards have been discussed above—the change of maximum population in secure facilities from twelve juveniles to twelve to twenty and the revision of Standard 7.5 D. barring intrusive searches of visitors. See Appendix for details of the revisions.

Standard 7.8 limits the use of mechanical and chemical restraints and weapons in the facility. Weapons are barred, chemical restraints strictly controlled, and mechanical restraints authorized during transportation only.

Nonsecure programs may require intermittent (overnight or weekend) or continuous residence. The most frequently used nonsecure placements are foster homes and group homes. A foster home is defined as the home of one or more persons who take in juveniles as temporary family members. The department retains ultimate responsibility for supervision of juveniles in foster homes and the juvenile's preferences should be considered in such placements. Foster parents should receive in-service training and support services from the department or private agency involved.

A group home is a community-based residence for housing between four and twelve juveniles under the sponsorship of a public or private agency. Whenever possible, the juveniles should attend local schools and use other community resources. If the group home provides services, the juvenile's informed consent should be obtained prior to participation. If participation in the program is required, the juvenile should be allowed a pre-placement stay and be granted a transfer if unwilling to take part in the program. In general, there should be at least one staff person on duty for every five juveniles and at least one staff person should sleep at the facility, providing twenty-four-hour staff coverage.

Other nonsecure settings are: rural programs, such as forestry camps, ranches, and farms; boarding schools or other settings that primarily provide for nonadjudicated children; and apartments, especially for juveniles of working age.

Requirements for secure programs are prescribed in Standard 7.11. Security refers to staff and resident safety and to prevention of escape. Security is ensured by physical features of the building and by staffing arrangements. Because the maximum size of the facility is twenty juveniles, there should be no electronic surveillance of residents by closed circuit television, listening systems, or other such devices.

Security classifications are recommended to allow juveniles placed in the lower security category opportunities to participate in outside activities. Criteria for the classification should be current and previous offenses, any history of violence or escapes from secure facilities, and findings in disciplinary proceedings, but *not* the extent to which the juvenile participates in services. Determination of the classification is made by the program director. The juvenile should be notified and given an opportunity to challenge the classification through the grievance mechanism. Lower security juveniles should take part in community educational, work release, and recreational activities; other juveniles should have equivalent activities inside the secure facility, including at least two hours of recreation each day, with the opportunity for strenuous physical exercise. Workloads should provide for at least one staff person with full-time supervisory responsibility on duty for approximately every four juveniles, with at least one staff person on duty and awake at night.

Furloughs for juveniles in the lower security category should be permitted at least one weekend every two months and for all juveniles at least five days during the month prior to discharge.

Isolation should be permitted only in accordance with the standards on discipline or as a temporary emergency measure for conduct that creates an imminent danger of physical harm to the juvenile or others. Emergency isolation should be reported immediately to the program director and, when necessary, to appropriate medical personnel. A plan should be devised for the earliest release from isolation or for care in a more suitable setting. Eight hours during the daytime is the maximum duration for isolation. A juvenile may be isolated as protective custody at the juvenile's own request, out of a legitimate fear for his or her safety. The program director should identify and resolve the problem giving rise to protective custody. Other restrictions on isolation are provided in Standard 7.11 as follows:

4. **When possible, isolation should be accomplished in the juvenile's own room. The program director should determine whether any items should be removed from the room during the period of isolation. Such decision should be based on whether or not such items may be used as instruments of self-injury and not as a punitive measure.**

5. **If the facility does not utilize individual rooms, a room may be specially designated. Such room should resemble, as nearly as possible, the ordinary rooms of the facility.**

6. **If a room specially designated as an isolation room is required, such room should be planned and located in the staff office area and not in the bedroom section of the facility.**

7. **No special diet or extraordinary sensory or physical deprivations should be imposed in addition to the room confinement. Reading materials and regular periods of indoor and outdoor exercise should be available.**

8. **All juveniles in isolation should be visited at least hourly by a specially designated and trained staff person, and should be provided one hour of recreation in every twenty-four-hour period of isolation.**

**When the isolation is an emergency measure growing out of violent behavior, a staff member should remain with the juvenile. If considerations of safety make it impossible for the staff member to remain, the staff member should maintain constant observation of the juvenile.**

**When the juvenile is in isolation at his or her own request, the regular staff visits should be designed to clearly identify and quickly resolve the problem that led to the request for isolation.**

9. **Each incident during the period of isolation, along with the reasons for and the resolution of the matter, should be recorded and subject to at least monthly review by the**

**program director and an individual or individuals assigned such a review function in the department.**

Standards on discipline are set forth in Part VIII. They are designed to apply to adjudicated juveniles placed in residential facilities, except foster homes. Disciplinary matters in foster homes should be governed by the law regulating parent-child relationships and any special laws in the jurisdiction applicable to foster home (or group home) placements.

The same principles of due process and proportionality applied to the court process and student disciplinary proceedings—that procedural safeguards be commensurate with the extent to which liberty may be deprived and that the severity of sanctions be proportionate to the seriousness of the offense—and of least restrictive alternative are adapted to the disciplinary system proposed for correctional institutions. The objectives of these provisions are stated in Standard 8.2.

**8.2 Objectives.**
**The objectives of these standards are:**
**A. to allow those charged with the custody and control of juveniles to reasonably regulate the behavior of those in their charge and to impose disciplinary measures congruent with the willful violation of the applicable regulations;**
**B. to promote fairness and regularity in the disciplinary system;**
**C. to separate major infractions from minor infractions and to prohibit the imposition of disciplinary measures in certain cases;**
**D. to promote the use of written regulations and to ensure that the juvenile know as precisely as possible what conduct is expected of him or her and what sanctions may be imposed;**
**E. to provide a procedural format for the imposition of disciplinary measures; and**
**F. to prohibit cruel and unusual punishment within juvenile correctional facilities.**

Violations of the regulations reasonably controlling the behavior of juvenile corrections residents are divided into major, minor, and petty infractions. Infractions that would constitute a felony should be processed as if the juvenile were not in a correctional facility. If the charge is not pursued by the jurisdiction, the felony should be treated as a major infraction within the facility. A minor infraction that also is an offense under the penal law (presumably a misdemeanor) may be reported at the discretion of the program director and processed by the state as if the juvenile were not in a correctional facility. Otherwise, it should be treated as a minor infraction within the facility. If an offense under penal law definitions is prosecuted or referred to family court, the disciplinary board should determine whether probable cause exists to believe the juvenile committed the offense and if so found, the program drector should determine whether restrictive measures are necessary to protect the juvenile or other residents or for institutional integrity. The least restrictive disciplinary measures should be used.

Standard 8.3 C. cites representative major infractions: murder, kidnapping, manslaughter, armed robbery, burglary, assault causing serious physical injury, rape, physical restraint of another with threat of serious harm, arson, tampering with a witness, bribery, escape by use of force, possession of a narcotic drug (not marijuana or its derivatives), inciting a riot, theft or destruction of property valued at $500 or more, and sexual abuse.

Minor infractions listed in Standard 8.4 B. include simple assault, escape without force, threatening physical harm, theft or destruction of property valued under $500, creating a disturbance, engaging in a riot, lying to a person in authority, willful and repeated disobedience of orders, reporting a false alarm, possessing or using alcohol or marijuana, and refusal to perform work assignments.

Petty infractions in Standard 8.5 B. include attempted escape or unauthorized absence for less than a day, refusal to attend school, creating a hazard, theft of property valued under $5, and violation of any other regulations not otherwise covered.

Certain behavior currently considered punishable in correctional institutions is expressly excluded from disciplinary action in Standard 8.6. However, subdivision A., which in the tentative draft only restricted sexual behavior forbidden by law, was expanded to include reasonable institutional regulations.

**8.6 Conduct that may not be subject to disciplinary action.**

**Juveniles should not be subject to disciplinary action for any of the following behavior:**

**A. sexual behavior that is not forbidden by statute or reasonable institutional regulations;**

**B. refusal to attend religious services;**

**C. refusal to conform in matters of personal appearance or dress to any institutional rule that is not related to health or safety;**

**D. refusal to permit a search of the person or of personal effects that is not authorized by these standards;**

**E. refusal to continue participation in any counselling, treat-**

ment, rehabilitation, or training program, with the exception of school or class attendance mandated by the compulsory school attendance law;

F. refusal to address staff in any particular manner or displaying what is viewed as a negative, hostile, or any other supposed attitude deemed undesirable;

G. possession of any printed or otherwise recorded material unless such possession is specifically forbidden by these standards;

H. refusal to eat a particular type of food;

I. refusal to behave in violation of the juvenile's religious beliefs;

J. refusal to participate in any study, research, or experiment;

K. refusal to take drugs designed to modify behavior or to submit to nonemergency, surgical interventions without consent.

Maximum sanctions permitted for the disciplinary process are graduated by the seriousness of the infraction in Standard 8.7 as follows: for *major infractions*—up to ten days room confinement, loss or non-accrual of good time credits, suspension of earning good time credits for up to thirty days, and suspension of privileges for up to thirty days; for *minor infractions*—up to five days room confinement, loss or non-accrual of good time credits not to exceed half of that currently earned, and suspension of privileges up to fifteen days; for *petty infractions*—reprimand and warning, suspension of privileges up to seven days. A second petty infraction may be treated as a minor infraction after advance written notice to the juvenile of such decision.

"Privileges" include access to movies, radio, television, telephone, recreational or athletic activities, outside activities, off-grounds privileges. Telephone access to the juvenile's family or attorney may not be denied. Other proscribed punishments are corporal punishment, special clothing or insignia, altered diet or sleeping patterns, hard labor, silence, or anything designed to cause contempt, ridicule, or physical pain. All time periods are bracketed in Standard 8.7 to indicate that those proposed are advisory only.

The disciplinary board conducts the hearing based on written reports of major or minor infractions. Petty infractions need not be dealt with in a formal hearing. The board should consist of five members—two employees of the facility, two from a rotating group of citizens who have volunteered to serve, and the fifth a non-voting chairperson. The procedural prerequisites to the imposition of sanctions for a major or a minor infraction are notice (orally, immediately after discovery of the alleged infraction, and written, within twenty-four hours); a hearing no later than seven days after service of notice; representation by any person selected by the juvenile; opportunity to hear the charge and admit or deny; the introduction, confrontation, and cross-examination of witnesses and evidence; and notification of a written decision based on clear and convincing evidence within twenty-four hours. The decision should include a finding of guilty or not guilty, the reasons for the decision, a summary of the evidence relied upon, the sanction to be imposed, and the reasons for the sanction. The revised standards are less liberal than the tentative draft with respect to the juvenile's right to call witnesses, present evidence, and confront and cross-examine witnesses, which were made subject to institutional safety and the discretion of correctional officials in amended Standard 8.9 D.

The program director should review major infractions automatically and minor infractions at the request of the juvenile. Petty infractions are not reviewable. The director has authority to reverse the board's finding of guilt or reduce the severity of the sanction. Appeals of the director's decision should be made to an independent review body under grievance mechanisms described in Standard 9.2.

Part IX deals with accountability, establishing standards for information systems, grievance procedures, monitoring, evaluation, and a planning process open to public scrutiny. Full accountability is said to depend upon a combination of mechanisms within and outside the department applied to all public and private programs and upon public access to information gathered by the mechanisms responsible for accountability.

The process especially suited to corrections is the grievance mechanism, whereby complaints about department programs, policies, personnel, or procedures can be expressed and resolved. Standard 9.2 C. states the principles to govern grievance mechanisms.

**1. Every resident assigned to any program unit should have the means to file a grievance and make use of any grievance procedure that is developed.**

**2. Each facility should design a mechanism appropriate to its physical set-up, the age and size of its population, and the focus of its program. The mechanism should be subject to review and approval by the department.**

**3. There should be available to any resident with an emergency grievance or problem, a course of action that can provide for immediate redress.**

**4. Elected residents and designated staff should participate in the development of procedures and in the operation of the grievance mechanism.**

5. The mechanism employed should be simple and the levels of review kept to a minimum.

6. Residents should be entitled to representation and other assistance at all levels, including informal resolution within the established procedure.

7. There should be brief time limits for the receipt of all responses to a grievance as well as for action that is required to relieve the grievance.

8. A course of action should be open to all parties to a grievance, staff and residents alike, for appealing a decision.

9. A juvenile should be guaranteed a speedy, written response to his or her grievance with reasons for the action taken. In the absence of such a response, there should be further recourse available to the juvenile.

10. Monitoring and evaluation of the entire operation by persons not connected with the facility should be required.

11. The procedure should include, as a final review, some form of independent review by a party or parties outside the department. Such review may be in the form of binding or nonbinding arbitration.

12. No reprisals should be permitted against anyone using the grievance mechanism.

13. The grievance mechanism should include an impartial method for determining whether a complaint falls within its jurisdiction.

14. Implementation of the grievance mechanism is a vital factor in its potential for success. This calls for administrative leadership and commitment, resident and staff involvement, a strong orientation and explanation program for new residents, and outside monitoring.

The standards for research and planning, information systems, and monitoring conform generally to those adopted in the separate volumes on those subjects to be discussed in the next part covering the work of Drafting Committee IV, Administration. Of particular interest here are the standards for establishing a research and planning division. The responsibilities of this division are described in Standard 9.3.

**9.3 Organization of research and planning within the department.**
A. Research and planning division.
The department should establish a research and planning division within its central office with organizational status

similar to that of other divisions within the department. The division should have responsibility for:

1. the assembly and processing of data concerning all department activities;

2. continuous monitoring of all programs;

3. ensuring program effectiveness;

4. short- and long-term planning for the department;

5. coordination with appropriate state agencies.

B. Information system.

The research and planning division should develop an information system designed to serve the department's data needs for administration, research, and planning. The data assembled should include:

1. basic characteristics of juveniles within the department's jurisdiction;

2. program descriptions and features;

3. departmental organizational arrangements such as local offices, field offices, and other units of administration;

4. characteristics of department personnel; and

5. fiscal data.

C. Monitoring activities.

The division should ensure program quality through the monitoring of all programs. Monitoring should include the compilation of basic data on all programs and regular visits to programs by monitoring teams. Monitoring should be designed to ensure compliance with the department's standards and the program's statement of purpose.

## 6.5 Architecture of Detention and Corrections Facilities.

The *Architecture of Facilities* volume is a rare addition to the literature of juvenile corrections and architecture. It reflects a combination of humane values, practical considerations, and technical skill unusual in any field. The priorities expressed in the standards, "stressing the primary matters relating to agency policy and operations, and the secondary and supportive role of facilities," are addressed to an architectural program that seeks to establish space needs and design characteristics for the administration of the programs within the facilities. The fundamental principle in these standards is the concept of normalization—that juveniles in detention or corrections facilities should live in an environment as close to normal as possible. The primary goal stated "is to develop an optimum environment for the normalization of the juvenile justice system through the use of community settings." Therefore, the emphasis is on small community settings with a minimum of hardware, using space and design combined with staff supervision to achieve management and physical security. The standards also rely on access to community resources in preference to duplication within the facility to the extent possible.

The standards for values and purposes are:

## 2.1 Normalization.

**Facilities for the juvenile justice system should be designed with the objective of creating environments which will encourage normalization.**

## 2.2 Small community-based facilities.

**Existing large custodial facilities for juvenile detention and corrections should be phased out and replaced with a network of smaller, community-based facilities.**

## 2.3 Flexible buildings.

**The design of facilities for correction and detention should not impede administrative or policy changes.**

## 2.4 Secure settings.

**Secure settings should provide security measures which:**

**A. instill a sense of security and well-being in facility residents; and**

**B. rely on increased staff coverage rather than building plant.**

## 2.5 Overcrowding.

**Overcrowding is generally a symptom of an operational problem and does not imply the need for new construction.**

## 2.6 Community norms.

**Community norms should be considered and analyzed in planning and locating facilities for detention or corrections.**

## 2.7 Personal space.

**The stress of life in a secure setting requires recognition of the individual's need for some degree of personalization of space, privacy, and territoriality.**

The information that should be included in the written document describing the architectural program for each facility is set forth in Standard 3.1.

A. statement of the general goals and purposes of the project;

B. description of the agency or organization to be served, including its tasks, statutory authority, operating procedures, services provided, and administrative structure;

C. description of the management model (Standard 1.6) which is used as the basis of the current and future operations;

D. impact statement that:

1. analyzes past and current workload and budget;

2. projects future workload, staffing, programs, and operating and capital budgets; and

3. assesses the impact of the proposed project on the overall operation of the agency;

E. justification of the project and its operating costs, exploring alternative management models and their impact on staffing, budget, and space requirements;

F. quantitative and qualititative description of space requirements for the proposed facility, including outdoor spaces, character, symbolism, and other descriptive factors;

G. outline of budget and time restrictions; and

H. study of alternate strategies to satisfy space requirements including leasing, renovation, and new construction.

Other requirements for an architectural program are the development of a broad data base concerning all those involved in the program, "adaptive architecture"—facilities providing a variety of spatial configurations adaptable to the changing needs of programs and operations, and conformity with all pertinent fire, safety, health, and building codes. Standard 3.4 states: "Building design should not present an expectation of abusive behavior and vandalism and invite challenge by residents, nor should it be assumed that every juvenile behaves in a violent and destructive manner." This standard is consistent with the definition of "soft architecture" in Standard 1.9: "A design attitude that results in spaces and buildings that do not present an expectation of destructive behavior." However, the standards for nonsecure or group homes and secure corrections and detention facilities allow for the wide range of security requirements for juveniles placed in different settings.

Part IV contains the standards for group homes. The other type of nonsecure placement, foster care, is not covered because it is assumed that the juvenile in foster care is living in a private family home.

A group home is defined as "a community-based residential dwelling for housing juveniles, under the sponsorship of a public or private agency." Maximum capacity is four to twelve juveniles. Every group home should be certified annually as complying with public safety codes and be inspected by the department at least twice annually for quality of upkeep and suitability of the facility for the program. There should be a governing body for the group home that includes community representatives. Group homes should be located in residential areas, near community resources and public transportation, and should be similar to residential buildings in those neighborhoods. Residents should be permitted to decorate their rooms. Ordinarily, the group home should not be the sole residence of staff members, to preserve the normality of the staff personnel in contact with the juveniles. There should be space for staff administration work and a room for secure storage of confidential records. Group homes should provide a pleasant environment, sufficient space, and suitable equipment to meet program goals.

Standards for secure corrections facilities are provided in Part V. Standard 5.1 defines the function of security in a secure corrections facility.

**5.1 Security.**

**Security in a secure corrections facility should recognize and balance the legitimate need for security and safety felt by staff and society with the residents' need for a setting that provides them with safety and a reasonable quality of life.**

The other standards in Part V are designed to create an equilibrium between the needs of the staff and society and the needs of the juvenile residents of the secure facility. In exterior appearance, the facility should resemble residential buildings in the vicinity. It should be located to facilitate the use of community services and continued contact with the juvenile's family and friends. The maximum capacity should be twenty, although this figure is bracketed to indicate that it is recommended but not necessarily expected to be achieved immediately. The facility should be planned like a large private house, with no control center. As in the group home standards, the facility should not be the sole residence of staff members and it should provide space for staff administration work, a room for secure storage of confidential records, and a pleasant environment, sufficient space, and suitable equipment to meet program goals. An isolation room, if required, should be planned in conjunction with staff offices. The commentary adds that confinement in isolation should be a last resort and that staff should always have the option of confining the juveniles to their own rooms and, if necessary, removing the chairs and tables. Built-in fixtures such as doors, locks, and windows should be domestic in character and encourage normalization.

The standards in Part VI for secure detention facilities are identical to those for secure corrections facilities with respect to general physical requirements, exterior appearance, fixtures, isolation rooms, staff administrative space, secure storage of confidential records, and prohibitions against control centers and permanent staff living quarters. The detention standards differ in their recognition that many of the residents are preadjudicative and therefore presumed innocent and that even adjudicated juveniles awaiting enforcement of a dispositional order are placed in the detention facility on a temporary, short-term basis.

Standard 6.1 describes a secure detention facility as characterized by physically restrictive construction and procedures intended to prevent an accused juvenile from departing at will. Other standards provide that security in the facility should be supportive rather than deterrent and that its internal organization should be clear and unambiguous to minimize uncertainty due to lack of orientaton. As in corrections facilities, the standards recommend that the facility be planned like a large house. Standard 6.3 provides that the capacity of a secure detention facility should be approximately twelve to twenty residents.

Standard 6.8 provides that entrance spaces and waiting rooms in the detention facility should reflect a concern for normalization, the presumption of innocence, and the fact that an appearance before an intake worker may not necessarily result in detention. Location of the facility should take the following factors into account, stated in Standard 6.4:

## 6.4 Location.

Location of secure detention facilities should take the following factors into account:

**A. facilitation of the maintenance of ties between residents and their community, family, and friends;**

**B. accessibility to mass transit and highways to facilitate visits by family and friends;**

**C. accessibility to courts to avoid excessive time spent in transit to and from the court and waiting in court;**

**D. proximity to concentrations of law offices to facilitate attorney-client meetings; and**
**E. use of community settings.**

Secure detention facilities should have interview rooms for residents to meet privately with attorneys and family. No vocational training facilities, chapel, or laundry facilities should be provided in a secure detention facility. The facilities should be certified annually to ensure compliance with safety codes and inspected at least four times a year to ascertain quality of maintenance and ensure against overcrowding. Certification also should include determination of the maximum number of residents the facility may hold.

# PART VII: ADMINISTRATION

## 7.1 Making the System Work.

In the preceding sections, we explored the deficiencies of the current system and presented the proposals for reform of the concepts, roles, procedures, and programs of juvenile courts and other agencies. Now we must look at the administrative problems—lack of planning; inadequate or unproductive monitoring and evaluation; abuse, misuse, and over-accumulation of records and information. These are not trivial defects. Juvenile court judges invariably attribute the impotence of the current system to a lack of resources, but that very inadequacy in large measure is chargeable to misguided administrative decisions. Millions of dollars have been poured into building and operating oversized, inhumane correctional institutions that neither correct juvenile delinquency nor provide security to the community or staff; into treatment programs that do not cure; into diversion programs that divert only briefly; into courts that are inferior in more than status; into probation departments that are too busy collecting data to supervise juveniles; and into voluntary agencies that duplicate unneeded facilities for risk-free placements but turn their backs on the tough cases, the "hard-to-place" aggressive adolescents.

Drafting Committee IV, Administration, has attempted to prevent those ills from infecting the healthy new system proposed by these standards. The volumes approved by the committee are:

*Monitoring*
*Planning for Juvenile Justice*
*Juvenile Records and Information Systems*

All three volumes were adopted by the House of Delegates of the American Bar Association with minimal revisions, as described below.

## 7.2 The Planning Process.

The standards treat planning as an integral part of the administration of juvenile justice. The introduction to *Planning for Juvenile*

*Justice* states the position that planning is a process of innovation and reform that should be performed by officials and practitioners in the system rather than "an emerging class of formally titled 'juvenile justice planners.' " Standard 1.1 provides as follows:

**1.1 Definition of Planning.**
**Planning should be employed within the juvenile justice agencies and among interest groups concerned with juvenile justice to mean the process of applying systematic thought to the future in such a way that a desired future state is conceived and a process for attaining that state is defined and initiated.**
**A. Planning, as defined above, is necessarily both an intellectual process and a political process; because it is future-oriented, it is also necessarily experimental, both in its intellectual methods and its political processes.**
**B. Planning should be a flexible process in which the plan and its implementation are constantly being modified to reflect changes in the purposes of the planners and the environment of planning.**

Standard 1.2 defines the coordination of juvenile justice services as "bringing services into harmony without reducing the authority of component agencies." Coordination of services is restricted to the following conditions:

**1. that it can be shown that greater economies of scale will more than compensate for the costs of coordination efforts;**
**2. that lack of coordination can be demonstrated to result in inequitable distribution of services or resources to juveniles; or**
**3. that clear understanding exists among the agencies to be coordinated concerning the function to be coordinated, the means by which coordination is to take place, and the specific benefit to be realized by each agency and by the client group.**

Most states will find condition 2 easy to satisfy. Inequitable distribution of services or resources to juveniles is one of the classic sins of the system. Conditions 1 and 3 may be less readily established.
Standard 1.3 defines "purposive" duplication of services and specifies conditions for permitting planned duplication as the existence of: a need for greater diversity of services; specialized conditions requiring provision of services on a modified basis for a minority of the

juveniles served by the system; or a particular problem regarded as meriting special attention when a successful model of service is absent. At this time it is difficult to envision a state in which all three conditions do not exist, but perhaps our ideal system will eliminate some of these conditions.

Standard 2.1 creates a juveniles' services agency as a line department at the highest level of the executive board of the state government. Its administrative functions are described as follows:

**Planning for services to juveniles; monitoring and evaluating the quality of services provided throughout the state; allocating state revenues dedicated to juveniles' services; setting standards for personnel practices and service quality; and conducting or administering experimental or demonstration programs; and programs for the most difficult juveniles and those with special needs.**

Standard 2.1 permits geographically centralized provision of *services* to juveniles only under the following conditions:

**1. regional juvenile justice service agencies responsible for the juvenile have attempted and failed to provide services within close geographical proximity to the juvenile's home; or**

**2. the juvenile is a member of a small group whose special needs are provided for through centrally operated programs which could not be provided in each region of the state and which can be demonstrated to be more effective than those programs administered locally.**

While reserving comment on the impact of Standard 2.1 on other standards, we shall consider two other standards, 2.2 and 2.4.

**2.2 Regional juvenile justice service agencies.**

**A. State legislatures should mandate the creation of regional juvenile justice service agencies as subdivisions of the juveniles' services agency. They should be organized at as great a level of geographic decentralization as is consistent with provision of an adequate range and quality of services.**

**B. Regional juvenile justice service agencies should perform the following functions: direct provision of services or treatment, acquisition of services from a purchase of services system, superintendency of community-based services, and coordina-**

tion with any county or local planning or operating agency in its geographical area. They may perform diversion, intake, or probation services.

C. Regional juvenile justice service agencies should be mandated to provide services or treatment to address the needs or behavior of all juvenile delinquents, juveniles who would have been regarded as status offenders, and neglected or abused juveniles. They may also have responsibility for providing services for all orphaned juveniles and all juveniles who, by reason of physical, psychological, or emotional problems, are deemed as being in need of direct care, custody, or supervision by the state.

D. Regional juvenile justice service agencies should be advised by a board composed of people concerned with and affected by the juvenile justice agencies, but not employed by them.

Standard 2.4 creates local juvenile justice boards in all cities and counties of each state with the following functions:

1. monitoring agencies of the purchase of services network located in their geographical areas;
2. supervising or operating juvenile justice services provided at the subregional level;
3. initiating and reviewing proposals for revision of the system of service provision in their areas.

Before we proceed further, a problem should be noted. The administrative scheme in the *Interim Status, The Juvenile Probation Function: Intake and Predisposition Investigative Services, Corrections Administration,* and *Youth Service Agencies* volumes relies on a statewide department in the executive branch for centralized administration and supervision of each public function (detention, probation, corrections), with local implementation, operation, and delivery or responsibility for delivery of service. Thus, the department of corrections has field or local offices, as does the department for probation intake and investigative services. In fact, the family court itself is part of a statewide system, but of the judicial branch of government. The youth service agencies are community-based and charged with the responsibility to provide or arrange for the provision of local social services to juveniles and their families. Therefore, what is the relationship of the agencies and boards created in the *Planning* volume to those other agencies?

While not suggesting that the various schemes are incapable of being reconciled, it is apparent that that task has not been accomplished. In fact, the initial directive in the introduction that planning should be the function of persons working in the system is controverted by the determinedly non-professional membership of the juvenile justice boards (persons "concerned with or affected by the juvenile justice system but not employed by agencies involved in the provision of juvenile justice services"). The purchase of service standards in Standard 2.3 do not alleviate the problem.

In the absence of clarification to the contrary, portions of the *Planning* standards conflict with standards in the other volumes, which assiduously avoided regional superstructures except in circumstances where geography and sparse populations or resources would make regional rather than local operation of facilities or services the only practical approach. See the *Interim Status* volume, commentary at page 47.

Other *Planning* standards are of general application. Standard 3.1 defines planning modes as follows:

**A. Agency planning should be defined as the process of planning the allocation of resources within an agency and the monitoring of its performance to aid innovation of methods of accomplishing the mandate of the agency. It is the overall planning process primarily concerned with maintaining the continued organizational effectiveness of the agency and the process by which the agency alters its mode of operation to adapt to changes in its environment.**

**B. Advocacy planning should be defined as the process of building a constituency for juvenile justice and promoting the shared interests of that constituency in funding, programmatic, and other decisions affecting juvenile justice. As such, it is largely directed outward, focusing on the process of consciously pursuing the interests of juveniles with regard to services.**

**C. Program planning should be defined as the application of the planning process to innovation of approaches to juvenile justice. It is a process cutting across agency and interest group constituencies and responsibilities and is not directed toward the maintenance of any particular organization.**

Three characteristics recommended for the planning process in Standard 3.5 B. are simplicity, focus, and flexibility.

The federal role in planning is described in detail in Standard 4.1.

4.1 The federal role.

A. Federal policy in juvenile justice should be concentrated in two areas: the development of new ideas, both in the form of basic research and through the process of evaluating reform strategies; and the funding of states, localities, and private agencies in support of programs oriented toward innovation.

B. Federal policy concerning juvenile justice should be planned through a process which provides maximum opportunity for participation by the states and which reflects, insofar as possible, the needs of the states.

C. Federal programs directed to the development of new ideas should include at least the following:

1. a national research institute;

2. a continuing program of monitoring and evaluation of all federally funded programs in juvenile justice;

3. appointment of commissions and task forces to address salient issues in juvenile justice as they arise.

D. Federal funds in direct support of juvenile justice agencies and programs should be administered and distributed by a single federal agency; other funds available to juveniles in the juvenile justice system should be planned and coordinated by that agency.

E. Federal juvenile justice policy should encourage reduction of the number of agencies in each jurisdiction, innovation in services and organizational structure, and new approaches to decisionmaking. Federal funding for juvenile justice should be allocated in such a way as to give incentives to states, localities, and private agencies to pursue these purposes.

F. Federal funds for juvenile justice planning and service delivery should be allocated to an agency having authority to perform the function for which the funds are designated, consistent with the mandate of the juveniles' services agency.

G. Federal funds should include money directly allocated for agency and program planning, and indirectly allocated to support advocacy planning through the funding of professional staff.

H. Priority for federal funding in the juvenile justice system should be placed in the following areas: planning and personnel to support planning, demonstration or pilot projects, and incentive awards for agencies to upgrade services or adopt innovations.

I. Federal funds allocated to state, local, and private agencies of juvenile justice should be allocated in support of locally planned and defined programs which respond to more general federally defined policy themes.

The state governors are urged in Standard 4.2 to employ their authority and influence to work toward improving the quality of juvenile justice planning, but even more concretely, to restructure lines of authority within the executive branch to conform to the standards and to exercise overall budgetary control to ensure that adequate and appropriate resources are available for juvenile justice. In Standard 4.3, similar recommendations are addressed to legislators both in Congress and in the states to develop proposals for juvenile justice reform.

## 7.3 Monitoring Programs for Juveniles.

The standards in the *Monitoring* volume are scrupulous in conforming to the concepts of the other volumes in the series, including those on planning. In the introduction to *Monitoring,* the following distinction is expressed, "If planning can be said to be future oriented, monitoring is concerned with the present." The monitoring process is further defined as an activity "concerned with whether and how policy is being carried out and...new policies are being developed and implemented." Standard 1.1 defines monitoring as the "process of overseeing and examining the operations of the various components of the juvenile justice system." The following activities are involved:

1. the determination of data and information needs and the generation or collection of needed data and information;
2. the identification of existing norms or standards for, and objectives of, the operations of various components of the system;
3. the evaluation of whether these operations are in compliance with the applicable standards and meet the stated objectives;
4. the assurance of compliance with standards;
5. the provision of data and evaluations for any necessary alteration of standards or modification of objectives; and
6. the dissemination of findings and conclusions resulting from the activities performed in 1. through 5. above.

Standard 1.2 sets forth the general goals of the monitoring process and monitoring mechanisms. It was amended by adding a new subdivision G. to specify prevention of discrimination as a monitoring goal.

**A. to ensure that all juveniles' substantive and procedural rights are protected, and that all pertinent laws, administrative rules and regulations, and executive or judicial policies pertaining to juveniles are continuously complied with in any executive or judicial process, program, or facility under state or other public or private aegis, within the juvenile justice system;**

**B. to evaluate the fairness, humaneness, availability, and effectiveness of any such executive or judicial process, program, or facility;**

**C. to identify and evaluate alternatives to all forms of coercive intervention in juveniles' lives, including but not limited to coercive intervention at the arrest, pretrial, trial, and disposition stages, and all forms of incarceration or institutionalization; and to conduct or cause to be conducted research on the efficacy of such alternatives;**

**D. to gather, evaluate, and disseminate information to components of the juvenile justice system and to the general public that provides the basis for remedies for illegal, unsound, unfair, or inhumane policies and practices, and that increases public awareness of policies and practices concerning juveniles; and to evaluate the speed, efficacy, and consequences of reform;**

**E. to evaluate the adequacy and effectiveness of existing standards and criteria that apply to decisions made in any executive or judicial process, program, or facility within the juvenile justice system; to identify and evaluate the needs for additional or more comprehensive standards and criteria; and to ensure the uniform application of standards;**

**F. to identify and evaluate the existing documentary, informational, and data bases for monitoring the juvenile justice system, and, if necessary, to develop and implement additional provisions to ensure that information gathering, data collection, written records, and record maintenance are adequate for monitoring purposes;**

**G. to prevent discrimination in the juvenile justice system on the basis of race, sex, age, language, or family background.**

Maximum access to, usage, and dissemination of information commensurate with the rights of privacy and confidentiality as balanced against the particular monitoring function is the common-sense guideline prescribed in Standard 1.6.

**A. Each jurisdiction should adopt laws and institute practices that will ensure that each monitoring mechanism:**

**1. is afforded the broadest possible access, relevant to its particular function and consistent with notions of privacy, to all appropriate information, records, data, and staff of the judicial or executive process, agency, program, or facility that is being monitored;**

**2. has necessary powers to conduct investigations, secure testimony and production of documents, and perform on-site inspections of agencies, facilities, and institutions. Such powers, however, should be no broader than is reasonably sufficient for, commensurate with, and essential to the given monitoring mechanism's performance of its functions.**

Appropriate methods of obtaining relevant information should include collection of pertinent reports, data, and records; on-site visits; interviews with staff and affected juveniles; and investigative hearings. The standard for monitoring activities involving records that contain identifying information is described in 1.6 B. 2. as follows:

**a. that fact alone should not be a basis for denying access to the records;**

**b. all necessary steps should first be taken by the agency to prevent disclosure of the identities of juveniles who are the subjects of the records;**

**c. if it is not possible to expunge identifying characteristics, access to the records should be denied the monitor;**

**d. under all circumstances monitors and agencies should be subject to the provisions of the** *Juvenile Records and Information Systems* **volume with respect to disclosure of the identities of the juveniles who are the subjects of the records, including any applicable civil and criminal penalties for improper collection, retention, or dissemination of information pertaining to juveniles.**

Standard 1.6 D. recommends regular and periodic publication and dissemination of reports, findings, and recommendations to the public, the legislature, agencies, programs, facilities, and other monitoring mechanisms, using all appropriate media to accomplish the widest possible dissemination. The caveat that the concept of confidentiality and individual privacy be observed is added but not amplified.

Appropriate powers granted to the monitoring mechanism to propose reforms and improvements and to enforce compliance with laws, rules, regulations, standards, and proposed reforms is defined in Standard 1.7 to include the authority:

**1. to draft and disseminate proposals for changes in legislation, administrative rules and regulations, executive or judicial policies, practices, and the like relating to any process, program, or facility for juveniles, based on information gathered pursuant to monitoring activities;**

**2. to require agencies responsible for any process, program, or facility for juveniles to produce plans or procedures to correct problems or improve policies and practices;**

**3. to appoint masters or ombudsmen to agencies or facilities, when necessary, to oversee the implementation of reforms or improvements in accordance with the plans developed;**

**4. to bring suit when remedies are not implemented or are implemented improperly.**

Monitoring focal points—the areas in which the monitoring mechanisms should concentrate—as covered in Standards 2.1 through 2.6 are discretionary decisions; guaranteed rights of any person under the jurisdiction of a component of the juvenile justice system; mandatory provisions, duties, and obligations of any component (agency, process, program, or facility) being monitored; organizational aspects and operational functions of the component; record and information bases for decision making, protection of rights, performance of mandatory duties and established procedures; and consumer or user (juveniles and families) participation in monitoring the services, programs, and facilities.

The balance of the standards expand upon the specific monitoring mechanisms enumerated in the general standards: attorneys, a state commission on juvenile advocacy, community advisory councils, legislative committees, ombudsmen, private citizen groups, the courts, and internal monitoring of the agencies themselves. Standard 1.3 A. was amended to add educators to the enumerated external monitoring mechanisms.

With respect to defense counsel or counsel for private parties, Standard 3.1 notes that primary responsibility for monitoring individual cases rests with the juvenile's counsel. Therefore, the legislature should give priority to funding programs that provide counsel for juveniles, including adequate funding for support services. Standard 3.2 recommends establishment of a lawyer's committee of the bar association composed of lawyers representing juveniles to monitor the activities of the juvenile justice agencies.

The monitoring duties of the proposed commission on juvenile advocacy, appointed by the governor and composed of no more than a bare majority of any one political party, are described in Standard 4.2 as including the evaluation of all aspects of the juvenile justice system within the state; drafting, disseminating, and conducting hearings on proposals for changes in the laws, policies, and practices governing the system; publishing periodic reports on its findings; appointing consultants to oversee the implementation of remedies affecting juveniles; and staffing temporarily any committees probing children's problems or issues. Its powers include bringing suit against an agency when proposed remedies are not being implemented properly. It should be noted that *Prosecution* Standard 7.2 imposes a duty on the juvenile prosecutor to monitor the effectiveness of dispositions imposed on adjudicated delinquents.

The community advisory councils created under Standard 5.1 are given the duty to report findings resulting from their monitoring function to the agencies, the community, and the commission on juvenile advocacy, but they have no enforcement powers.

Legislative committees to monitor the juvenile justice system are given broad powers in Standard 6.3, to hold hearings, conduct investigations, subpoena witnesses or records, impose sanctions for failure to comply with the committees' directives, publish reports and findings, and other appropriate legislative functions, which would include the important duties of drafting and reviewing legislation and appropriations affecting the juvenile justice system.

An ombudsman is defined in Standard 7.1 as a government official who investigates complaints by private citizens against government agencies, specifically public and private juvenile agencies. The need for an ombudsman in a particular agency should be based on the following criteria:

**1. the degree of visibility of the decision makers, decisions, and activities of the agency to other mechanisms;**

**2. the frequency and adequacy of the monitoring of the decision makers, decisions, and activities of the agency by other mechanisms;**

**3. the availability, promptness, and adequacy of review for any person aggrieved by a decision or activity of the agency;**

4. the degree of harm that might occur to an aggrieved person resulting from a decision or activity not subject to prompt and immediate investigation and review;

5. the existence and adequacy of remedies available to a person aggrieved by a decision or activity of the agency; and

6. the responsiveness of the agency in the past in correcting and eliminating discovered abuses of discretion or improper actions.

The ombudsman's powers are limited to investigating complaints and recommending action. They do not include taking direct action to carry out the recommendations. The ombudsman would be appointed by the commission on juvenile advocacy, whose duty it would be to receive the reports and act on the recommendations. If no commission exists, an ombudsman's office should be established.

Standards 8.1 and 8.2 on private sector monitoring include independent research and evaluation activities and juveniles' rights advocacy organizations.

The standards for the courts as a monitoring mechanism are broadly inclusive, covering the range of the courts' traditional activities that might provide an opportunity to observe the operation of the juvenile justice system, as well as the invocation of inherent powers to require individuals or agencies within its jurisdiction "to adopt and comply with practices designed to provide a basis for monitoring." Standard 9.2 on the juvenile court refers to the judges' duty to inspect facilities and to appoint an officer of the court with full-time responsibility for monitoring activities. Standard 9.3 on the appellate process does not appear to extend monitoring beyond appeals of final orders of the juvenile court and publication of all decisions relating to such appeals. Civil court monitoring under Standard 9.4 includes appointment of a master to monitor the implementation of court orders in appropriate cases.

The final mechanism for monitoring the juvenile justice system is self-monitoring by the agencies. The general principles governing internal monitoring activities are covered in Standard 10.1.

A. Self-monitoring activities conducted by juvenile justice agencies should be performed in accordance with the applicable provisions of these standards.

B. Each agency should monitor its activities on a continuous basis to ensure that it is discharging its duties and obligations and observing mandatory provisions in accordance with the standards applicable to its functions.

C. Each agency should:

1. identify the key decisions it makes with respect to the processing of juveniles and their parents under its authority;

2. develop criteria and guidelines to be applied by agency personnel to the decision-making process, when the exercise of discretion is permitted; and

3. closely scrutinize the decisions made by its personnel to ensure that guidelines and criteria are being properly applied.

D. Each agency should ensure that rules or regulations requiring documentation of discretionary decisions, sufficient for monitoring requirements, are developed and complied with in order to facilitate both the agency's self-monitoring activities and the monitoring activities conducted by other mechanisms. Such documentation should be specific and should include:

1. the reasons and supporting facts relied upon for the decision;

2. the options considered; and

3. the reasons for rejecting any and all less intrusive and less coercive options.

E. Each agency should prepare frequent, periodic reports, summarizing the activities of and the actions taken by the agency, and evaluating these and the agency's organizational and administrative functions in terms of efficiency in cost and time involved, results obtained, objectives achieved, compliance with rules, regulations, criteria, or standards, and other similar considerations. These reports should be distributed to the appropriate supervising authority, if any, to the appropriate external, independent monitoring mechanisms, and to the public through publication by any appropriate media.

F. Each agency should assist and cooperate fully with mechanisms assigned to monitor the agency. Each agency should promptly implement the recommendations of such monitoring mechanisms.

## 7.4 Records and Information Systems.

The *Juvenile Records and Information Systems* volume is impressive, both for quality and sheer bulk. The twenty-two standards, and multiple subdivisions thereof, are arranged in four parts: general standards (I to V); specific standards for social and psychological histories (VI to X); specific standards for juvenile court reports (XI to XVIII); and standards for police records (XIX to XXII). Parts II and III are intended to supplement Part I. Part IV provides self-contained standards pertaining to police, as law enforcement agencies were excluded from the coverage of the first three parts.

### 7.4.1. General standards on juvenile records.

The definitions in Standards 1.1 through 1.11 are essential to an understanding of the standards in this volume and in the other volumes in the series. Standard 1.1 defines a juvenile agency as any public or private agency providing clinical, evaluative, counseling, medical, educational, or residential services to a juvenile *and* any court (other than one for divorce or adoptions) with legal authority to issue orders pertaining to a juvenile's custody or liberty. Thus we see an express exception from coverage for those outcasts of our family court, divorce and adoption. It also might be recalled that the *Monitoring* volume treated all courts as external monitoring mechanisms, whereas this and other volumes include juvenile courts in the definition of a juvenile agency.

A juvenile in Standard 1.2 is any person who is under the age of eighteen or who as a result of a delinquency or neglect petition is subject to confinement, probation, release, or other reduction of liberty.

Standard 1.3 limits juvenile records to records in the custody of a juvenile agency and *in which the juvenile may be identified*. Parents are defined under Standards 1.4 and 1.5 to include a "surrogate parent"—a legal guardian or an adult who has voluntarily assumed the role of parent, but not an agency or institution or employee thereof.

In Standards 1.6, 1.7, and 1.8, "indirect access" is distinguished from access and direct access as including the right to receive information but *not* the rights to view or photocopy the actual record; "access" as the right to view and photocopy the record but *not* the right to enter the place where the record is stored; and "direct access" as encompassing the right to enter the storage place and withdraw the record so that it may be observed by an authorized person for an authorized purpose.

A centralized information system is described in Standard 1.11 as one in which two or more juvenile agencies participate for information pertaining to identifiable juveniles.

Standards 2.1 to 2.8 establish mechanisms to protect against the improper collection, retention, or dissemination of a juvenile record or information pertaining to identifiable juveniles. The mechanisms prescribed are: for each jurisdiction to establish a juveniles' privacy committee and to promulgate statutes creating tort liability as a civil remedy and a misdemeanor as a criminal remedy; for juvenile agencies to adopt administrative sanctions for violation of any law or rule of the agency, procedures for correction of records, periodic audits to verify adequate controls to ensure accuracy and completeness of records, training programs and operations manuals for agency personnel; and for statutes providing that information collected or retained by an approved researcher or evaluator is privileged.

The watchdog mechanism with enforcement powers is the privacy committee created by Standard 2.1, as follows:

**2.1 Juveniles' privacy committee.**

**A. Each jurisdiction should establish by statute at least one juveniles' privacy committee. The members of the committee should include persons who have knowledge and expertise in juvenile advocacy, delivery of services to juveniles, information systems, and criminal justice agency activities affecting juveniles.**

**B. The committee should have the authority to examine and evaluate juvenile records and information issues pertaining to juveniles and the right to conduct such inquiries and investigations as it deems necessary.**

**C. The committee should periodically make recommendations concerning privacy, juvenile records, and information practices and policies pertaining to juveniles.**

**D. The committee should have the authority to receive automation statements submitted by juvenile agencies pursuant to Standard 4.6, in order to computerize juvenile records.**

**E. The committee should have the authority to receive proposals submitted by juvenile agencies to establish a centralized information system.**

**F. The committee should have the authority to commence civil actions against juvenile agencies for declaratory judgments, cease and desist orders, and other appropriate injunctive relief in cases involving the failure to promulgate written rules and regulations pursuant to Standard 2.2 or the improper collection, retention, or dissemination of a juvenile record or identifiable information pertaining to juveniles.**

Some concepts for agencies to take into account in promulgating rules and regulations governing the *collection* of information appear in Standard 3.1:

**A. too much as well as too little information can inhibit the process of decision;**

**B. the need for information increases as the options available to the decision maker increase and decreases as the available options decrease; and**

**C. information that is collected is often misused, misinterpreted, or not used.**

The only permissible purposes for which an agency should collect information are limited in Standard 3.2 to making lawful decisions pertaining to juveniles, managing or evaluating the agency, and approved research. Standards for collection of information pertaining to an identifiable juvenile require, in Standard 3.3, that:

**A. reasonable safeguards have been established to protect against the misuse, misinterpretation, and improper dissemination of the information;**

**B. the information is both relevant and necessary to a proper purpose for collecting the information;**

**C. the information will be utilized within a reasonable period of time for a proper purpose;**

**D. an evaluation (conducted pursuant to Standard 3.4) indicates that it would be reasonable to rely upon the type of information for the purposes for which it is collected;**

**E. the cost of collecting the information, considered in relation to the significance of the purpose for collecting the information, does not appear to be excessive;**

**F. the collection of the information does not involve an invasion of privacy; and**

**G. it is reasonable to expect that the information collected will be accurate.**

Standard 3.4 requires agencies to prepare periodic written evaluations of their information collection practices and policies, which should be available as public records.

If information collected for research or evaluation concerns identifiable juveniles, Standard 3.5 requires the written consent of juveniles over the age of fifteen and their parents. Standard 3.6 requires that an agency should collect no information of a personal nature from a juvenile over the age of ten, without first informing the juvenile of those who have a right of access to the information. A parent should be so informed if the juvenile is not over the age of ten.

Standards 4.1 to 4.7 cover information *retention*. Retention of information is a separate decision from the initial decision to collect the information. Standard 4.2 for the retention of information reads:

A. the information is collectible, as set forth in Standard 3.3;

B. the information is accurate;

C. it is reasonable to expect that the information will be utilized at a later time;

D. reasonable safeguards have been established to protect against the misuse, misinterpretation, and improper dissemination of the information; and

E. it is likely that retaining the information in written or other retrievable form will ensure that the information will be recalled more accurately; or

F. the information has been collected as a part of a formal judicial or administrative proceeding.

An agency should not retain a juvenile record without making a reasonable effort to notify the juvenile and the juvenile's parent, if the parent has a right of access to the record. Such notice should include information that there is a right to challenge the accuracy of the record. Standard 4.3 was amended to change "information" to "record" to indicate that the duty of the record retainer is to notify as to the existence of a record and not the information contained therein.

Standard 4.5 on limited use of labels provides:

**A juvenile record should not include summary conclusions or labels describing an identified juvenile's behavioral, social, medical, or psychological history or predicting an identified juvenile's future behavior, capacity, or attitudes unless the underlying factual basis, meaning, and implications are explained in terms that are understandable to a nonprofessional person, and their use is necessary.**

As might be guessed, the restrictions on retention of information in computers are extensive, including submission of an "automation statement" to the juvenile's privacy committee for evaluation and comment, a requirement that identifiable data be objective and factual and not subjective or predictive, and that juveniles be identified by an arbitrary nonduplicating number instead of by name.

Centralized record-keeping also is limited, specifically to the minimum data necessary to identify the juvenile, the names of the agencies that have provided or will provide services to the juvenile or family, and the dates on which those services were or will be provided.

Standards 5.1 through 5.7 cover *access* to juvenile records. Direct access by agency personnel should be limited to the minimum number necessary of persons specifically designated by the agency's chief administrator, and no access should be permitted except for the purpose of providing services or for other proper agency purposes. Juveniles and their parents and attorneys should be given access to their records unless the information is likely to cause harm or, if the information was obtained in connection with services the juvenile had a legal right to receive without parental consent, the record should not be disclosed to the parents without the juvenile's full informed written consent.

Access by third persons to a juvenile record is strictly restricted to situations of informed consent, such consent to be obtained from juveniles over the age of ten and their parents if the parents have a right of access and from juveniles alone if emancipated or over the age of fifteen, if the information has been reevaluated within the past ninety days and found accurate, or if there is a statement of the last date of review and a warning that conditions may have changed since that date, if disclosure is appropriate, and if the person signs a nondisclosure agreement. These restrictions on access by third persons do not apply if a compelling health and safety need exists and disclosure is made to a court for the purpose of obtaining consent. Standard 5.4 was amended to add the statement and warning concerning the last date of review as an alternative to ninety-day review, and to limit the conditions for disclosure from a "bona fide emergency" to a "compelling health and safety need."

Anyone who seeks access for research or evaluation must file a written application with the juvenile agency and a copy with the privacy committee. The agency should approve the application if the applicant has adequate training and qualifications for the project and the project is for valid educational, scientific, or other public purposes, the anonymity of the juveniles will be preserved, and no information will be reproduced, except for internal purposes, or disclosed to an unauthorized person. Final reports of the projects should be a public record and should be presented so that juveniles cannot be identified. If an application is disapproved, the applicant should have the right to appeal to a court of general jurisdiction.

Standard 5.7 specifies that access should not be provided to a law enforcement agency unless required consent is obtained *or* a judge determines, after *in camera* examination of the record, that such access is relevant and necessary. Standard 5.7 A. originally read in the conjunctive, but "and" was changed to "or" concerning access to a law enforcement agency.

Juvenile records should only be produced for a legal proceeding pursuant to a subpoena.

Juvenile records, except juvenile court records, should not be admissible unless the juvenile or parents consent as required above and the record or information is otherwise admissible, or a judge determines, after *in camera* examination of the record, that it is not all or part of a social or psychological history (prepared by or for an agency other than a juvenile court), that it is relevant and necessary, and that admission is warranted despite the juvenile's expectation of privacy.

Standard 5.8 requires rules and regulations providing for periodic *destruction* of juvenile records based on such criteria as: death of the subject, age of the record, likelihood that the record will not be useful to the agency or juvenile in the future, and the benefits from retention are outweighed by risk of harm to the juvenile if it is improperly disseminated. Whenever possible, the agency should give the juvenile an opportunity to get a copy of the record before it is destroyed, if retention by the juvenile might be useful.

### 7.4.2 Social and psychological histories.

To some extent, the standards governing social histories reiterate the general standards covered in section 7.4.1 and will be treated accordingly.

Standard 6.1 defines a social or psychological history as information retained in a retrievable form by a juvenile agency, pertaining to an identifiable juvenile's family, social, or psychological background, for the purposes of: providing counseling; deciding whether to confer or deny a service, a placement, or other benefit to the juvenile; predicting whether the juvenile will engage in future antisocial conduct; and determining the disposition of a juvenile case before or after adjudication as a delinquent or neglected juvenile.

Anyone familiar with the proposed standards will be alerted to the care, if not reluctance, with which social and psychological material will be permitted to be disseminated. Positions challenging the value of predictive judgments, rejecting the presumption that services, placements, or other interventions are benefits unless voluntarily accepted, and resisting the accumulation and use in the decision-making process of social information that may be subjective, irrelevant, or hearsay compel the records and information standards to impose tight restrictions on collection, retention, and use of social and psychological histories.

The duty to inform a juvenile over the age of ten and a parent of the preparation of the history before information is collected for that purpose is covered in Standard 7.1. The juvenile must be informed of the purposes of the history, the persons and agencies likely to have access and those likely to be contacted to provide information, the persons who will prepare the history and their qualifications, and the juvenile's and others' right to deny consent to its preparation. The parent should be given the same information, unless the agency preparing the information is not a juvenile court or is not acting for a juvenile court and the history is to be prepared in connection with provision of counseling, psychological, psychiatric, or medical services that the juvenile has a legal right to receive without parental consent. Standard 7.2 requires prior consent to preparation of the history from juveniles who are emancipated or over the age of fifteen, or if the history is being prepared in connection with services that the juvenile has a legal right to receive without parental consent, and from a parent if the services may only be provided with parental consent, unless the history is being prepared by or for an agency other than a juvenile court.

Standard 8.1 requires agencies to account for and ensure the security of social histories.

Access to social histories is restricted by Standard 9.1 to juveniles, their parents, and attorneys, as provided in the general standards, requiring that the history be translated into their native language if it is not English and that professional language or information that may not be understood be explained to them. The contents are confidential and should not be disclosed without informed consent. If the history was prepared for another agency or is released to a third person, it should not be released in summary form. A detailed explanation of any diagnosis or conclusion should be included and labels may be used only in accordance with the general standards.

Standard 10.1 describes the agency's duty to destroy the history if the agency is not an institution or court that has custody or control of the juvenile and the juvenile has become eighteen years of age, unless the juvenile objects within thirty days of receiving written notice. If the juvenile is subject to the custody or control of a court or institution beyond the age of eighteen, the history should be destroyed within 180 days of the juvenile's release from custody or control. If the agency has closed the case, it may destroy the history and all reference to it prior to the juvenile's eighteenth birthday. The juvenile should receive upon request a copy of the history prior to destruction. After destroying the history, the agency should notify all other agencies to which copies were sent that all references in their files should be destroyed immediately.

### 7.4.3 Juvenile court records.

Standards 11.1 through 18.4 pertaining to juvenile court records cover the records of legal proceedings and probation records. Standards

11.1 and 11.2 require the legislature of each jurisdiction to enact a comprehensive statute regulating juvenile courts' collection, retention, dissemination, and use of information and records.

Each juvenile court is required to maintain complete records of all proceedings involving juveniles, including summary records, case indexes, case files, and statistical records. Records of proceedings should be kept separate from probation records.

The summary record of the proceedings should be limited to objective data, including the nature of the complaint, a summary of all formal proceedings, and the results thereof. It should *not* include probation records, subjective or evaluative information, or data of an identifying nature, such as the name and address of a juvenile or parent. It should be assigned a number when the matter is first referred to the court, which should appear on all subsequent court records pertaining to the juvenile. Summary records of active and closed cases should be maintained separately in a secure place separate from adult court records.

Indexes to active and closed cases also should be kept separate and secure. Case indexes should be maintained alphabetically by the juvenile's name, and should include only the name, address, and age of the juvenile, the parent's name and address, and the file number referred to above. The court personnel who are permitted direct access to case indexes should be designated in writing by the court and the number limited. The official indexes should be the only system for access to the records.

The case file on each case should include all formal documents, such as the complaint or petition, summaries, warrants, motions, legal memoranda, judicial orders or decrees, but not social histories. Case files of active and closed cases should be maintained separately and securely.

Each court should prepare a monthly and annual statistical report of all juvenile proceedings, with maximum aggregate data, using standardized forms developed by the chief justice of the highest court to ensure uniformity.

All probation records should be placed in a temporary or a permanent probation file. Probation records of active and closed cases should be kept separately and securely. A temporary probation file should contain all unverified or unevaluated information being collected for an active case and all the probation officer's working papers and notes. All information collected and retained in the temporary file should be destroyed within three months after collection or within ten days after the case has been closed, whichever is sooner. The permanent probation file should contain only information determined by a probation officer to be verified and accurate and should be the only file or information provided to a judge by a probation officer for case disposition purposes. Before reporting to the court, the probation officer should review and explain the contents of the report and permanent file with the juvenile, parents, and attorney unless disclosure is likely to cause harm; they should be informed that they have the right and be given the opportunity to make additions or corrections to the report. The court has the duty to regulate information practices of outside agencies through written rules and regulations protecting the confidentiality and security of the court records.

Juvenile records should not be public records. Access and use should be strictly controlled to limit the risk that disclosure will result in misuse or misinterpretation of information, denial of opportunities and benefits to juveniles, or interference with the purposes of official intervention. Access to case files should be limited to the juvenile, parents, attorney, prosecutor, a party and his or her attorney, judge, probation or other professional person assigned to the case, researcher granted access under the general standards, and designated court personnel for authorized internal administrative purposes. Access to summary records should be limited to those persons permitted access to the case file plus the state correctional agency if the juvenile is detained or otherwise subject to its custody or control, the state department of motor vehicles if access is limited to information on traffic offenses for regulating car licensing, and a law enforcement agency for execution of an arrest warrant or other compulsory process or for a current investigation. Direct access to or disclosure of information from a summary record is prohibited except as provided above; indirect access may be provided with written consent of the juvenile and parents if disclosure of summary information is necessary to secure services or a benefit for the juvenile. The same access rules for case files and summary records apply to permanent probation files. Waiver of access rules is prohibited—consent of the juvenile, parent, or attorney is insufficient to authorize access to persons not expressly authorized under these standards. Any person other than the juvenile, parent, and attorney to whom a juvenile record is to be disclosed should be required to execute a nondisclosure agreement barring disclosure to an unauthorized person.

Rules and regulations should be promulgated for a procedure by which a juvenile or representative may challenge the correctness of a record and for notice to the juvenile of the availability of such a procedure.

The standards on destruction of juvenile court records provide that all unnecessary information in records that identify the juvenile should be destroyed. In cases involving delinquency complaints, all identifying records should be destroyed when the application for the complaint is denied, the complaint or petition is dismissed, or the juvenile is adjudicated not delinquent. In cases of adjudicated delinquents, all identifying records should be destroyed when no subsequent proceeding is pending, the juvenile has been discharged from the supervision of the court or the correctional agency, two years have elapsed from the date of such discharge, and the juvenile has not been adjudicated delinquent for a felony offense. In neglect cases, all identifying records should be destroyed when no subsequent proceeding is pending on a neglect or delinquency petition, the juvenile is no longer subject to a disposition order, and the youngest sibling is over sixteen. All other agencies (police, corrections, probation, etc.) that the court has reason to believe have received a copy of any portion of the record destroyed or possess any notation of the record in their own records should be notified of the destruction and required to destroy any copies or notations of the record. Before destruction, the court should offer the juvenile a copy. After destruction, the court should send the juvenile a written notice that he or she has no record with respect to the matter involved and if it involved delinquency, the juvenile may inform anyone that he or she was not arrested or adjudicated delinquent, unless called as a witness in a criminal or delinquency case and the juvenile is required by the judge to disclose that he or she was adjudicated delinquent. Whenever a juvenile's record is destroyed, the proceeding may be deemed to have never occurred and the juvenile may so inform any person or organization.

Standard 18.1 on use of juvenile records by third persons provides that:

**Public and private employers, licensing authorities, credit companies, insurance companies, banks, and educational institutions should be prohibited from inquiring, directly or indirectly, and from seeking any information relating to whether a person has been arrested as a juvenile, charged with committing a delinquent act, adjudicated delinquent, or sentenced to a juvenile institution, except the state agency or department responsible for juvenile justice may be authorized to inquire and seek such information pertaining to persons being considered for positions requiring ex-offenders.**

The exception concerning jobs for ex-offenders was added to revised Standard 18.1.

With respect to application forms, Standard 18.2 states:

**All applications for licenses, employment, credit, insurance, or schooling, used by a licensing authority, employer, credit company, insurance company, bank, or educational institution, which seek information concerning the arrests or convictions or**

criminal history of the applicant should include the following statement: "It is unlawful for a licensing authority, employer, credit company, insurance company, bank, or educational institution to ask you, directly or indirectly, whether you have been arrested as a juvenile, charged with committing a delinquent act, adjudicated a delinquent, or sentenced to a juvenile institution. If you have been asked to disclose such information, you should report that fact to the state attorney general. If you have a juvenile record, you may answer that you have never been arrested, charged, or adjudicated delinquent for committing a delinquent act or sentenced to a juvenile institution."

If a person not authorized to receive record information seeks it, the person to whom the request is made should reply that no record exists. If the information is sought on behalf of an employer, credit company, insurance company, bank, licensing authority, or educational institution, the person to whom the request was made should report the matter to the state attorney general.

As to admissibility in evidence of juvenile court records, Standard 18.4 C. was amended to provide that evidence could not be rendered admissible or inadmissible in a criminal trial by its introduction during a waiver hearing. Standard 18.4 provides as follows:

An adjudication of any juvenile as a delinquent, or the disposition ordered upon such an adjudication, or any information or record obtained in any case involving such a proceeding, should not be lawful or proper evidence against such juvenile for any purpose in any proceeding except:

A. in subsequent proceedings against the same juvenile for purposes of disposition or sentencing, if the record of the prior proceeding has not been destroyed;

B. in an appeal of the same case, information or records obtained for or utilized in the initial trial of the matter should be admissible upon appeal, if the information or record is otherwise lawful and proper evidence; and

C. in a criminal trial involving the same matter after waiver of juvenile court jurisdiction. Evidence not otherwise admissible in a criminal trial is not made admissible by its being introduced at the waiver hearing.

### 7.4.4 Police records.

The standards for police records contained in Standards 19.1 through 22.1 are intended to apply to criminal history records pertaining to juveniles and not to cover all questions of police information systems and practices concerning juveniles.

The general standard on rules and regulations requires each law enforcement agency to promulgate rules and regulations on collection, retention, and dissemination of records pertaining to juveniles, taking into account the need of law enforcement agencies for detailed and accurate information concerning crimes committed by juveniles and police contacts with juveniles, the risk that information may be misused and misinterpreted, and the need of juveniles to mature into adulthood without the stigma of a police record. All information on arrest, detention, and disposition of a case involving a juvenile should be complete, accurate, and up to date. A person or persons responsible for the collection, retention, and dissemination of law enforcement records pertaining to juveniles should be designated. The records should be kept in a secure place separate from adult records. The agencies should keep a record of all persons and organizations to whom information is released.

Standard 19.6 includes detailed provisions on the taking, retaining, using, filing, and destroying of juveniles' fingerprints and photographs. In general, if the crime charged is a felony, police may take prints but the card and all copies should be destroyed if the juvenile is not adjudicated delinquent for the alleged felony and it may be retained if the juvenile is adjudicated. Juveniles in custody may be photographed for criminal identification only if necessary for a pending investigation and the photographs should be destroyed unless the juvenile is found delinquent. Willful violation of this standard would be a misdemeanor.

Monthly and annual statistical reports with maximum aggregate data on crimes committed by juveniles should be prepared. Standardized forms should be developed for collecting and reporting data to insure uniformity. The juveniles' privacy committee established in Standard 2.1 should have authority with respect to law enforcement records pertaining to juvenile arrest, detention, and disposition.

Police records and files should not be public records, but juveniles, their parents, and their attorneys should be given access to all such records. Standard 20.3 covers disclosure to third persons as follows:

**A. Information contained in law enforcement records and files pertaining to juveniles may be disclosed to:**

    **1. law enforcement officers of any jurisdiction for law enforcement purposes;**

    **2. a probation officer, judge, or prosecutor for purposes of executing the responsibilities of his or her position in a matter relating to the juvenile who is the subject of the record;**

3. the state juvenile correctional agency if the juvenile is currently committed to the agency;

4. a person to whom it is necessary to disclose information for the limited purposes of investigating a crime, apprehending a juvenile, or determining whether to detain a juvenile;

5. a person who meets the criteria of Standards 5.6 and 5.7.

B. Information contained in law enforcement records and files pertaining to a juvenile should not be released to law enforcement officers of another jurisdiction unless the juvenile was adjudicated delinquent or convicted of a crime or unless there is an outstanding arrest warrant for the juvenile.

C. Information that is released pertaining to a juvenile should include the disposition or current status of the case.

When information concerning a juvenile is to be disclosed to a police agency outside of the jurisdiction, that agency should be advised that the information may be disclosed only to police personnel, probation officers, judges, and prosecutors currently concerned with the juvenile and that a nondisclosure agreement must be executed by the agency.

The standards for responses to police record inquiries are the same as those for court records. The agency should adopt rules and regulations permitting juveniles or their representatives to challenge the correctness of police records.

Standard 22.1 describes the procedure and timing of destruction of police records.

Upon receipt of notice from a juvenile court that a juvenile record has been destroyed or if a juvenile is arrested or detained and has not been referred to a court, a law enforcement agency should destroy all information pertaining to the matter in all records and files, except that if the chief law enforcement officer of the agency, or his or her designee, certifies in writing that certain information is needed for a pending investigation involving the commission of a felony, that information, and information identifying the juvenile, may be retained in an intelligence file until the investigation is terminated or for one additional year, whichever is sooner.

# PART VIII: FUTURE IMPACT OF THE JUVENILE JUSTICE STANDARDS

## 8.1 Great Expectations.

Now that the IJA-ABA Joint Commission, its executive committee, and the ABA have completed the task of devising a comprehensive series of standards for juvenile justice, the proponents of the standards must enter a new phase. The preceding chapters of this book have described the background and accomplishments of the Juvenile Justice Standards Project. The balance of the volume will focus on the author's personal analysis of the current situation, including the factors contributing to the anticipated reception of the standards and suggestions for future plans to achieve maximum impact.

The vast quantities of money, time, energy, and skill that went into the formulation of the juvenile justice standards were not expended as an academic exercise, nor were the volumes of standards and commentary published merely to enrich the literature in the field. After the project assessed the problems in the system, the goal became the reform of the juvenile justice system as a whole—a revolution, not just another phase of the evolution.

If they are to accomplish so ambitious a mission, the standards cannot be permitted to languish on library shelves. They must be adopted and implemented, with an impact that is immediate and eloquent. Patchwork, incremental improvements, a sprinkling of statutory revisions and new rules, will not suffice.

Studies of the national impact of the ABA Criminal Justice Standards Project have shown us the hazards that await a gradual implementation. As time elapses, new issues arise, old problems require reevaluation, and unforeseen decisions, federal rules, or new funding sources create situations the standards may never have addressed. The proposed brave new world can become outdated without ever having arrived. And the untenable concepts, violations of basic rights, and ineffective mechanisms that permeate the existing system can be papered over with diversionary modifications. Thus, the status quo manages to survive the threat of fundamental change.

275

The best defense against gradualism and its inevitable erosion of broad systemic reforms is to acquaint influential persons and organizations with the essential elements in the standards and mobilize them into forceful action. Time must be recognized as an enemy. Time has not improved the system from the point of view of the children it was designed to help or the community to be protected. After ten years of intensive and meticulous efforts to develop a new system, after drafting, deliberating, revising, and finally approving a comprehensive set of standards to govern that system, the time has arrived to move forward courageously and complete the process. This chapter will be devoted to discussing the steps to be taken, the strategies to be pursued, and the pitfalls to be avoided. We will conclude with an evaluation of the standards and an estimate of their prospects for national acceptance.

## 8.2 Pre-implementation Action.

Several crucial steps remain before adequately financed and officially supported action to implement the standards can commence.

At the time the first edition of this summary volume was completed (March 1977), all of the volumes had been approved by the IJA-ABA Joint Commission and all were in page proof form. The *Counsel for Private Parties* volume had been published in soft cover as a tentative draft and was about to be distributed. The publication phase was due to be completed by July 1977.

Therefore, all substantive issues had been resolved within the project but outside reactions were still sparse and necessarily ill-informed. There had been some preliminary press coverage based on several news releases and informational materials prepared by the project staff. Members of the staff, the drafting committee, and the Commission, as well as the reporters, had participated in various symposia, conferences, lectures, and other meetings concerned with juvenile justice throughout the life of the project. Some were called upon to testify before legislative committees. Many requests for technical assistance from a variety of civic organizations and reform groups were received by the project staff and other participants, who complied within the limits of available time and resources. Some articles were written and published, such as "Of Juvenile Justice and Injustice," by the Honorable Irving R. Kaufman, then Chief Judge of the Second Circuit of the United States Court of Appeals and Chairman of the Commission, which appeared in the *ABA Journal* in 1976.

Thus, a great deal of advance information did filter out during the five years in which the standards were formulated and the volumes drafted. Unfortunately, most of it was fragmented, tentative, and incomplete. And some was inaccurate. Early drafts were "pirated" and circulated, leading to confusion as the drafts were revised.

Distribution of the volumes began to dispel the confusion and misunderstanding. By introducing the persons involved in the operation of the juvenile justice system and other concerned individuals and organizations to the actual contents and purposes of the proposed standards, rational discussion was initiated. Members of the ABA sections on criminal justice, family law, individual rights and responsibilities, young lawyers, judicial administration, and a special committee of the House of Delegates were among those to whom copies of the published volumes were sent. The National Council of Juvenile and Family Court Judges, National Association of Social Workers, National District Attorneys Association, and the multitude of local, state, and national organizations of judges, probation workers, police, public defenders, prosecutors, corrections officers, and other juvenile justice specialists also were on the mailing lists for the published volumes. Their interest was legitimate and intense. The professions had direct or indirect representation in the preparation of the volumes through membership on the Commission, the drafting committees, or working groups. However, their views did not always prevail. Some practitioners in the juvenile justice system objected to the proposed standards—not surprisingly, since it is they who were most immediately affected by changes in the system. Their responses to the published standards were transmitted to a project representative at the Institute of Judicial Administration and conveyed to the executive committee of the Commission. Revised standards, expanded commentary, or some other corrective or clarifying action were considered by the executive committee, and instructions for final revisions were issued. As discussed more fully in Part II, the ABA House of Delegates debated their position at the 1979 and 1980 midyear meetings and approved twenty volumes of proposed standards. All twenty-three final editions now are ready for distribution by the publisher. The next step must be the creation of an adequately funded project or task force to plan and supervise the implementation of the IJA-ABA Standards.

The most important function remaining for those who will be responsible for the implementation of the standards is to prepare the community to understand and accept them. This educational process should be well planned, making maximum use of both the popular media and the professional communications network—law review commentaries; juvenile justice newsletters; journals published by various academic disciplines, such as psychology, education, and sociology; conferences; testimony before Congressional, state legislative, regional, and local bodies; meetings with public and voluntary agencies and with judicial authorities; and panel discussions. A lecture is a useful educational tool, but the question and answer session that follows usually is doubly beneficial because it exposes to the lecturer and audience alike the standards or concepts people have found objectionable and provides the lecturer with a forum to reply in a manner that may resolve doubts or misapprehensions.

There can be no doubt that adoption of the standards by the ABA House of Delegates has been a primary goal for implementation of the standards. Although publication and propagation of the volumes could produce significant impact on the prevailing system without endorsement by the House of Delegates, the task is greatly advanced by official ABA adoption. State by state implementation strategy must be planned and executed, but the expert procedures and mechanisms developed by the ABA, as well as the professional authoritativeness attached to its formal approval, should facilitate the process.

On the other hand, it would be a serious error, and not an uncommon one, to assume that standards adopted by the ABA House of Delegates are accorded automatic acceptance. Implementation is a long and arduous trail, requiring unremitting efforts at every level and branch of the government and in the private sector. The following section deals with the implementation process now that the final approved versions of the volumes are available.

## 8.3 Implementation.

The ABA Section of Criminal Justice prepared a pamphlet entitled *How to Implement Criminal Justice Standards* under a grant from the United States Department of Justice Law Enforcement Assistance Administration (LEAA). The pamphlet describes a four-step implementation strategy and three case studies of the effectiveness of the strategy in the states of Arizona, Arkansas, and Florida. It also provides a chart of the number of reported decisions in which each of the seventeen volumes of the ABA Standards for Criminal Justice was cited, as a measure of the degree of acceptance of the standards by the courts as of November 1975. The majority (ten) of the criminal justice standards volumes were published in 1968, with three more released in 1970, two in 1971, and one each in 1972 and 1973.

An additional source of information on the impact of the criminal justice standards is a project undertaken by the Institute of Judicial Administration pursuant to a grant from the same federal funding source. This project conducted a survey of the impact of five selected volumes of standards in various states as reflected in legislation enacted or court rules adopted on the subject since the draft was released, changes in the law observed by a reporter within each state responding to a uniform questionnaire, discernible trends, and important studies and law review articles pertaining to the standards. The questionnaire used was designed to disclose the extent of congruence between principal features of the standards studied and current state legislation, rules, and practice.

It should be noted that the three states studied in the ABA pamphlet showed significantly greater impact through adoption of the criminal justice standards by means of revised codes or court rules than those covered in the IJA survey. Whether the difference is in form or substance will be considered in this analysis. However, our concern here is not to measure the impact of the criminal justice standards but the lessons to be learned from that experience to assist us in designing a strategy for the implementation of the juvenile justice standards.

The four steps that constitute the state implementation strategy described in the ABA pamphlet are as follows:

1. Preparation of a state comparative analysis. The analysis compares each proposed standard with the subject state's statutes, pertinent constitutional provisions, court rules, case law, and legal practice. It also indicates which standards have been implemented and the action needed to be taken to bring the state's laws into conformity with the standards. The pamphlet calls the analysis a blueprint or planning tool and suggests that it may be useful as a bench book for local judges.

2. Appointment of task forces of key leaders to coordinate implementation activity within the state. In practice, after the National Advisory Commission on Criminal Justice Standards and Goals task force reports were completed, state supervisory commissions for standards and goals were established to work with the state planning agencies under LEAA grants. Task forces were created within the supervisory commission, generally to cover specific subject areas of the NAC and ABA standards and goals.

3. Goal-setting and strategy development. The pamphlet recommends "a high degree of interaction between [the task force] and all existing criminal justice planning and action programs. *One of the greatest weaknesses that has been observed in the Section's implementation project has been the lack of communication among various criminal justice components.*" The italics appear in the pamphlet, to reflect its emphasis on the agencies and practitioners working together to develop implementation strategies.

4. Education of practitioners in the system and the public about the standards. Suggested educational techniques are continuing legal

education programs, judicial conferences, training academies, seminars, cassettes, films, articles, video tapes, lobbying, and a media workshop for journalists and editors. Among efforts to gain citizen support, the pamphlet refers to materials prepared by the ABA Section of Criminal Justice, including an audio-video tape on the history of the standards and a booklet, "How to Mobilize Citizen Support for Criminal Justice Improvement: A Guide for Civic and Religious Leaders."

The ABA pamphlet provides evidence of success of the prescribed implementation efforts. It reports 3,664 citations of the criminal justice standards in appellate court decisions as of November 1975. The three case studies describe the methods pursued to effectuate the four-step strategy. In all three states these efforts led to new rules of criminal procedure and statutory revisions reflecting substantial incorporation of the standards.

By contrast, the IJA impact survey of the ABA Standards for Criminal Justice presents a more complicated set of observations and conclusions. Possibly the variations result from the differences in methodology. The ABA pamphlet discusses states specifically selected for concentrated implementation efforts supported by grants from LEAA state planning agencies and from the Section itself, whereas the IJA project focused on seven of the standards in detail: *Sentencing Alternatives and Procedures, Trial by Jury, Pleas of Guilty, Joinder and Severance, Criminal Appeals, Post-Conviction Remedies,* and *Probation.* It may be that the standards chosen for special attention accounted for the more intricate analysis of the influence of the standards on the state laws. The IJA project considered the interposition of other factors: the Uniform Rules of Criminal Procedure of the National Conference of Commissioners on Uniform State Laws, the American Law Institute (ALI) Model Penal Code, the National Advisory Commission (NAC) on Criminal Justice Standards and Goals, relevant Supreme Court and state appellate court decisions, treatises by leading authorities, and other indicia of national trends affecting changes in the criminal law. The individual reports on each of the selected standards tend to cautious comments, such as the following with respect to *Post-Conviction Remedies:* "Activity in the courts seems to be frequently consonant with the Standards, but direct linkages are not frequently noted." *Id.* at 50.

The problem of competing uniform codes is evidenced in the report on *Sentencing Alternatives and Procedures,* because the ALI Model Penal Code provisions on sentencing and corrections were issued prior to the ABA Standards. The report states, "Consequently, without explicit statements by the drafters in the respective states, it would be difficult to determine whether the ABA Standards were even considered when wholesale revisions of state penal codes tracking the Model Penal Code were adopted." *Id.* at 2. But even when the states purport to comply with features of the standards, it may be more form than substance, as stated in the report: "The format may be adopted and the substance of reform may never be attempted, much less achieved." *Id.* at 5.

The additional problem of piecemeal or patchwork adoption of the standards is referred to in several of the reports. The report on *Pleas of Guilty* expresses this concern effectively as follows:

> Because the ABA Standards...are a comprehensive approach to the subject it is arguable that an omission of any of the basic notions set out in the standards would constitute a failure to comply with them and would result in a state simply selecting isolated bits to incorporate into its law or practice. When what is omitted are the Standards' basic policy statements which give meaning to its technical requirements, then the failure is all the more obvious. *Id.* at 4.

It would be inaccurate to leave the impression that the five reports that constitute the IJA study of the impact of the ABA Criminal Justice Standards concentrate on failures in implementation. The reports discuss many instances of major impact demonstrated by legislative enactment of new criminal codes, rules of criminal procedure, developments in case law, formation of state study groups to compare state laws with the standards, or even simply "advancing understanding" about the nature of a criminal law procedure. Where evidence of direct influence of the standards is elusive, the reports usually find indirect influence or the combined effect of multiple factors that include the ABA standards.

Nevertheless, the ABA pamphlet and the IJA survey reports suggest some of the dangers to circumvent in the activities anticipated in connection with implementation strategies for the juvenile justice standards.

## 8.4 The Pitfalls.

In reviewing the implementation and impact experiences relating to the ABA Criminal Justice Standards, numerous potential difficulties that may affect the proposed juvenile justice standards become apparent. By bringing these difficulties to the surface and exposing them to the consideration of the persons and organizations who will be responsible for federal, state by state, and local implementation of the standards, some of the pitfalls may be avoided.

## 8.4.1. Competing standards and goals.

There were at least three prominent national juvenile justice standards projects: the IJA-ABA Juvenile Justice Standards Project, the National Advisory Commission on Criminal Justice Standards and Goals Task Force on Juvenile Justice and Delinquency Prevention (Task Force), and the National Advisory Committee on Juvenile Justice and Delinquency Prevention (NAC). The Juvenile Justice and Delinquency Prevention Act of 1974 (JJDP Act) administered by the Office of Juvenile Justice and Delinquency Prevention (OJJDP) of the LEAA of the Department of Justice established the NAC Task Force on Juvenile Justice and Delinquency Prevention, from which the NAC Standards Committee was drawn. LEAA also was one of the funding sources for the IJA-ABA project. LEAA further participated in the task of formulating juvenile justice standards by providing for grants to the states to support their development of state juvenile justice standards and goals as guidelines to local implementation of the JJDP Act. The confusion created by these duplicative efforts is just as real as it is apparent. Few people in the system are able to distinguish among the various national and state standards projects, although they differ in many important respects.

There would be little gained by attempting to clarify here the lines of demarcation in the principles governing the projects. This summary volume will have earned sufficient tribute if it succeeds in presenting the IJA-ABA standards clearly. However, it should be noted that the IJA-ABA project began its work in 1971. The Task Force was formed in 1975, and the NAC Standards Committee was appointed in March 1975, meeting for the first time on July 18, 1975. Many of the reporters, drafting committee members, and Commission members who had been working on the IJA-ABA standards were invited to join the JJDP projects. Some of the IJA-ABA standards have been adopted almost totally (e.g., the original abuse and neglect standards). Others were prepared without reference to the IJA-ABA standards (e.g., the police standards). Many overlap; many conflict.

Although many of the standards do coincide, the departures are significant. Delinquency prevention, except as an ultimate and greatly cherished consequence of providing voluntary services and of an effective juvenile justice system, is not one of the permissible criteria for decision making in the IJA-ABA standards because of the project's policy of rejecting the reliability of predictive behavior judgments. Other standards projects oppose the JJSP positions on proportionality in sanctions and removal of status offenses from the jurisdiction of the court; such projects generally place greater emphasis on rehabilitative and treatment goals than JJSP.

Several reports have been published, including the Report of the Task Force in 1976 and the NAC Report in July 1980. In a study for the American Justice Institute, funded by OJJDP, a comparative analysis was prepared of *four* sets of juvenile justice standards—NAC, Task Force, IJA-ABA, and CAC (Commission on Accreditation for Corrections)—examining the way each group treats such matters as diversion, separation, deinstitutionalization, reducing commitments, and community-based alternatives. For example, with respect to delinquency prevention, a chart summarizes the position of each group as follows: NAC—"Places substantial emphasis on delinquency prevention efforts;" Task Force—"Devotes considerable attention to delinquency prevention;" and CAC—"Because of the correctional focus of the project, does not address the issue." The IJA-ABA entry quotes the statement in the preceding paragraph on delinquency prevention. On other issues, like the separation of juveniles from adults in facilities, the groups are very similar.

The problem is the existence of a diversity of projects promulgating standards for juvenile justice and the debilitating effect that has on the prospective impact of the IJA-ABA standards. It is a contributing factor to the other three "pitfalls": inadequate comprehension of the substance of the standards; planning and funding problems; and excessive time for implementation. Therefore, it is imperative that the IJA-ABA standards are presented affirmatively in a forthright, unambiguous, and recognizable manner. Controversial positions should not be buried under the mass of voluminous detail so that the package can be "sold" as a whole. The stature and prestige of many of the proponents would warrant trusting acceptance from co-professionals and the general public. But it would be a mistake to seek adoption by the state legislatures, Congress, or the courts on the basis of simple faith when there is so much to understand and endorse. The standards require intelligent, *informed* support.

The only viable way to combat the danger of losing impact because of confusion with other standards is to persuade the system and the citizenry that the IJA-ABA standards merit adoption. The underlying principles and the specific positions must be presented in an identifiable format, in a massive drive to educate and proselyte individuals and groups concerning a new approach to juvenile justice. Controversy and the threat of change should not be shirked. The public generally recognizes the inadequacy of the current system, but not the causes. The fear and envy of youth, the comfort and piety of paternalism, the huge sums invested in the existing agencies and institutions, the temptations of self-righteousness, and the outrage of crime victims blind the community to the basic inequity and irrationality governing juvenile justice today. The IJA-ABA standards are not a religion to be preached from a pulpit or a philosophy to govern us in our daily decisions. They are concepts and guidelines dealing with a single facet of our society—the rights and obligations of juveniles. Standards for intervention, court roles and procedures, treatment and corrections, and the administration of the system only are relevant to a common understanding of what we have a right to demand from juveniles and what they have a right to demand from us.

### 8.4.2 Inadequately understood contents.

The standards might be seen as creating an intricate design, parts of which can be removed without destroying the design, while others are indispensable. The features that produce the intricacy, the design, and the indispensable parts must be communicated to the community.

The steps described as the implementation strategy in the ABA pamphlet—a state comparative analysis, task force, development of goals and strategy, and education—are valuable tools but are incomplete. They fail to acknowledge certain realities affecting a community in the struggle to implement reform: the dynamics of inertia, conflict, and priorities. Resistance to change, whether active or passive, is the most difficult barrier to overcome. It is reasonable to anticipate that many judges and probation workers may not want their jobs to be changed. Agencies may not want their programs to be challenged. Correctional authorities may not want their facilities to be condemned or their discretion curtailed. Public interest lawyers suing the state on right to treatment theories may not want the concepts they are relying upon as the basis for favorable court rulings to be eliminated, at least not while their actions are pending.

These participants in the current system have reason to feel threatened by a total overhaul. They have a right to be provided with accurate and persuasive material to convince them that the proposed reform is necessary.

Equally important is assuring the legislature, civic organizations, and general public of the need for broad statutory reform. Testimony before legislative committees, conferences to which key legislators are invited, panel discussions, and media coverage should be arranged carefully to prepare them and create a climate conducive to proposed enactments that otherwise might seem excessively disruptive.

Trends do not get set by themselves. Articles in magazines, professional journals, and law reviews sometimes start trends. If so, they can lead to "recent developments," produce case law, become part of programs for civic reform, and if they are really effective, they may even be included in the governor's annual State of the State message and become part of the governor's legislative program. In other words, a successful educational program could make the proposed standards for juvenile justice fashionable. But that presupposes popular acceptance of the basic concepts being promoted. The process of gaining acceptance for as complex a scheme as the standards may not be easily perfected. But the more that is said, read, and heard about the standards, the closer we can come to having an impact on public opinion.

Legislative enactments or court rules adopting part of the standards might not reflect real impact at all. As in the IJA survey of the ABA Criminal Justice Standards, mere congruence of new rules or statutory revisions with the standards could represent a variety of factors without leading to reform of the system. Impact—adoption of the fundamental principles and pattern of the standards—is not possible until all positions have been discussed and potential consequences explored. Unless the concepts behind the standards are understood, they will not have the desired impact on the system.

For example, a draft report by the Institute of Policy Analysis, *Legislative History, Philosophy and Rationale of the Washington (State) Juvenile Justice Code,* describes that state's new code, including an elaborate sentencing schedule, with points allocated according to the severity of the offense, prior offenses, and age of the youth, and says,

> Although in many ways, the approach is similar to that found in the IJA/ABA standards, this similarity is attributable to the fact that both represent an application of the principles of the justice philosophy to the juvenile system. (Persons involved in developing the offender sections of the Washington law were not aware of the relevant volumes prepared by the IJA/ABA Joint Commission until after the law was passed.) (page 51)

The drafters of the Washington code clearly were aware of the *Noncriminal Misbehavior* volume and it influenced them deeply. Unfortunately, they did not read the *Dispositions, Youth Service Agencies,* or *Juvenile Probation Function* volumes. Much of their new code relies on a concept of diversion "to hold youths accountable" which is called voluntary "in that the youths are permitted at any time to request the formal court process...." Failure to complete the diversion agreement results in a petition filed on the original offense. Offenses for which the juvenile was diverted are counted in a subsequent criminal history. Finally, the juvenile court is not required to provide counsel to juveniles eligible for diversion, but only to advise them of their right to counsel. Less than 2 percent request legal counsel prior to signing a diversion agreement.

### 8.4.3 Planning and funding problems.

One of the declared purposes of the Juvenile Justice and Delinquency Prevention Act of 1974 as amended is "to develop and encourage the implementation of national standards for the administration of juvenile justice, including recommendations for administrative, budgeting, and legislative action at the Federal, State and local level to facilitate the adoption of such standards." That may appear to solve the project's implementation funding problems. However, the Act is expressly oriented to ". . . effective juvenile justice and delinquency prevention and rehabilitation programs. . . ." Therefore, it is reasonable to expect the NAC standards to be the national standards that will be implemented under the JJDP Act. The net effect of adopting those standards would be the codification of the better features of the current system, perpetuating the view that delinquency prevention through treatment is the principal function of the juvenile justice system, a position rejected by the IJA-ABA standards.

An example of the kind of reform supported by the Act and the national and state standards that will implement it is a provision that has created some dismay throughout the system. It requires that in order to receive the formula grants that support the state planning agency juvenile programs under the Omnibus Crime Control and Safe Streets Act of 1968, each state plan must provide within three years after submission of the plan that juveniles who are charged with or who have committed offenses that would not be criminal if committed by an adult, shall not be placed in juvenile detention or correctional facilities, but must be placed in shelter facilities.

That provision has been interpreted as barring placement of status offenders in secure facilities for detention or correction before and after adjudication. It appears progressive and humane, but what does it mean? Juveniles being held as runaways, truants, and behavior problems may not be placed in secure facilities. But these juveniles are known to be prone to run away if controls are imposed. How is the state to hold them? Under some state laws, violation of the dispositional order converts a status offender to a delinquent, which would enable the court to place the juvenile, who originally came within its jurisdiction because of defiance of adult authority, in a secure institution for committing the delinquent act of disobeying the court's order. States which do not construe absconding from a nonsecure placement as a delinquent act will have a complicated and expensive administrative problem of enforcement. Possibly their reaction will be to make certain that their "nonsecure" facilities and shelters become increasingly difficult to leave. Otherwise their continued jurisdiction over status offenders may become meaningless and ineffectual, if not totally unenforceable. The 1980 amendments to the JJDP Act expressly allow juveniles who violate a valid court order to be placed in secure detention or correction facilities (Section 233 (a) (12) (A)).

Admittedly, it is preferable for juveniles to be placed in shelters than in prisons called training schools or in jails or large detention facilities called juvenile halls. But if the goal purports to be delinquency prevention and rehabilitation, the results of this latest reform will be as abysmal as other misguided concepts that have led to "removing" children who have not committed crimes in order to help them.

On November 14, 1980 the OJJDP Administrator issued a "Policy Statement on Juvenile Justice Standards" in which he declared the official position regarding implementation of the various sets of standards as follows:

> While no set will receive exclusive endorsement, the standards developed by the National Advisory Committee for Juvenile Justice and Delinquency Prevention (NAC) will receive special attention....
>
> Consequently, the focus was shifted from endorsing a particular group(s)' standards to directing attention to the role of standards *in achieving some of the major objectives of the JJDP Act.* (Emphasis added.)

OJJDP proceeded to draft a Request for Proposal to establish national resource centers *to implement the JJDP Act.* The ABA then initiated a new Planning Task Force on the Implementation of the Juvenile Justice Standards and prepared a concept paper for an ABA Resource Center for Juvenile Standards, to be located in the Washington, D.C. office of the Criminal Justice Section. The proposed center would not focus exclusively on implementing the IJA-ABA standards or even on the twenty ABA-approved volumes, but it would "target" selected areas of the juvenile justice system as affected by the relevant national standards proposals. The three areas selected for priority attention were court organization and administration, due process, and the conflict between the rehabilitative and punishment models in juvenile court dispositions.

As for JJSP, the project began to reduce its activities after the 1980 midyear meeting of the ABA House of Delegates, with IJA gradually assuming the responsibilities for completing the few remaining tasks—revision and publication of the *Abuse and Neglect* standards and of this second edition of the summary volume. No funds have been allocated for the implementation of the IJA-ABA standards as of the present time, June 1981.

If the IJA-ABA juvenile justice standards are not implemented by Juvenile Justice and Delinquency Prevention Act grants, the funding problem becomes more acute. Well-funded competing standards, supported by a legislative mandate to submit a state plan consistent with the rehabilitative, treatment, and prevention goals of the Act present a further obstacle to the adoption of the IJA-ABA standards.

But it can be done. There are other sources of funding. There are foundations, charitable organizations, and civic reform groups, as well as a variety of public and private agencies. Enlightenment through education and persuasion can inspire public opinion to reexamine the goals of treatment and rehabilitation, appropriate as they may be in some situations, as the foundation of the system of juvenile justice. The principles and procedures in the IJA-ABA standards can prevail if the proper forum is provided for a full and fair consideration of the various proposals.

Without funding, planning cannot begin. The first step must be to arrange for adequate financial support of the implementation strategies to be adopted. Once that is accomplished, plans to promote the standards must begin by bringing together influential persons and organizations to develop strategies on the federal, state, and local levels. An executive committee of the Commission is the most logical body to organize these activities. Planning should begin there and fan out across the nation. The more people become acquainted with the standards, the greater the likelihood of impact. These standards can withstand the closest scrutiny. Implementation plans should emphasize methods of disseminating and explaining the contents of the volumes and the principles on which they are based.

### 8.4.4 Passage of time.

The IJA impact study of the ABA Criminal Justice Standards and the annals of reform movements indicate that the impact of any new proposal becomes dissipated as time passes. Bits and pieces get adopted, appellate decisions are affected, rules are revised, but the design disappears. Fundamental change must be dramatic. It must have its moment in history. The evolution of the juvenile justice system thus far has been gradual and incremental. Add psychological testing here, computers there. But that is not what these standards require. Invalid assumptions must be abandoned, a moratorium on the construction of new juvenile facilities declared, the structure and jurisdiction of the court revised, personnel retrained, programs changed, roles reexamined, statements of purpose rewritten, new policies and practices adopted, and juvenile justice funds reallocated.

That cannot happen gradually. A totally new system should be put into effect. Each state should establish an advisory board to reform its juvenile justice system. After one or two years of operation, the effect of the new system should be studied and necessary adjustments made. Anything less is an abandonment of the monumental work of these years. Merely prohibiting secure placements or developing a scheme of determinate dispositions is not enough. Nor does a right to representation by counsel mean much if counsel's function is to advise the juvenile in choosing between going into a treatment program or a correctional institution until the juvenile becomes an adult. Implementation should include ongoing monitoring of the impact of changes in the system. For example, in many states, deinstitutionalization of status offenders has produced a movement to find alternative methods of locking up disruptive children. Misuse of "voluntary" commitments to mental hospitals by parents and the state (as guardian of children declared wards of the court) and unwarranted removals under broadly defined dependency statutes have begun to replace status offense filings. Voluntary placements of older children also have been used as disciplinary measures, with the concurrence of the courts. Furthermore, a disturbing trend toward harsh punitive dispositions for designated offenses has not been tempered by more humane approaches to less serious offenses. Thus, the dangers of piecemeal incorporation of isolated standards must be anticipated.

The proponents of the IJA-ABA standards have an invaluable asset—a series of twenty-three volumes packed with treasures: studies, statistics, decisions, references, well-defined positions, and carefully reasoned justifications. If implemented intelligently, the future impact of the juvenile justice standards could be impressive. There could be a new system of justice, providing respect for the rights of juveniles, protection of the personal and property interests of the community, and safeguards to ensure a fair balance among the legitimate concerns of juveniles, families, and the state.

## 8.5 Conclusion: The New System.

The standards are not perfect. Some definitions and procedures overlap or conflict. The activities and duties of the agencies in one volume may appear to lack coordination with those of the agencies in another. The report recipient agency in the *Abuse and Neglect* volume may run afoul of the *Youth Service Agencies* standards, which in turn seem blithely unaware of the existence of the local juvenile justice boards in the *Planning for Juvenile Justice* volume. The words "parent" and "agency" encompass broader categories in some volumes than in others. And other differences could be identified.

But those cross-volume discrepancies are not substantial or important. Far more important is the incredible consistency of the principles underlying the twenty-three volumes in their approach to the respective roles of juveniles and parents, the expanded role of counsel, the restraints on the exercise of official discretion, the emphasis on community care and small humane facilities, the repudiation of predictive interventions to prevent delinquency, the participation of juveniles in decisions, the protection of privacy and confidentiality in preference to broad data collection, the accountability of juvenile courts and agencies, the safeguards against intervention in the absence of a substantial risk of specified harm, the recognition of the need for normal developmental growth, and the stress on a right to voluntary involvement in service or treatment programs. The presumption of innocence, family autonomy, rights of minors, proportionality of sanctions to the seriousness of the offense, determinate dispositions, least restrictive alternative, open hearings at the option of the respondent, written decisions subject to review and appeal, rigorously prescribed but not easily waived juvenile court proceedings—those are the concepts governing all of the volumes.

The same general pattern can be seen in the procedures for administrative sanctions in correctional agencies and schools as those provided for juvenile court. The same point of view with respect to juveniles in relation to social institutions pervades the volumes on police, probation intake and investigative services, youth service agencies, counsel for private parties, prosecution, and schools. The same general criteria for appropriate facilities are expressed in the standards on architecture, correctional administration, dispositions, and interim status.

This summary volume has attempted to cover the total undertaking of the IJA-ABA Juvenile Justice Standards Project. It has traced the development of the juvenile justice system and the issues that emerged, the reasons for establishing the project, the process of formulating the standards, the content of the standards drafted under the supervision of each of the four drafting committees, the revisions made after the volumes were distributed and reviewed, the steps remaining for implementation of the standards, and the impact anticipated if the standards are adopted.

There has been frequent reference to a new, reformed juvenile justice system. We have sought to describe its characteristics and to make it familiar to the readers of this volume. But to gain full understanding of the standards, one must read the volumes themselves. Each set of standards is accompanied by a commentary that presents the background and justification for the specific standards. This summary volume has made no pretense of providing a substitute for the original work of the reporters, committees, and Commission members who labored to achieve their primary objective—the promulgation of comprehensive standards to govern society's handling of the problems of youth. They have produced a brilliant new response to a perennial social problem. It is fair, honest, and thorough. It deserves to be adopted throughout the nation.

# Bibliography

..E. Abt and I.R. Stuart, eds., *Social Psychology and Discretionary Law* (1979).

Academy for Contemporary Problems, *Readings in Public Policy: Major Issues in Juvenile Justice Information and Training* (1981).

R. Hale Andrews, Jr. and Andrew H. Cohn, "Ungovernability: The Unjustifiable Jurisdiction," 83 *Yale L.J.* 1383 (1974).

W. Bailey and J. Pyfer, Jr., "Deprivation of Liberty and Right to Treatment," 7 *Clearinghouse Rev.* 519 (1974).

*Bartley v. Kremens, vacated as moot,* 431 U.S. 119 (1977), 402 F. Supp. 1039 (E.D. Pa. 1975).

Council of Voluntary Child Care Agencies, "Services to PINS and Adolescents: The Voluntary Agencies' Perspective" (1973).

P. Clute, "How to Implement Criminal Justice Standards" (American Bar Association Section of Criminal Justice 1976).

N. Dorsen and D. Rezneck, *"In re Gault* and the Future of Juvenile Law," 1 *Fam. L.Q.* 34 (1967).

E. Ferster and T. Courtless, "Pre-Dispositional Data, Role of Counsel and Decisions in a Juvenile Court," 7 *Law & Soc. Rev.* 195 (1972).

B. Flicker, *Summary Report,* Conference on New York City Juvenile Justice Resources (IJA-LEAA, May 1974).

S. Fox, *Cases and Materials on Modern Juvenile Justice* (1972).

S. Fox, "Juvenile Justice Reform: An Historical Perspective," 22 *Stan. L. Rev.* 1187 (1970).

S. Fox, "Prosecutors in the Juvenile Court: A Statutory Proposal," 8 *Harv. J. Legis.* 33 (1970).

S. Fox, "The Reform of Juvenile Justice: The Child's Right to Punishment," *Juv. Justice* 2 (Aug. 1974).

W. Friedlander, *Introduction to Social Welfare* (3rd ed. 1968).

B.J. George, Jr., "Gault and the Juvenile Court Revolution" (Institute of Continuing Legal Education 1968).

J. Goldstein, A. Freud, and A. Solnit, *Beyond the Best Interests of the Child* (1973).

Institute of Judicial Administration, "The Ellery C. Decision: A Case Study of Judicial Regulation of Juvenile Status Offenders" (1975).

Institute of Judicial Administration, "The Law Officer Project in the Family Court of New York City: An Evaluation (October 1973).

IJA-ABA Juvenile Justice Standards Project (1977).
  M. Altman, rptr., *Juvenile Records and Information Systems.*
  J. Areen, rptr., *Youth Service Agencies.*
  S. Bing and L. Brown, rptrs., *Monitoring.*
  E. Bittner and S. Krantz, rptrs., *Police Handling of Juvenile Problems.*
  L. Buckle and S. Buckle, rptrs., *Planning for Juvenile Justice.*
  R. Burt and M. Wald, rptrs., *Abuse and Neglect.*
  W. Buss and S. Goldstein, rptrs., *Schools and Education.*
  F. Cohen, rptr., *Dispositional Procedures.*
  R. Dawson, rptr., *Adjudication.*
  B. Feld and R. Levy, rptrs., *Rights of Minors.*
  S. Fisher, rptr., *Pretrial Court Proceedings.*
  D. Freed, J.L. Schultz, and T. Terrell, rptrs., *Interim Status: The Release, Control, and Detention of Accused Juvenile Offenders Between Arrest and Disposition.*
  J. Gittler, rptr., *The Juvenile Probation Function: Intake and Predisposition Investigative Services.*
  A. Gough, rptr., *Noncriminal Misbehavior.*
  A. Greenberg, rptr., *Architecture of Facilities.*
  J. Junker, rptr., *Juvenile Delinquency and Sanctions.*
  J. Manak, rptr., *Prosecution.*
  M. Moran, rptr., *Appeals and Collateral Review.*
  T. Rubin, rptr., *Court Organization and Administration.*
  A. Rutherford and F. Cohen, rptrs., *Corrections Administration.*
  L. Singer, rptr., *Dispositions.*
  L. Teitelbaum, rptr., *Counsel for Private Parties.*
  C. Whitebread, rptr., *Transfer Between Courts.*
IJA Survey of the Standards Relating to Criminal Justice (unpublished reports).
  B. Agata, "Sentencing Alternatives and Procedures" (January 1976).
  J. Fishman, "Survey of the ABA Standards Relating to Probation" (May 1975).
  G. Hirsch, "Jury Trial" (n.d.).
  M. Mahan, "Report on the Joinder and Severance Standards" (May 1975).
  M. Mahan, "Standards Relating to Criminal Appeals" (January 1976).
  C. Reitz, "Standards Relating to Post-Conviction Remedies" (February 1977).
  D. Rotenberg, "The Progress of Plea Bargaining: The ABA Standards and Beyond" (n.d.).
*In re Ellery C.,* 32 N.Y. 2d 588 (1973).
*In re Gault,* 387 U.S. 1 (1967).
*In re Winship,* 397 U.S. 358 (1970).
*Jackson v. Indiana,* 406 U.S. 715 (1972).
Juvenile Justice and Delinquency Prevention Act of 1974, 18 U.S.C. 5031 *et seq.*
I. Kaufman, "Of Juvenile Justice and Injustice," 62 *A.B.A.J.* 730 (1976).
*Kent v. United States,* 383 U.S. 541 (1966).

G. Konopka, "The Needs, Rights and Responsibilities of Youth," 55 *Child Welfare* 173 (1976).

LEAA, "Children in Custody: A Report on the Juvenile Detention and Correctional Facility Census of 1971" (U.S. Department of Justice, 1974).

*Lake v. Cameron,* 364 F.2d 657 (D.C. Cir. 1966).

*Lessard v. Schmidt,* 349 F. Supp. 1078 (1972).

M. Levin and R. Sarri, "Juvenile Delinquency: A Comparative Analysis of Legal Codes in the United States" (National Assessment of Juvenile Corrections, 1974).

M. Luger, "Tomorrow's Training Schools: Problems, Progress, and Challenges," 19 *Crime & Delinq.* 545 (1973).

J. Mack, "The Juvenile Court," 23 *Harv. L. Rev.* 104 (1909).

C. Malmquist, "Juvenile Detention: Right and Adequacy of Treatment Issues," 7 *Law & Soc. Rev.* 159 (1972).

*Martarella v. Kelley,* 349 F. Supp. 575 (S.D.N.Y. 1972).

*McKeiver v. Pennsylvania,* 403 U.S. 528 (1971).

*Morales v. Turman,* 535 F.2d 864 (5th Cir. 1976), 383 F. Supp. 53 (E.D. Tex. 1974).

D. Moynihan, *The Politics of a Guaranteed Income* (1973).

National Advisory Commission on Criminal Justice Standards and Goals, "Courts" (1973).

National Advisory Commission on Criminal Justice Standards and Goals, *Report of the Task Force on Juvenile Justice and Delinquency Prevention* (1976).

National Advisory Committee on Juvenile Justice and Delinquency Prevention, *Report of the NAC for Juvenile Justice and Delinquency Prevention Standards for the Administration of Justice* (1980).

National Conference of Commissioners on State Laws, "Uniform Juvenile Court Act" (1968).

P. Nejelski and J. La Pook, "Monitoring the Juvenile Justice System: How Can You Tell Where You're Going, If You Don't Know Where You've Been?" 12 *Am. Crim. L. Rev.* 9 (1974).

Note, "Developments in the Law—The Constitution and the Family," 93 *Harv. L. Rev.* 1156 (1980).

D. Papalia and S. Olds, *A Child's World: Infancy Through Adolescence* (1975).

*Parham v. J.R.,* 442 U.S. 584 (1979).

*Pennhurst v. Halderman,* 49 U.S.L.W. 4363 (April 20, 1981) *rev'g* 612 F.2d 84 (3d Cir. 1979).

F. Piven and R. Cloward, *Regulating the Poor: The Functions of Public Welfare* (1971).

A. Platt, *The Child Savers: The Invention of Delinquency* (2nd ed. 1972).

E. Powers, *The Basic Structure of the Administration of Justice in Massachusetts* (6th ed., Massachusetts Correctional Association 1973) (Supp. No. 2, 1974; Supp. No. 3, 1976).

President's Commission on Law Enforcement and Administration of Justice, *Task Force Report: Juvenile Delinquency and Youth Crime* (1967).

J. Rawls, *A Theory of Justice* (1971).

M. Rosenheim, ed., *Justice for the Child* (1962).

D. Rothman, *The Discovery of the Asylum* (1971).

*Rouse v. Cameron,* 373 F.2d 451 (D.C. Cir. 1966).

E. Ryerson, *The Best Laid Plans: America's Juvenile Court Experiment.* (1978).

A. Schneider, D. Schram, J. McKelvy, and D. Griswold, *Legislative History, Philosophy and Rationale of the Washington (State) Juvenile Justice Code* (NIJJ Draft 1981).

J.L. Schultz, "The Cycle of Juvenile Court History," 19 *Crime & Delinq.* 457 (1973).

E. Schur, *Radical Nonintervention: Rethinking the Delinquency Problem* (1973).

C. Silberman, *Crisis in the Classroom: The Remaking of American Education* (1970).

P.A. Strasburg, *Violent Delinquents: A Report to the Ford Foundation from the Vera Institute of Justice* (1978).

J. Strouse, *Up Against the Law: The Legal Rights of People Under 21* (1970).

Subcommittee on Detention and Placement for Children for the Subcommittee on Liaison with Public and Private Agencies of the Departmental Committees of the Appellate Divisions, 1st and 2nd Departments (New York) "Designation of Facilities for the Questioning, Detention and 'Holding' of Children Under the Family Court Act" (1972).

D. Sullivan and L. Siegel, "How Police Use Information to Make Decisions," 18 *Crime & Delinq.* 253 (1972).

A. Sussman, "Psychological Testing and Juvenile Justice: An Invalid Judicial Function," 10 *Crim. L. Bull.* 117 (1974).

A. Sussman and S. Cohen, *Reporting Child Abuse and Neglect: Guidelines for Legislation* (1975).

A. Sussman and M. Guggenheim, *The Rights of Parents,* ACLU Handbook (1980).

*Symposium: Juvenile Justice Standards Project,* 52 *N.Y.U.L. Rev.* 1014 (1977)

R. Tappan, *Juvenile Delinquency* (1949).

R. Titmuss, *Commitment to Welfare* (1968).

U.S. Department of Justice, Law Enforcement Assistance Administration, National Institute for Juvenile Justice and Delinquency Prevention, "National Evaluation Design for the Deinstitutionalization of Status Offender Program: Report of the Advisory Committee to the Administrator on Standards for the Administration of Juvenile Justice" (September 6 1975).

R. Vinter, G. Downs, and J. Hall, "Juvenile Corrections in the States Residential Programs and Deinstitutionalization: A Preliminary Report" (National Assessment of Juvenile Corrections, 1975).

*Wilder v. Bernstein,* 499 F. Supp. 980 (S.D.N.Y. 1980).

*Wilder v. Sugarman,* 385 F. Supp. 1013 (S.D.N.Y. 1974).

*Wyatt v. Stickney,* 344 F. Supp. 373 (M.D. Ala. 1972), *aff'd* 503 F.2d 1305 (5th Cir. 1974).

*Youngberg v. Romeo,* No. 80-1429, *cert. granted* 49 U.S.L.W. 3851, May 19 1981.

# Appendix
## of
## Revisions in the 1977 Tentative Drafts

### STANDARDS RELATING TO ABUSE AND NEGLECT

1. The Introduction was revised slightly to show the change in emphasis, which now mandates retaining parental rights and restoring custody unless the court finds the child would be harmed, rather than the original version authorizing termination or removal unless it would be detrimental to the child.

2. Standard 2.1 D. was amended to add to the definition of sexual abuse situations in which the parents knew or should have known the child was being sexually abused by another and failed to take appropriate action.

Commentary was revised to include a reference to the federal Child Abuse Prevention and Treatment and Adoption Reform Act, barring the commercial use and exploitation of children.

3. Standard 2.2 was amended by changing the phrase "to assume jurisdiction" to "to justify intervention."

4. Standard 3.3 was amended by deleting the portions pertaining to procedures in Part V, which have been revised substantially. See Items 7 to 11 below. The standard was amended further by adding a provision that a warrant must be obtained if the report recipient agency wishes to interview or investigate the parents or custodians or take custody of the child against the wishes of the parents or custodians.

Commentary was revised accordingly.

5. Standard 3.5 was amended to make hearings challenging reports of abuse nonpublic unless interested persons show they should be public.

6. Standard 4.3 on court review of emergency temporary custody was amended to conform to revisions in Part V on court proceedings. Provision for court-approved investigation prior to the filing of a petition was eliminated.

Commentary was revised accordingly.

7. Standard 5.1 was amended to incorporate the procedures for intake review of complaints in *The Juvenile Probation Function* volume and eliminate inconsistent or duplicative provisions.

The standard was amended further by adding new preadjudication proceedings derived from the *Pretrial Court Procedures* and *Adjudication* volumes. New standards barring access to social and investigative reports prior to an adjudication of endangerment, as in delinquency proceedings, and abrogating certain privileged communications also were added.

Commentary was revised accordingly.

8. Standard 5.2, providing for a preadjudication investigation of the petition, was amended by moving it from Part V to Part VI, thereby transforming the process into a predisposition investigation and report, as in delinquency proceedings. See Item 12 below.

Commentary was revised accordingly.

9. Standard 5.3 on postinvestigation proceedings was amended by deleting the references to the preadjudication investigation and postinvestigation hearing and combining the remaining provisions with new Standard 5.2 on preadjudication proceedings.

New Standard 5.3 was drafted to include standards for both contested and uncontested proceedings. The new procedures for hearings on uncontested petitions were based on the standards for judicial scrutiny of admissions in delinquency proceedings in the *Adjudication* volume. Standards for recording proceedings and for preserving and expunging records also were added.

Commentary was revised accordingly.

10. New Standard 5.4 on findings of law and fact following the hearing was added.

11. New Standard 5.5 on appeals was added.

12. New Standard 6.1 on predisposition investigation and reports was added. Standard 6.1 A. provides for an investigation by the probation department after an adjudication of endangerment. Standard 6.1 B. stipulates the information to be included in the predisposition report. Standard 6.1 C. requires that the report be distributed to the court and to all parties to the proceeding. Standards 6.1 B. and C. derive from former Standards 5.2 F. 1. and 2.

13. Standard 6.1 was changed to Standard 6.2 and amended to specify time limitations for the dispositional hearing, differentiated according to whether the child is in custody or at home.

14. Standard 6.2 was amended and combined with former Standard 6.1 to constitute new Standard 6.2.

15. Standard 6.3 was amended by changing subsection A. 5 from "placement" of a homemaker in the home to ordering the state or parents to employ a homemaker. New subsection C. was added to express the state's responsibility to provide an adequate level of services.

Commentary was revised accordingly.

16. Standard 6.4 was amended by adding to the general goal for all dispositions the principle of least restrictive alternative and deleting a condition to the prohibition against removal where the environment is beyond the parents' control.

17. Standard 6.5 A. was amended to eliminate references to a plan for services when a child is left in the home to be submitted *after* the dispositional hearing.

18. Standard 6.5 B. 3. was amended by adding a preference for placement with the child's relatives.

19. Standard 6.6 was amended by adding custodians to the caption, deleting termination of parental rights as a disposition following an adjudication of endangerment, and adding a new subsection D. barring removal from foster parents in certain situations.

20. Standard 7.1 was amended by adding grievance officers to those authorized to request court review prior to the six-month review. All time periods *except* the six-month review were bracketed.

21. Standard 7.5 D. was amended to change the warning to parents that termination may occur at the next review hearing to a warning of possible termination in a proceeding under Part VIII.

Commentary was revised accordingly.

22. New Standard 8.1 was added to provide for separate court proceedings as a prerequisite to termination of parental rights.

23. New Standard 8.2 was added to cover voluntary termination or relinquishment of parental rights. The standard is based in large part on the Model Act to Free Children for Permanent Placement (hereinafter, Model Act), Section 3.

24. New Standard 8.3 on involuntary termination was added. The procedures are essentially the same as the procedures for endangerment proceedings. The bases for termination in subsection C. were derived in part from the Model Act, Section 4, as modified by general principles underlying the standards in this and other volumes in the series.

25. Former Standards 8.1, 8.2, and 8.3 were deleted.

26. Standard 8.4 was amended by deleting the reference to former Standard 8.2.

27. New Standard 8.5 on dispositional proceedings was added. Subsection A., providing for the information to be included in the predispositional report, was based on the Model Act, Section 13(c).

28. New Standard 8.6 was added to provide for an interlocutory order for termination of parental rights. Voluntary termination also was covered by this standard.

29. Former Standard 8.5 was changed to Standard 8.7. Standard 8.7 B. was amended by adding the concept of making the original interlocutory order final when adoption or guardianship has been

effected and by adding the alternative orders of extending the duration of the interlocutory order or returning custody and parental rights to the parents if no permanent placement has been found.

30. Standard 10.4 G. was amended by changing one year as the period of placement that precedes possible termination of parental rights to eighteen months *if* the parents have failed to maintain contact for three years. See new Standard 8.3 C. 6.

31. Standard 10.5 was amended to add a preference for placement as chosen by the parents and child, in the absence of good cause to the contrary.

Commentary was revised accordingly.

32. Commentary to Standard 2.1 A. was revised by adding the comment that "serious" is used in the standard to connote "significant" physical injury.

33. Commentary to Standard 2.1 C. was revised to note that significant clinically demonstrable emotional harm caused by parental action or neglect could be grounds for official intervention.

34. Commentary to Standard 3.2 C. was revised by adding a reference to abuses by foster care agencies with respect to improper or overlong placements of reported children.

35. Commentary to Standard 4.1 A. was revised to require agencies that take custody of a child to act immediately to safeguard the child and report to the court.

36. Commentary to Parts V, VI, and VIII was revised and expanded to cover the amendments, deletions, and additions to the standards in those parts.

37. Commentary to Standard 6.3 C. was amended further by adding a discussion of placement in a residential treatment center as a disposition for an endangered child, with cautionary observations on the child's right to the least restrictive placement and to refuse nonemergency services. Purchase of services also was discussed.

38. Commentary to Standard 6.5 was revised to add the stricture that an agency's financial considerations should not be permitted to prolong placements. A further recommendation was that the agency's plan include training for foster parents.

39. Commentary to Standard 10.4 C. was revised to provide that the agency should refer cases to the juvenile court in which parents exercise their right to resume custody of their children more than twice within a thirty-day period.

40. Commentary to Standard 10.8 was revised to reflect the changes in the standards for termination of parental rights in Part VIII and in the underlying principles of that part.

# STANDARDS RELATING TO ADJUDICATION

1. Standard 2.2 A. was revised by deleting provisions for amendment of the petition by the prosecutor with the permission of the juvenile court prior to tender of a plea admitting an allegation or by the close of the government's case, and substituting a provision that amendment should be governed by the same rules that apply to amendment of a charge in a criminal proceeding.

Commentary was revised to state the view that the new standard is consistent with the basic position that juvenile court proceedings should provide as much protection to an accused juvenile as criminal court proceedings would to an adult defendant.

2. Standard 3.3 B. was amended by adding dispositional concessions to the matters subject to negotiation in plea agreements.

3. Standard 4.1 B. was amended by inserting brackets around the number "six," the recommended minimum number of persons to constitute a jury.

Commentary was revised to explain that the authorized size of a jury in a juvenile court proceeding should be the same as in an equivalent criminal proceeding.

The commentary was amended further to note that the standard provides for a demand by the respondent to invoke the right to a jury trial, which right can be waived, confirming the non-mandatory nature of a jury trial.

4. Commentary to Standard 2.4 B. was revised by adding a comment explaining the exclusion of a *nolo contendere* plea from the standards, on the ground that the plea would not admit or deny the allegations in the petition and therefore would not meet the criteria for plea terminology—that it be unambiguous and simple for juveniles to understand.

5. Commentary to Standard 3.1 was revised to add a cross-reference to Standard 4.4 and to assert the need to prove prejudice before disqualifying a judge who has inquired into social factors in determining that the respondent lacked the mental capacity to plead.

6. Commentary to Standard 5.3 C. was revised to add the observation that juvenile court adjudications may be admissible at the sentencing stage of criminal court proceedings for some purposes, but inadmissible for other purposes.

The commentary was revised further by the addition of cross-references to other volumes in which prior adjudications are factors in decisions affecting the juvenile's status at the various stages of juvenile court proceedings.

7. Commentary to Standard 6.1 was revised by distinguishing between the respondent's election to waive the right to a public trial and an absolute right to a closed trial, with a cross-reference to Standard 6.2.

## STANDARDS RELATING TO APPEALS
## AND COLLATERAL REVIEW

1. Standard 2.1 C. was amended by adding "except when the juvenile requests that such order not become final." The standard was amended further by bracketing sixty.
2. Standard 6.3 was amended by bracketing six.
3. Commentary to Standard 2.1 C. was revised by noting that local practices will govern the tolling of time limitations caused by motions to modify or vacate a court order. A reference to the exception added to the standard also was included in the revised commentary.
4. Commentary to Standard 2.2 B. was revised by describing the position of the Legal Services and Defender Attorneys Juvenile Justice Consortium in opposition to the provision authorizing parents, custodians, or guardians to appeal a court order.

## STANDARDS RELATING TO ARCHITECTURE
## OF FACILITIES

1. Standard 6.15 was amended to delete laundry facilities as follows: "No vocational training or chapel should be provided in a secure detention facility."
2. The commentary to Standard 6.15 was revised to delete the reference to laundry and the commentary to Standard 6.16 was revised to add a new subsection, L., captioned "Laundry facilities," discussing the factors to consider in determining whether laundry equipment should be installed in a secure detention facility.

## STANDARDS RELATING TO CORRECTIONS
## ADMINISTRATION

1. Standard 3.2 F. 2 was amended by adding training and promotion to appointment as areas for affirmative action to achieve equivalence for women and men.
2. Standard 4.10 F. was amended to incorporate the restriction

proposed by Commissioners Wald and Polier to require that stimulant, tranquilizing, and psychotropic drugs be used only when the department has a procedure for monitoring their effects by a licensed physician who is independent of the department. A footnote describing that restriction and the inability of the volume's editorial committee to resolve the independent monitoring requirement was deleted.

3. Standard 4.10 G. 1. was amended to authorize the court to approve the use of techniques that manipulate the environment of consenting juveniles under sixteen if parental consent is denied or unavailable.

Commentary was revised accordingly.

4. Standard 7.2 was amended to change the maximum size of residential facilities from twenty to twelve to twenty and to bracket twelve to twenty, in conformity with *Architecture of Facilities* Standard 6.3.

Commentary was revised accordingly.

5. Standard 7.6 D. was amended to eliminate the prohibition against routine searches of visitors and the requirement that the director have probable cause to believe the visitor may possess contraband, following which the director could delay the visit to apply for a search warrant or obtain the visitor's written consent to the search. As amended, the standard permits nonintrusive routine searches, intrusive searches based on consent or probable cause, and other searches based on reasonable cause to believe contraband is present. The amendment arises from the principle that constitutional safeguards afforded adult prisoners apply equally to juveniles in correctional institutions except for additional protections compelled by the special needs of juveniles.

Commentary was revised accordingly.

6. Standard 7.11 A. 1. was amended by changing the maximum size of a secure facility from twenty to twelve to twenty to conform to *Architecture of Facilities* Standard 6.3. See Item 4 above.

Commentary was revised accordingly.

7. Standard 8.6 A. was amended to expand the provision which would permit disciplinary action for sexual behavior forbidden by law to include behavior forbidden by statute or reasonable institutional regulations. This amendment conformed the standard to the definition of "law" in the commentary.

Commentary was revised to reflect the more explicit language of the amendment.

8. Standard 8.9 D. was amended to make the juvenile's right at disciplinary hearings to call witnesses and present evidence conditional on the effect not being unduly hazardous to institutional safety

or correctional goals and to subject the juvenile's right to confront and cross-examine adverse witnesses to the discretion of the correctional officials.

9. Commentary to Standard 4.9 was revised to note that the right to medical treatment as part of a safe, human, caring environment should include the opportunity to obtain advice concerning abortions, consistent with the juvenile's right to abortions discussed in *Planned Parenthood v. Danforth.*

10. Commentary to Standard 4.14 A. 2. was revised to state that housekeeping work performed by adjudicated delinquents must be of the kind that would be performed by the juvenile in his or her own home.

11. Commentary to Standard 5.2 D. was revised to discuss the ABA Section of Family Law's proposal that all findings of willful noncompliance with dispositional orders give rise to a new dispositional hearing, contrary to the provision in the standard which limits new hearings to cases in which the court preliminarily determines that the next most severe disposition may be imposed.

12. Commentary to Standard 7.6 K. was revised to add a cross-reference to the principle which was applied to determine the constitutional safeguards properly afforded to juveniles in connection with visitor searches by correctional officials in Standard 7.6 D. (see Item 5 above) and to apply it to searches of the juvenile's person, room, area, and property.

13. Commentary to Standard 7.10 D. was revised to expand the discussion of classification of nonsecure residential settings other than foster homes as group homes, especially with respect to residential treatment programs.

## STANDARDS RELATING TO COUNSEL FOR PRIVATE PARTIES

1. Standard 3.l(b) (ii) [c] [2] was amended by deleting "other than himself or herself."

Commentary was revised by adding a statement that the standard does not preclude appointment of juvenile's counsel as guardian ad litem.

2. Standard 6.1 was amended by changing "subjudicial" to "nonjudicial."

3. Standard 10.3(a) was amended by changing "should ordinarily" to "may."

Commentary was revised by noting that trial counsel should be retained unless appellate specialists are available.

4. Commentary to Standard 2.1(a) was revised by adding a reference to the position of the Legal Services and Defender Attorneys Juvenile Justice Standards Consortium (hereafter, Consortium) that state and local governments and legal services offices should be responsible for the provision of legal services in juvenile and family courts.

5. Commentary to Standard 2.2(a) was revised by adding a statement prepared by the Consortium describing a system for providing representation through a combined defender, neighborhood legal services, and appointed counsel plan.

6. Commentary to Standard 2.3 was revised by adding a distinction between unwaivable right to counsel at judicial proceedings and waivable right to counsel at post-adjudication administrative proceedings, with a cross-reference to *Corrections Administration* Standard 8.9 C.

7. Commentary to Standard 3.2 was revised by adding a comment on possible conflicts of interest between siblings who are represented by the same counsel in dependency or neglect proceedings and on the need for separate counsel if conflict exists.

8. Commentary to Standard 6.3(b) was revised by expanding the discussion of the strict safeguards imposed by the standards to protect juveniles who deny guilt from being persuaded to plead guilty to lesser charges or otherwise participate through counsel in plea negotiations. Cross-references to *Adjudication* and *Prosecution* standards were added.

# STANDARDS RELATING TO COURT ORGANIZATION AND ADMINISTRATION

1. Standard 1.1 D. was amended by deleting "nonjudicial" to conform to *The Juvenile Probation Function* Standard 2.4 D., which bars nonjudicial probation as a permissible intake disposition.

Commentary was revised accordingly.

2. Standard 1.2 was amended by bracketing juvenile intake and probation services, to make administration of such services by the executive branch of government permissive instead of mandatory.

Commentary was revised to indicate the controversy concerning this issue.

3. Standard 2.1 C. was amended by bracketing rotation of judges, as agreed at the ABA House of Delegates meeting in February 1980.

Commentary was revised accordingly.

4. Standard 2.3 was amended by bracketing four as the minimum number of judges in a family court division warranting a full-time

court administrator, to make the recommended minimum discretionary with the jurisdiction.

5. Commentary to Standard 1.1 A. was revised by adding a cross-reference to volumes dealing with the jurisdiction of family court.

6. Commentary to Standard 1.1 B. was revised to add a statement that the same judge should not preside at detention and adjudication hearings, if possible, and a discussion of the problem of a one-judge court.

## STANDARDS RELATING TO DISPOSITIONAL PROCEDURES

1. Standard 2.3 D. 2. was amended by substituting "juvenile prosecutor" for "attorney for the state."

2. Standard 2.4 D. was amended by substituting "juvenile prosecutor" for "attorney representing the state."

Commentary was revised accordingly.

3. Standard 3.1 was amended by adding "or their attorney" to reflect the parents' right to be represented by counsel at the dispositional hearing.

The standard was amended further by substituting "juvenile prosecutor" for "an attorney for the state."

Commentary to Standard 3.1 was revised by adding a reference to parents' waivable right to counsel at dispositional proceedings.

4. Standard 6.1 was amended by adding new subdivision A., requiring a disposition agreement to be introduced in open court and approved by the judge. Former subdivisions A. and B. were changed to B. and C., respectively.

5. Standards 6.3 B. and 6.3 D. were amended by substituting "juvenile prosecutor" for "attorney for the state."

6. Commentary to Standard 6.2 was revised by adding a statement that the court also may subpoena witnesses to testify at the hearing.

7. Commentary to Standard 7.1 B. was revised by adding a cross-reference to *Dispositions* Standard 5.1, describing the provision for a motion to reduce a disposition claimed to be illegal or unduly harsh or inequitable.

## STANDARDS RELATING TO DISPOSITIONS

1. Standard 2.2 was amended by changing "should be governed by" to "include consideration of."

2. Standard 5.3 was amended by adding brackets around "5."

3. Commentary to Standard 1.2 D. was revised by adding a comment that juveniles should be fully informed of their right to be provided with or to refuse services.

4. Commentary to Standard 1.2 G. was revised by adding a statement that state legislatures should exert efforts to ensure availability of necessary resources.

5. Commentary to Standard 2.1 was revised by adding a statement that the dispositional criteria recited in the standard inherently take into consideration the need for public safety in selecting the least restrictive disposition appropriate in the case.

6. Commentary to Standard 3.2 B. 1. was revised by adding discussion distinguishing a separate civil action brought by the victim for damages inflicted by the juvenile from enforcement of a restitution order by juvenile court.

7. Commentary to Standard 4.2 was revised by adding a statement on the need for juveniles to be fully informed of their rights and obligations in connection with their participation or refusal to participate in programs.

## STANDARDS RELATING TO INTERIM STATUS

1. Standard 3.1 was amended by inserting the word "generally" as a clarification, to heighten the meaning of the second sentence of the standard. Thus the first sentence is a statement of the general policy against restraints on the freedom of accused juveniles and the second sentence is a specific instruction to prefer unconditional release in each case.

2. Standard 3.3 was amended by adding a new section, E., which makes further interrogation or investigation an enumerated prohibited purpose of interim control or detention.

3. Standard 4.3 was amended by creating the alternative of stating on the record the evidence and authorized purpose on which a decision other than release is based.

4. Standard 5.3 F. was amended by changing the time limit for release or transportation to a facility to two to four hours and bracketing that time frame.

Commentary was revised to express the executive committee's continued preference for a two-hour time limit, describing the amendment as a recognition of the possible impracticality of the more rigorous standard for some communities.

5. Standard 5.6 was amended by bracketing "less than one year," thereby making it possible to apply mandatory release under that

standard to felony charges. The standard was amended further by substituting "evidence as defined in the standard" for "clear and convincing evidence." "First or second degree murder" was changed to "a class one juvenile offense involving violence" for cases in which the seriousness of the offense can be a sufficient ground for continued custody. Finally, the factor of being under the jurisdiction of the court while in interim release, on probation, or on parole (the "one-bite rule") was eliminated.

Commentary was revised accordingly.

6. Standard 6.1 was amended to conform to *Corrections Administration* Standard 2.1 with respect to providing for a statewide agency while recognizing the role of local agencies in situations in which geographic or political considerations place certain administrative responsibilities within the jurisdiction of local government.

7. Standard 6.6 A. 1. was amended in the same manner as Standard 5.6, described in item 5 above, with respect to exceptions to the mandatory release provisions, by changing a charge of first or second degree murder to a class one juvenile offense and eliminating the "one-bite rule."

Commentary was revised accordingly. The General Introduction also was revised to reflect the changes in Standard 6.6 A. 1.

8. Standard 7.7 was amended to authorize continued custody of the court when justified under the standards despite improper detention by the intake or arresting officer.

9. Standard 7.8 was amended by bracketing sixty days and changing the provision recommending a new judge at the trial from one "other than the one who refused to release the juvenile from detention" to one "other than the one who presided at the detention hearing."

10. Standard 7.9 A. was amended by adding a requirement that at the expiration of the time for execution of the dispositional order, the judge must execute the order forthwith, or explain on the record the reasons for the delay, or release the minor.

11. Standard 7.10 was amended by bracketing all time limits and adding a provision permitting extension of the time for execution of a disposition if requested by the juvenile in order to obtain a better placement.

Commentary was revised to note that since the extension would be for the juvenile's benefit, it should be at the juvenile's option.

12. Standard 8.1 was amended by distinguishing between the nonwaivable right to separate counsel for a child and the right of the parents to request court-appointed counsel in cases of conflict of interest between juveniles and their parents. This provision gives parents the choice of knowingly waiving their right to counsel.

13. Standard 8.3 was amended by deleting a provision that the adequacy of an appointed attorney's efforts to avoid or relax the conditions of detention should be an important component of the fee set by the court, because the fee should be based on the attorney's performance of *all* obligations to the client.

14. Standard 10.5 was amended by changing the maximum population of a detention facility from twelve juveniles to twelve to twenty and bracketing "twelve to twenty," to conform to *Architecture of Facilities* Standard 6.3. The standard was amended further by adding the phrase "in any calendar year" to the specified maximum time during which a mandatory ceiling on detained juveniles may be exceeded temporarily.

Commentary was revised by adding a cross-reference to *Architecture of Facilities* Standard 6.3.

15. Standard 10.8 was amended to add additional factors of staff qualification and training and staffing patterns and deployment of staff resources to the enumerated factors to consider in an inventory of secure detention facilities, since they are indicative of the quality of custodial care and supervision in the facilities.

16. Standard 11.1 A. was amended by bracketing "executive" to indicate continued preference for executive control of interim status administration, accompanied by a recognition of the possibility that some jurisdictions may choose judicial control of intake, investigation, and probation functions.

Commentary was revised accordingly.

17. Commentary to Standard 3.2 B. was revised to indicate that the provision for detention to reduce the likelihood that the juvenile may inflict serious bodily harm encompasses serious crimes against property which involve a substantial risk of serious bodily harm, such as arson or bombing.

18. Commentary to Standard 4.5 A. 1. c. was revised to note that tests of competency to stand trial may be given only after providing adequate notice and opportunity to be heard.

19. Commentary to Standard 5.3 C. was revised to include a cross-reference to *Pretrial Court Proceedings* Standards 5.1 and 6.1 and to expand the discussion of nonwaivability of the right to counsel, as distinguished from the right to have counsel present, and of the limited admissibility of statements made to intake officers.

20. Commentary to Standard 5.4 was revised to provide that juveniles may be held in designated facilities in communities which do not have separate juvenile detention facilities if arrangements are made to insure that juveniles will not come into contact with adult detainees.

21. Commentary to Standard 10.7 was revised to expand discussion

of the detained juveniles' rights, particularly with respect to attorney conferences, telephone access, and restrictions on mail searches for contraband. A cross-reference to the rights of confined juveniles in the *Corrections Administration* volume was added.

22. Commentary to Standard 11.1 A. was revised by referring to the controversy concerning the relative merits of programs administered by public agencies and those provided by contracting with private nonprofit organizations.

## STANDARDS RELATING TO JUVENILE DELINQUENCY AND SANCTIONS

1. Standard 1.3 was amended by adding "have the discretion to" in order to clarify the intention that the judge's decision to dismiss is discretionary under the circumstances described in the standard.

2. Standard 2.4, which eliminated delinquency liability for private offenses, was deleted on the ground that the definition of delinquency offenses in Standard 2.2 is sufficient.

3. Standard 4.1 (Part IV), which defined sexual offenses and assent by a juvenile to sexual behavior according to the ages of the participating juveniles, was deleted on the ground that each state's penal code should govern, as in other juvenile offenses.

4. Standard 5.2 (formerly 6.2) was amended by increasing the maximum custodial sanction from twenty-four to thirty-six months for a class one juvenile offense and from twelve to eighteen months for a class two juvenile offense. All time periods were bracketed, but the principle of establishing a graduated scale of specific maximum sanctions proportionate to the corresponding penalties in the state penal code was not affected.

Also, a new Standard 5.2 C. was added, authorizing the imposition of successive sanctions specifying a custodial and noncustodial disposition, provided that the total duration does not exceed the maximum term prescribed for the custodial sanction for the offense, in conformity with *Dispositions* Standard 3.3 C.

Commentary was revised accordingly.

5. Standard 5.4 (formerly 6.4) was amended by bracketing the twenty-first birthday as the date by which juvenile court orders imposing sanctions must terminate.

6. Commentary to Standard 1.1 was revised by adding a reference to rehabilitation in connection with recognizing the unique features of young persons as a purpose of the juvenile delinquency code, thereby coordinating with the *Dispositions* Standard 1.1 statement of the

purpose of the juvenile correctional system, which includes "developing individual responsibility for lawful behavior."

7. Commentary to Standard 1.2 was revised by adding a notation that the ABA Section of Family Law recommended deletion of the provision on burden of proof, whereas the Section of Criminal Law did not oppose the standard.

## STANDARDS RELATING TO THE JUVENILE PROBATION FUNCTION

1. Standard 2.4 E. 7. was amended by bracketing the three-month period for filing a petition.

2. Standard 2.5 A. 7. was amended by bracketing the three-month period for filing a petition.

3. Standard 3.3 E. 2. was amended by adding the requirement that summaries of prior contacts with the system include the dispositions made and the reasons given for the disposition following each such contact.

4. Standard 4.2 was amended by bracketing executive agency administration of intake and predisposition investigative services.

Commentary was revised to explain that the brackets were added in response to vigorous opposition from representatives of juvenile and family court judges and others to executive control of such services, thereby making the designation of the executive agency precatory rather than mandatory.

5. Standard 5.1 C. was amended to add equivalent experience as an alternative to the stated minimum educational requirements for personnel from areas in which applicants with the educational qualifications are not available.

Commentary was revised accordingly.

6. Standard 5.2 A. was amended to bar arbitrary discharge of intake and investigating officers during the probationary period as well as after its completion.

Commentary was revised accordingly.

7. Commentary to Standards 2.11 A. and B. was revised to note the recommendations of the ABA Section of Criminal Law and Young Lawyers Division, whereby the former urged deletion of the provisions in order to give officers the freedom to conduct their investigation as they chose, but the latter disagreed, on the ground that the standards provide sufficient latitude for the investigating officers. The executive committee of the joint commission voted to retain the standards as written, endorsing the position of the Young Lawyers Division.

## STANDARDS RELATING TO JUVENILE RECORDS AND INFORMATION SYSTEMS

1. Standards 4.3 A., B., and C. were amended by changing "record" to "information" so that notice of record retention need refer only to the record and need not specify the information contained therein.

2. Standard 5.4 was amended by adding the qualifying phrase, "except as modified by Standards 5.3, 5.6, and 5.7." Subdivision E. was amended by adding an alternative to reevaluation every ninety days: a statement of the most recent review of the record and a warning that conditions may have changed since that review. Subdivision H. was amended by substituting for "a bona fide emergency" the requirement that a compelling health or safety need exists, in order to narrow the conditions for disclosure without consent.

3. Standard 5.7 A. was amended by adding "or" between subdivisions 1. and 2. to clarify the intention that the provisions be in the disjunctive, as set forth in the commentary.

4. Standard 18.1 was amended to add an exception to the prohibition against the use of juvenile records by third persons by expressly authorizing inquiries by the state youth authority when candidates are being considered for positions requiring ex-offenders.

5. Standard 18.4 C. was amended to permit juvenile records to be admitted in a criminal trial after waiver of juvenile court jurisdiction, provided the evidence is otherwise admissible in criminal trials.

Commentary was revised accordingly, including a statement that evidence should not be rendered inadmissible by its introduction during a waiver hearing.

6. Commentary to Standard 2.6 was revised by indicating that the requirement in the standard that each juvenile agency establish a procedure to correct a record and to give notice to juveniles and their families of the availability of such procedure is satisfied by written notice of their rights to access and to challenge the records, if the notice gives sufficient procedural information to enable them to initiate the process.

## STANDARDS RELATING TO MONITORING

1. Standard 1.2 was amended to add new subdivision G., thereby including the prevention of discrimination as a specific goal of the monitoring process.

2. Commentary to Standard 1.2 was revised to add a brief discussion of the need to prevent the intrusion of discriminatory factors in official decision-making in the juvenile justice system.

3. Standard 1.3 A. was amended to include educators among independent, external monitoring mechanisms.

4. Commentary to Standard 1.3 A. was revised to restrict the educators qualified to serve as external monitors to those not employed by the school system.

5. Commentary to Standard 1.6 A. was revised by adding to footnote 42 a cross-reference to the discussion of the relationship between the *Monitoring* standards and the *Juvenile Records and Information Systems* standards that appears in the commentary to Standard 1.6 B.

6. Commentary to Standard 3.1 was revised by adding a discussion of the monitoring function performed by juvenile prosecutors.

7. Commentary to Standard 3.3 was revised to add a reference to self-monitoring of counsel representing juveniles and a cross-reference to *Counsel for Private Parties* Standard 2.1 (a) (iii).

8. Commentary to Standard 4.1 was revised to require appointees or employees of the state commission on juvenile advocacy to be compensated at a salary and rank commensurate with their responsibilities.

## STANDARDS RELATING TO PLANNING FOR JUVENILE JUSTICE

1. The standards were not amended.

2. Commentary to Standard 2.4 C. was revised to add the sentence, "Special efforts should be made to include local parents and juveniles in the planning process as representatives of client or community interests."

## STANDARDS RELATING TO POLICE HANDLING OF JUVENILE PROBLEMS

1. Standard 2.2 was amended by adding a phrase making the standard for retention of police records subject to the relevant standards in *Juvenile Records and Information Systems*.

2. Standard 3.4 was amended by changing "interest" to "action."

3. Standard 3.5 was deleted and the text was added to the commentary to Standard 3.2.

Commentary to Standard 3.5 was deleted.

4. Commentary to Standard 2.3 was revised by adding a cross-reference to Standard 4.3.

5. Commentary to Standard 2.4 was revised by adding a clarification that the prohibition against the police initiating their own

deterrence or treatment programs is not intended to proscribe police recreational, athletic, or educational programs for the community.

6. Commentary to Standard 2.5 was revised by conforming the text in the quotation of *Interim Status* Standard 5.6, as published in the tentative draft, to the approved version, by bracketing "less than one year," changing "clear and convincing evidence" to "the evidence as defined below," substituting "a class one juvenile offense involving a crime of violence" for "first or second degree murder," and deleting Standard 5.6 B. 3.

The commentary was revised further by expanding the reference to the policy against detaining juveniles in adult facilities discussed in the commentary to *Interim Status* Standard 5.4, to include the addition to the revised commentary, i.e., that juvenile court authorities in small communities shall have the duty to designate facilities to be used for juvenile detention in which such juveniles will not be in contact with adult detainees.

7. Commentary to Standard 3.2 was revised by inserting the text of former Standard 3.5, as noted in Item 3 above.

The commentary was revised further by adding cross-references to *Interim Status* Standard 5.3 and *Pretrial Court Proceedings* Standards 5.1, 6.1, and 6.2, which deal with limitations on the juvenile's capacity to waive constitutional rights before trial, based on the juvenile's presumed susceptibility to official pressure, especially while in police custody.

## STANDARDS RELATING TO PRETRIAL COURT PROCEEDINGS

1. Standard 2.1 B. was amended by adding a provision that the judge's personal explanation of the written notice of the juvenile's rights should be in open court at the prescribed hearing.

2. Standard 2.2 B. was amended by adding to the rights to be explained by the judge the right to a trial by jury.

3. Standard 3.10 was amended to restrict the medical and scientific reports to be disclosed to the petitioner to those intended to be introduced in evidence.

Commentary was revised accordingly.

4. Standard 5.1 C. was amended to permit juvenile's counsel to waive the right to bar statements or other information derived from statements made by the juvenile to an intake officer or social service worker without the advice of counsel.

Commentary was revised to correct the statement that the standard is drawn practically verbatim from the U.S. Children's Bureau Model

Family Court Act § 26, since it no longer applies to the revised standard.

5. Standard 6.8 A. was amended to add a limitation on the parent's right to free counsel by a cross-reference to Standard 6.5.

Commentary was revised by deleting a comment that the standard would free the parent's right to counsel from dependence on the exercise of judicial discretion.

6. Standard 6.9 A. was amended by changing the appointment of counsel for indigent parents from a mandatory to a discretionary obligation of the court.

Commentary was revised by adding a discussion of the position that parents' right to counsel is discretionary at the adjudicatory proceeding and mandatory at all other proceedings. It also notes that an adult's right to counsel is waivable in delinquency proceedings, whereas the juvenile's right to counsel is nonwaivable.

7. Commentary to Standard 1.3 was revised by adding a clarifying statement that particularity in setting forth the allegations in the petition should not preclude the customary requirement that the pleadings be brief and succinct.

8. Commentary to Standard 1.7 was revised to add a provision that parents who waive service by knowingly submitting to the proceeding without objection should be provided with a copy of the petition at the proceeding.

9. Commentary to Standard 3.3 A. was revised to add a reference to the greater safeguards required for pretrial investigation of juvenile offenses, as compared to adult criminals, with cross-references to such provisions in the *Police, Records and Information,* and *Interim Status* volumes.

The commentary also was revised to add a comment that the results of a lineup or similar identification procedures should be subject to discovery by respondent's counsel, as in criminal proceedings.

10. Commentary to Standard 4.1 was revised by adding a comparison of provisions covering probable cause hearings in the *Prosecution, Interim Status,* and *Transfer Between Courts* volumes.

11. Commentary to Standard 6.6 C. was revised by adding a statement that a corrections agency having custody of a juvenile is not intended to come within the definition of "parent" for the purposes of this standard.

## STANDARDS RELATING TO PROSECUTION

1. Standard 2.2 B. was amended to change the criterion for the salary of juvenile prosecutors and their staff from that paid by leading

law firms to a range commensurate with other government attorneys, as provided in *Counsel for Private Parties* Standard 2.1 (b) (iv).

Commentary was revised accordingly.

2. Standard 4.3 A. 3. was amended by reducing the minimum age for transfer to criminal court from sixteen to fifteen, adding class two offenses, and limiting the prerequisite of a prior record to class two offenses, to conform to revisions in *Transfer Between Courts* standards.

Commentary was revised accordingly.

3. Standard 4.4 was amended to add brackets to time limits for filing a petition (forty-eight hours if in custody, five days if not in custody).

4. Standard 4.5 A. was amended to permit dismissal of a petition by the court on the juvenile's motion without the prosecutor's consent.

5. Standard 5.1 A. was amended to authorize plea agreements concerning dispositions in addition to the charges that may be filed.

Commentary was revised accordingly.

6. Standard 6.3 A. was amended to delete the condition that the juvenile be subject to a disposition ·involving loss of liberty as a prerequisite to the prosecutor having the burden of proving the allegations beyond a reasonable doubt.

Commentary was revised accordingly.

7. Commentary to Standard 4.3 B. was revised to add a cross-reference to *Pretrial Court Proceedings* Standards 3.1 to 3.9, on discovery to the provision covering the prosecutor's duty to disclose.

8. Commentary to Standard 5.3 was revised by adding a note that the standard requiring independent evidence to support a plea does not preclude a reduced charge in exchange for a partial admission.

9. Commentary to Standard 7.2 B. was revised to require prosecutors to make reasonable efforts to notify parents of unsatisfactory implementation of dispositional orders, unless the class is too large for notice to be practicable.

10. Commentary to Standard 8.2 A. was revised by adding a notation that investigations of violations of probation orders should include consultation with the juvenile's probation officer.


## STANDARDS RELATING TO RIGHTS OF MINORS


1. The Introduction was revised by deleting the last paragraph describing the contents of Part VII and substituting a new paragraph explaining the rationale for eliminating the subject of first amendment rights from the coverage of the volume.

2. Standard 3.2 was amended by deleting the phrase pertaining to

the style of life which the child had been accorded as a factor in determining the scope of support.

Commentary to Standard 3.2 was revised to delete discussion of perpetuating life style and other patterns of family life as relevant to determining the scope of the support obligation.

3. Standard 3.3 E. was amended by expanding the provision for criminal prosecution for parental failure to support: protection of children under twelve was expanded to include children under sixteen. Sixteen was then bracketed to allow some discretion in states' adoption of an age ceiling.

4. Standard 3.4 B. 1. was amended to add an exception that would continue the support obligation for children living separately after a finding of endangerment.

Commentary was revised to discuss the addition.

5. Standard 4.4 was amended to add "emancipated" to describe minors living separate and apart and managing their own affairs.

6. Standard 4.6 A. was amended to bracket age sixteen in the description of mature minors.

Commentary was revised to explain that the amendment is designed to emphasize the minor's capacity to understand, rather than his or her mere chronological age, for informed consent to treatment.

7. Standard 4.6. B. was amended to make the provision on notifying a mature minor's parents of medical treatment expressly subject to Standard 4.2 B., in which the physician must seek the minor's consent to notify parents of specified medical treatments.

8. Standards 4.7 B. and 4.8 B. were amended to change "physician" to "person or agency" providing treatment.

9. Standard 7.1 (Part VII) was deleted in its entirety, as discussed in Item 1 above.

10. Commentary to Standard 2.1 on emancipation was revised to add a reference to the ABA Young Lawyers Division and Family Law Section's support of Commissioner Wald's dissent to family function as an exception to tort liability.

It was also revised to describe the Family Law Section's position on specific grounds for emancipation.

11. Commentary to Standard 3.3 was revised to define "suitable" in a vendor's right to recover for goods or services "suitable" to the child's or family's economic situation.

12. Commentary to Standard 3.4 A. was revised to endorse the position of the ABA Family Law Section on extending the parental support obligation beyond the age of majority when the child is enrolled in high school or an equivalent degree program.

13. Commentary to Standard 4.1 was revised to insert a discussion of the minor's right to refuse treatment.

14. Commentary to Standard 4.2 was revised to add a cross-reference to *Abuse and Neglect* Standard 6.6 B. on continued parental right to consent to medical treatment when the child is removed temporarily from the home.

Further revision added that any disclosures made by a minor to a physician during medical counseling be protected as privileged communications.

15. Commentary to Standard 4.9 was revised to add a recommendation that states adopt uniform licensing requirements for psychotherapists.

## STANDARDS RELATING TO TRANSFER BETWEEN COURTS

1. Standards 1.1 B. and 1.1 C. were amended by reducing the minimum age for criminal court jurisdiction from over fifteen to over fourteen years of age at the time the offense is alleged to have occurred.

The commentaries to Standards 1.1 B. and 1.1 C. also were revised to include fifteen-year-old juveniles among those under eighteen who could be subject to waiver of juvenile court jurisdiction.

2. Standard 1.2 A. was amended by bracketing thirty-six months to comply with the policy adopted by the executive committee of making recommended time limitations permissive rather than mandatory.

The commentary to Standard 1.2 A. also was revised to place brackets around three years, the recommended maximum duration for juvenile court dispositions.

3. The commentary to Standard 1.2 B. was revised to add two sentences at the end of the last paragraph to expand the cross-reference to the provisions in the *Dispositions* volume that modify a disposition by applying *Dispositions* Standard 5.4 to revocation of probation.

4. Standards 2.1 A. through 2.1 E. were amended to bracket all numbers representing time limits, adding class two juvenile offenses to the category of charges for which waiver of juvenile court jurisdiction would be possible, and reducing to fifteen the age at which the alleged juvenile offense must have been committed for waiver to be possible.

The commentaries to Standards 2.1 A. through 2.1 E. were revised to reflect the above changes.

5. Standard 2.2 A. 1. was amended to add class two offenses to the provision requiring a finding of probable cause as a prerequisite to waiver.

The commentary also was revised to add class two offenses.

6. Standard 2.2 C. was amended by adding class two offenses to the provisions on necessary findings for waiver, by requiring a finding of a prior record of adjudication for class two offenses only, and by adding a cross-reference to Standard 2.1 E. providing that the court's finding that the juvenile is not a proper person for juvenile court handling must be in writing.

The commentary to Standard 2.2 C. was revised accordingly.

7. Standard 2.2 D. was amended to include class two offenses in the provision on the substitution of a finding of probable cause in subsequent juvenile court proceedings but not in any subsequent criminal proceeding.

8. Standards 2.3 A. and B. were amended to bracket five court days for notice of the waiver hearing.

9. Standard 2.3 C. was amended to add to the provision that the court pay expert witness fees and expenses a clause making payment subject to the court finding the expert testimony necessary.

The commentary was revised to include the same caveat.

10. Standard 2.3 E. was amended to add class two offenses to the provision placing the burden of proof of probable cause and of the juvenile's unfitness for juvenile court handling on the prosecutor.

Commentary to Standard 2.3 E. was revised to add to the discussion of the juvenile's right to challenge prosecution evidence a cross-reference to the right to compulsory process in *Dispositional Procedures* Standard 6.2, *Juvenile Records and Information Systems* Standard 5.7 B., and *Pretrial Court Proceedings* Standard 1.5 F.

11. Standard 2.3 I. was amended to delete "criminal," thereby extending the inadmissibility of admissions by the juvenile during the waiver hearing to both juvenile and criminal proceedings, and to add an exception for perjury proceedings.

12. Standard 2.4 was amended to bracket the seven days for filing appeals.

Commentary to Standard 2.4 was revised to add a cross-reference to *Appeals and Collateral Review* Standard 2.2, which authorizes appeal of the waiver decision by either party.

## STANDARDS RELATING TO YOUTH SERVICE AGENCIES

1. Standard 4.11 was amended to include a cross-reference to Standard 5.1.

2. Standard 4.12 was amended to restrict privileged communications during participation in youth service agency programs to

confidential disclosures made to intake, counseling, and supervisory personnel.

3. Standard 6.2 was amended to add specific cross-references to *Juvenile Records and Information Systems* Standards 5.1 to 5.8.

4. Commentary to Standard 6.2 was added to stress the fact that this standard applies only to access to case files by designated agency staff and the client. Further dissemination of information in the files is governed by *Juvenile Records and Information Systems* Standards 5.1 to 5.8.